TO BE LEARNED IS GOOD

Latter-day Saint photographer Charles Ellis Johnson captured this striking image of Orson Pratt's scientific observatory, constructed just south of the Salt Lake Temple around 1869. The temple and the observatory are emblematic of the Latter-day Saint impulse to reconcile heavenly and earthly concerns, to interweave the intellectual and spiritual. "Exterior observatory, circa 1900," Church Archives, The Church of Jesus Christ of Latter-day Saints.

Essays on
Faith and
Scholarship
in Honor of
RICHARD
LYMAN
BUSHMAN

TO BE LEARNED IS GOOD

Edited by

J. SPENCER FLUHMAN • KATHLEEN FLAKE • JED WOODWORTH

NEAL A. MAXWELL
INSTITUTE *for*
RELIGIOUS SCHOLARSHIP

Brigham Young University
Provo, Utah

Permissions. No portion of this book may be reproduced by any means or process without the formal written consent of the publisher. Direct all permissions requests to Permissions Manager, Neal A. Maxwell Institute for Religious Scholarship, Brigham Young University, Provo, UT 84602.

Library of Congress Cataloging-in-Publication Data

Names: Bushman, Richard L., honouree. | Fluhman, J. Spencer, editor. | Flake, Kathleen, editor. | Woodworth, Jed, editor.
Title: "To be learned is good" : essays on faith and scholarship in honor of Richard Lyman Bushman / edited by J. Spencer Fluhman, Kathleen Flake, and Jed Woodworth.
Other titles: Essays on faith and scholarship in honor of Richard Lyman Bushman
Description: Provo, Utah : Neal A. Maxwell Institute for Religious Scholarship, Brigham Young University, [2017]
Identifiers: LCCN 2017038676 (print) | LCCN 2017036354 (ebook) | ISBN 9780842530224 (print : alk. paper) | ISBN 9780842530231 (e-book) | ISBN 9780842530248 (Kindle)
Subjects: LCSH: Mormon Church—History—Study and teaching. | Church of Jesus Christ of Latter-day Saints—History—Study and teaching. | Mormons—Historiography. | LCGFT: Festschriften.
Classification: LCC BX8611 .T6 2017 (ebook) | LCC BX8611 (print) | DDC 289.3/32—dc23
LC record available at https://lccn.loc.gov/2017038676

♾ This paper meets the requirements of ANSI/NISO Z39.48-1992 (Permanence of Paper).

Cover design by Heather G. Ward
Interior design by Emily V. Strong
Endpaper design by Daniel O. McClellan

Printed in the United States of America

CONTENTS

SECTION 4
Can Historians Quest after Religious Truth?

SECTION 5
Scholarship in Its Purest and Best Form?

EDITORS' PREFACE

This volume reflects the vibrant exchanges from a memorable scholars' colloquium in June 2016 in honor of friend and mentor Richard Lyman Bushman. Credit for originating the idea of such a gathering belongs to M. Gerald Bradford, former executive director of the Neal A. Maxwell Institute for Religious Scholarship at Brigham Young University. We are grateful to him and to all who contributed to this celebration of and elaboration on the themes that have animated Richard's thought and work.

Richard's scholarly work speaks for itself. His formidable list of publications appears as an appendix to this collection. In addition to honoring his intellectual contribution to his fields of study, however, this colloquium celebrated his contribution to his colleagues and students: his work as mentor and friend. This volume applauds in particular his attention and care for a generation of Latter-day Saint protégés. In characteristic fashion, when we sought his approval for a festschrift, he demurred, protesting he had been praised enough. Eventually, he agreed on the condition that the undertaking focus on the intersections between the life of the mind and the life of faith and that, not least, this be done from the point of view of LDS scholars.

What follows, then, are essays and introductions that embody Richard's own priorities and passions. They are scholarly, rigorous, and faithful. They probe meaning and significance through reflection, experience, and comparison. They mingle voices from various perspectives across the spectrum of Christian and Jewish faith traditions and from those who practice no religion at all. In their twin commitments to academic and religious worlds, they reflect our vibrant and productive moment in LDS intellectual life that Richard himself helped to create and shape. In some ways, Richard's influence pervades the work of contemporary LDS scholars but was established one seminar, one workshop, one student at a time. We are grateful recipients of his friendship and intellectual and spiritual gifts, and we hope the conference out of which this volume arises contributes to that legacy.

We are grateful not only to those who contributed their scholarly time and talent to this enterprise but also and no less to those whose financial generosity made it possible. While the Neal A. Maxwell Institute hosted the colloquium and proudly publishes this collection, several academic partners served as cosponsors and underwriters: the Charles Redd Center for Western Studies at Brigham Young University, the Church History Department of The Church of Jesus Christ of Latter-day Saints, the Howard W. Hunter Chair of Mormon Studies at Claremont Graduate University, the Laura F. Willes Center for Book of Mormon Studies at BYU's Neal A. Maxwell Institute, the Leonard J. Arrington Chair of Mormon History and Culture at Utah State University, the Obert C. and Grace A. Tanner Humanities Center at the University of Utah, Religious Education at Brigham Young University, the Religious Studies Program at Utah Valley University, and the Richard Lyman

Bushman Professorship of Mormon Studies at the University of Virginia. In addition, we thank several private donors for their generous financial support of the colloquium: H. Brent and Bonnie Jean Beesley, David A. and Linda C. Nearon, and Tom and Cheryl Quinn.

J. Spencer Fluhman
Kathleen Flake
Jed Woodworth
July 2017

1 | HISTORIANS ARE NEVER INNOCENTS

WHAT CONSTRAINS OUR UNDERSTANDING OF THE PAST?

Section Introduction

DAVID D. HALL

Several years ago, I opened a folder on my laptop to which I gave the name "corrections." It is where I store examples of one historian correcting another—not historians in general, but those who study Tudor-Stuart Britain circa 1540–1660 and the early decades of New England history (ca. 1620–1660), the twin periods I am presently engaged in trying to understand. Much was new to me when I took up the challenge of absorbing large quantities of British history, including what its interpreters regarded as unsettled or in dispute. Hence, for my purposes, the practical benefit of noting the disagreements or corrections that litter this scholarship.

It may seem naive to compile a folder of this kind, naive because doing so implies the possibility of achieving an error-free description of religious politics in Tudor-Stuart England and early New England. There is no such animal. As Terryl L.

Givens emphasizes in his paper for this conference, historians bring a great deal more to the task of understanding the past than a knowledge of the facts. They bring their own politics or, to borrow one of Givens's key words, their "prejudices," that is, assumptions about what really matters and how history should serve some larger purpose—perhaps by legitimizing policies and practices or, more commonly these days, by exposing the darker side of the past. Historians write apologies (in the older sense of that term) for what has happened, but I add to this description the fact that historians also excel at unmasking the hidden or unsuspected. In either mode, historians are never innocents who transmit the past "as it really was," to quote a well-known nineteenth-century aphorism.

This truth must be accompanied by another: the capacity of historians to recognize the prejudices (to use Givens's word again) that inform another person's understanding of the past. In the course of reediting a manuscript of the late sixteenth-century Welsh radical Puritan John Penry, the historian of English nonconformity Albert Peel characterized one of Penry's previous biographers as "a fiery Welshman, his partisanship was keen, even fierce; and he was particularly happy if he could find anything which would enable him to damn a bishop." This is straightforward, as are the many demonstrations of how denominational and theological allegiances—or, in the case of the British historian E. P. Thompson, his reaction to the Methodism he experienced growing up—have shaped a historian's work for better or for worse. Professional historians are trained to detect half-hidden assumptions that become taken for granted, passing from one context to another and never seriously questioned. An excellent example of scholarship that exposes this process is Curtis J. Evans's *The Burden of Black*

Religion (1998), which traces the long life of the trope or figure of the African American as naturally religious.

There is a deeper point to make about the interplay between our own subject position and the past. Revising what we take for granted can be prompted by the discovery of fresh evidence, as has happened for historians of early Mormonism. Or it can be driven by something more mysterious and impersonal, the coming and going of larger frameworks or paradigms. The arrival of women's history in the 1970s is one of many examples of paradigm shifts within the past half century. Meanwhile, much older paradigms persist, although possibly less compelling than when they were novel. Every historian depends on structures of this kind to connect his or her work to what others are doing and to identify the questions that matter the most.

What happens to "the truth," a term that figures in Mauro Properzi's dialectical model of philosophical and theological work, amid the ebb and flow of competing paradigms? And what happens, in particular, to truth as defined and cherished by a religious community? From the earliest centuries of Christianity to the present day, historians have wrestled with this question. Are they empowered to adjudicate truth claims? Not really. Anne Hutchinson's assertion in 1637 Massachusetts that God was speaking directly to her cannot be challenged or corroborated on the basis of historical evidence. Not that most of her contemporaries accepted her testimony; to the contrary, they characterized her as an "enthusiast" (i.e., mistaking the merely natural for the divine). Nor can historians adjudicate the dispute between Catholics and Protestants at the time of the Protestant Reformation about the meaning of idolatry or what was truly apostolic. All we can do (unless we are engaged in acts of apology) is to describe the manner in which faith communities engage in meaning-making and embody those meanings in, say, ritual practice. Yet I hastily add that historians can and must interrogate all such moments of meaning-making. Are these as coherent as a faith tradition may assume they are? Given that the words someone is using are always freighted with how those same words have been used by others, can we detect valences of meaning that may have eluded the actors or churches or traditions we are studying? In the period of time I study, orthodoxy mattered, as did an appropriate interpretation of scripture. Yet we have learned that all attempts at orthodoxy were leaky at best and, at worst, confused or self-contradictory. Ditto how scripture was being cited; in hotter moments of the Westminster Assembly (1643–49), its members mocked how others were citing the Bible. Surprises of this kind proliferate—finding, for example, that John Calvin incorporated two quite different understandings of the sacrament of baptism in his monumental *Institutes*. In his case as in so many others, system gives way to negotiations and a blurring of boundaries.

For good reason, historians do not set themselves the goal of achieving consensus when they study the past. Nor, in most cases, do they set themselves the goal of validating a particular understanding of politics, religion, literature, and the like, although their own sympathies may tilt them in one direction or another. Consider the people I have spent a long time studying, the Puritans of early modern Britain and early America. They are not around any longer to protest how they are treated, but their descendants in the nineteenth century fought among themselves and with outsiders over the nature of the historical record. Were the Puritans intolerant theocrats or makers of a remarkably democratic church order? Advocates of a paralyzing Calvinism or armed with a repertory of devotional practices that enabled some people to practice a richer version of their faith? Or possibly both at one and the same time? And to whom does the answer matter, all of us as students of the American past or only those who (feebly, perhaps) look back fondly on the *Mayflower* and the *Arbella*?

Philip Barlow endorses the proposition that character, by which he means our deepest moral and aesthetic orientation, guides how we work as historians. This argument is reminiscent of Jonathan Edwards's understanding of the freedom of the will: we are free in the special sense of being guided by our deepest inclinations. I endorse this proposition in light of my own personal history; my emphasis in what I have written about Edwards on his failure to understand the yearning of his congregation to incorporate their children into the covenant is rooted in challenges I have experienced. Yet I remind myself that an emphasis on character can trap us in the same way that Edwards's insistence on sincerity trapped him. As his fellow minister and grandfather Solomon Stoddard put it, what infallible sign does God give us that x is saved and y is not? Religious experience is astonishingly complex and varied—and sometimes at odds with official norms. So is character. I hope it is more than mere cynicism on my part to point out that historians with a public identity as moral beings can and do make up stories about the past. Granting character a role, therefore, may generate more questions than answers.

Givens, Barlow, and Properzi have each enabled us to recognize the interplay between faith and history as deeply rooted in matters that are extrahistorical or touch on the relationship between formal truth and the play of culture. They remind us that writing history that satisfies the ethics of a discipline as well as the ethos of a faith community can be problematic. But as Barlow and Givens have already demonstrated in their own work, this tension can also be remarkably fruitful.

"WE GAIN KNOWLEDGE NO FASTER THAN WE ARE SAVED"

The Epistemic Dimension of Character

PHILIP L. BARLOW

Two score and seven years ago, one of our intellectual fathers brought forth on this continent a new conception of historical method, dedicated to the proposition that Mormon scholars might meld their religious perspectives and a theory of history to better understand the workings of peoples and nations.

Richard Bushman's essay "Faithful History" appeared in an early issue of *Dialogue: A Journal of Mormon Thought*, one year after the trustees of Columbia University awarded him the Bancroft Prize for *From Puritan to Yankee*, the book its jury judged the best of the year in American history and diplomacy.[1] The essay anticipated by three decades George Marsden's work that treated related themes and culminated in his book *The Outrageous Idea of Christian Scholarship* (1997),[2] which incited a debate that spilled beyond academic circles into public outlets such as the *New York Times*.

While several aspects of Bushman's essay remain richly provocative, it is his concluding thought I wish to engage here. He asserts that one cannot improve as a historian without improving as a person. This is because moral insight, spiritual commitment, and critical intelligence entwine. Then comes his last line, inspired by Joseph Smith's well-known teaching that "man is saved no faster than he gets knowledge."[3] Bushman's inversion reads, "We gain knowledge no faster than we are saved."[4]

Is this true?

One must allow a measure of poetic license in this formulation, noting also that its Mormon author was addressing a Mormon audience. Bushman did not imply that secular scholars were incapable of rigorous scholarship. Rather, he invited Latter-day Saint scholars to imagine history through God's eyes in order to provide a different frame of analysis.[5]

My own rumination on this notion—*we gain knowledge no faster than we are saved*—is experimental. I shall shape it by proposing that *there is an epistemic component to each of our character traits*. I am about to zoom in the lens by sketching specific ways in which this may work in practice.

Note that I am not arguing that one's sight is colored by one's gender, race, class, location, or era. Scholars have had a half century and more to establish that. Nor am I writing of the alleged "moral turn" in the practice of history during the past decade or so. "Moral history" can mean, variously, a "moral attitude" or judgment on the part of the historian, or a study in choices and actions historical actors made or refrained from, or the attempt to re-create "the moral tone of a particular time and place."[6] All this could naturally prove relevant to my wider purposes, but it is not my immediate theme. Neither am I alluding simply to a scholar's values. While related, the topic I address is more elemental and personal than either values or ethics, something beneath even one's conscious self-identity, from which one's ethics and values tend to flow. I speak, rather, of one's character, whether or not one is conscious of its components.

I confess that I am drawn to the notion that character impinges on what and how we can know. That is, if a scholar shows courage or cowardice, she is not thereby merely admirable or deplorable, but her traits also condition what she is capable of seeing or sensing, what she is even equipped to look for. Because this thought resonates with me, I am also suspicious of it, lest Freud rightly dispense with me as prey to wish fulfillment. Moreover, because I do not personally know very much, the thesis that we gain knowledge no sooner than we are saved may imply that I am wicked!

Additional objections spring to mind; I will mention four. Some will chafe at the thesis as inherently maudlin, pious, or excessively self-conscious. They may insist that our attention rest strictly on our topic, not on the scholar treating it, whether ad hominem or pro hominem. If our interest is to discern the origins of the Korean War or what made the Puritans tick, who cares if the author of an argument cheats on his wife? While this objection may give us pause before judging the work of others, my interest lies in prompting thought about our own selves as scholars. A maudlin by-product would be an errant result, not one dictated by exploring personal epistemology.

A second challenge is that the proposal that character and attitude are epistemic may seem sectarian, luring us to conceptual cul-de-sacs, proffering too much religion in the *study* of religion. This is a legitimate danger, but is again a danger of distortion rather than a negation of our thesis. There is nothing inherently sectarian about examining what influences how one thinks.

Third, the idea that character affects perspective may seem self-evident, not worth bothering about. After a generation of postmodern preaching, who needs more talk of the self? Yet while the abstract principle may strike some as intuitive, human character, identity, motivation, and psychology applied to scholarly tasks are a labyrinth, requiring reflection.

Finally, other objections may have more merit. Rather than being self-evident, the corollary that poor character constricts insight may be hard to prove or simply be wrong. Impressive creations of music, art, sport, and science do not seem to hinge on moral rectitude—why should scholarship? Beyond this, positive epistemic *advantages* to otherwise contrary traits may surface. Would we read Mark Twain more dearly had he been a cheery fellow? Was it not precisely Twain's curmudgeonly squint toward religion that allowed Huck Finn to cash in his ticket to heaven rather than cash in his slave friend, Jim? And what of the yet more pronounced misanthrope H. L. Mencken? Was he not both grouchy and (hyperbolically) correct in proclaiming, "No virtuous man—that is, virtuous in the Y.M.C.A. sense—has ever painted a picture worth looking at, or written a symphony worth hearing, or a book worth reading, and it is highly improbable that the thing has ever been done by a virtuous woman."[7]

There is, then, potential substance to this objection. Without doubt, useful scholarship and provocative art have come from problematic characters.

Given such qualifications, we might attempt an exegesis of, or an amendment to, Bushman's last sentence: "We gain knowledge no sooner than we are saved." An exegesis would pivot on what we mean by "knowledge" and by "saved." A provisional reconstruction might read: *We gain a certain class of historical knowledge* (redeeming knowledge? the sort of knowledge that matters most? "wisdom"?) *no sooner than we are good enough, evolved enough, and redeemed enough to be able to imagine, search for, recognize, apprehend, and apply it.* Alas, like any exegesis, this reach for precision is cumbersome. Compressed, our amendment might read: *We gain wisdom no sooner than we are good.*

But this pales and mars Bushman's poetic play with Joseph Smith's prose. And "good" is not quite "saved," much less "holy." In the end I defer to Bushman's original cast, if granted the henceforth silent complications noted to this point. I embrace the idea and believe the iteration of it I am musing on is not an incidental concern. Indeed, contemporary philosophers have developed a strand devoted to such inquiry: "virtue epistemology,"[8] besieged with technical nomenclature. Given our compressed space, however, I shall draw my example not from philosophy but from science. If the dynamics of character sometimes condition even the results of science, we can more readily see how they may apply in the study of history, religion, and culture.

The botanist Barbara McClintock was awarded the Nobel Prize in 1983 for work with maize, by which she revolutionized ideas about genetics, with implications for evolutionary processes. Recognition of her accomplishment was tardy: she was a woman in a man's profession, and skepticism of her breakthrough research in the 1940s and 50s induced her to stop publishing her data in 1953. By then, "McClintockian" had become code for "unscientific" in some circles. Not until the 1960s and 70s did other scientists come to better understand her work and confirm her demonstrations of certain startling mechanisms of genetic change.

McClintock's way of practicing science, her way of thinking about her subject and of relating to her corn plants and her critics, suggests something of her character and imagination as well as her intellect and results. In what seemed science fiction in an era before stem cells, McClintock proclaimed, decades ago, "With the tools and the knowledge, I could turn a developing snail's egg into an elephant. It is not so much a matter of chemicals because snails and elephants do not differ that much; it is a matter of timing the action of genes."[9] Her critics thought her crazy as a goat, but, she said, "When you know you're right, you don't care. . . . You know sooner or later it will come out in the wash."[10]

McClintock's relationship to her maize was intimate, caring—one might even say *loving*—if that will not embarrass the tough-minded. This caring induced an extraordinary attention, a kind of deep listening, that teased into the open things otherwise obscure. Listen to a medley of her reflections I've culled from disparate sources: "There is no question that plants have [all] kinds of sensitivities. . . . But just because they sit there, anybody walking down the road considers them just a plastic area to look at, [as if] they're not really alive." To the contrary, "plants are extraordinary. For instance, . . . if you pinch a leaf of a plant you set off electric pulses. You can't touch a plant without setting off an electric pulse. . . . They do a lot of responding to their environment. They can do almost anything you can think of."[11] Indeed, "the ability of a cell to sense these broken ends, to direct them toward each other, and then to unite them so that the union of the two DNA strands is correctly oriented, is a particularly revealing example of the sensitivity of cells. . . . They make wise decisions and act upon them."[12]

What enabled this botanist to see further and deeper than her colleagues? Brains and ambition do not alone explain it. McClintock's own explanation was disarmingly simple. Repeatedly she discloses that one must have the time to look, the patience to "hear what the material has to say to you," the openness to "let it come to you." Above all, one must have "a feeling for the organism." "I start with the seedling, and I don't want to leave it. I don't feel I really know the story if I don't watch the plant all the way along. So I know every plant in the field. I know them intimately, and I find it a great pleasure to know them."[13] McClintock insisted that she could write the biography of each of her plants.[14]

I suspect that, for her, the veil grew thin between metaphor and literality in her methodological descriptions and prescriptions. I think that is true also of the distinction between her now-uncontested genius and the specific character traits and attitude through which she forged her method. Those traits include curiosity, imagination, courage, independence, confidence in relation to her critics, and, toward her subjects, an uncommon species of humility, patience, caring, and that deep listening and discerning, born of respect, affection, and persistence.

Transposed to the humanities, such sensitivities and attributes may yield knowledge and understanding. I have concluded, for example, that I am smarter when I am grateful—smarter within myself, rather than as compared to others. When I am grateful, I am *grace-ful*, more aware of grace, of the proximate or transcendent giftedness behind all things. This awareness prompts wonder at every phenomenon: the color green, perhaps, or my very breath or the way a dandelion or a river or a day is made. When grateful, I take these things less for granted and I attend to them differently—each person, each moment. I am more aware, sentient in wider dimensions, than when I am ungrateful and comparatively oblivious. In gratitude I experience the world differently. I may ask different questions of what I perceive, including matters of history, human behavior, and other academic arenas.

Similar epistemic enrichment may attach to humility. For the vast majority of ancient Greeks and Romans, *humilis* and its analogues primarily meant "low," not "humble." It meant "lowly, low-lying, low-growing, shallow, vulgar, stunted, common, colloquial, poor, obscure, insignificant, base, mean, small-minded, cheap." Those who spoke variants of this word intended no compliment and certainly no advantage in how we apprehend things. Only as Christianity made its mark on Western language and culture did the word assume meanings like "grounded," "of the earth," and the admiring connotations of our modern "humility." More than degrading, the act of washing a peasant's feet would have been inconceivable by the conventional standards of classical Greece and Rome. We have no record of Caesar Augustus washing anyone's body parts.[15] I dare surmise that a Christian king or pope or abbess or ordinary disciple who washed the feet of a peasant in imitation of Christ was better able to *see* the peasant. Any history such a disciple might have undertaken would have been affected by that sight.

This assertion, like Barbara McClintock's example, suggests that scholars may do well to endure a periodic look in the mirror. What qualities of mind, soul, and self do we discern there, filtering what we imbibe of the world? However, finding other than surface forms and conventions in a mirror is more difficult than first appears. Augustine demonstrated as much in the fifth century by inventing autobiography, as surely as Isaac Newton invented calculus when he faced problems that the mathematics of his day did not allow him to solve. At least in the Western tradition, Augustine produced the first *self-life-writing* possessed of a real interior, an exploration of the self, one that went beyond boasts of travel and conquest.

This first autobiography, the *Confessions*, took the form of an extended, self-probing prayer addressed to God. What led to this profound creative act was its author's search for God, accompanied by an existential crisis. Part of this crisis involved a *time wound*: Augustine sensed and reasoned that the past does not exist, except in memory, while the future does not yet exist save by anticipation. Moreover, the present exists in only a most peculiar way, for it has no duration or "extension." By the time one can think about the present, it is the past. By the time one gets to the second syllable in pronouncing the word *present*, the first syllable is but memory. "Where, and when, am I?" Augustine wondered.

Ultimately, and in imitation of God's creative Word, as he believed, Augustine "called himself into being" through his autobiographical birth. The "self" he both discovered and shaped in the process was one that abided in an infinitely extended present (the "eternal now") that grappled with an imagined past and future. Augustine understood that in order to know something of God and the world, he must know something of himself.[16] His was a *serious* look in the mirror, one whose depth would not be approximated again for a millennium.

Now, a mirror has its own traits and dangers. It can distort. It can divert. One may there find Narcissus or other hauntings. But whether or not one notices and makes critical use of it, the mirror helps compose the window through which thinkers and scholars discern past and present "reality," offering their portraits to the world.

It is not that we flawed humans, secular and religious, are incapable of scholarship and insight. It is rather that, comparing ourselves with only ourselves, there remains a realm, a mode, and a kind of truth in which our character affects the degree of grace-offered light that enters us. In the words of seventeenth-century philosopher John Smith:

> To seek our divinity merely in books and writings, is "to seek the living among the dead:" we do but in vain seek God many times in these where his truth too often is not so much enshrined as entombed. No, seek for God within thine own soul. . . . [T]hat which enables us to know and understand aright the things of God, must be a living principle of holiness within us. . . .
>
> Divine truth is better understood as it unfolds itself in the purity of men's hearts and lives, than in all those subtle niceties into which curious wits may lay it forth. . . .
>
> . . . Some men have too bad hearts to have good heads. . . . He that will find truth must seek it with a free judgment and a sanctified mind.[17]

Notes

1. The article was reprinted in George D. Smith, ed., *Faithful History: Essays on Writing Mormon History* (Salt Lake City: Signature Books, 1992), 1–17. It was originally published in *Dialogue: A Journal of Mormon Thought* 4 (Winter 1969): 11–25.

2. George Marsden, *The Outrageous Idea of Christian Scholarship* (New York: Oxford University Press, 1997). Marsden did not

restrict his vision of Christian scholarship in the academy to theology or study of religious practice; he envisioned engagement with history, economics, law, ethics, the arts, and the natural sciences. He argued that the university disparages faith-informed scholarship in ways it does not impose on Freudian, Marxist, or other pre-theoretical orientations and that all scholars, despite their personal orientations, must marshal their academic interpretations on publicly accessible grounds, evidence, and principles. He further maintained that scholars ought not attempt to ghettoize their religious identity any more than their race or gender, and he provided examples of how Christian doctrines of creation, incarnation, and the roots of the human condition can foster scholarly views on the origins of the universe and human rights and economic fairness that may help better society at least as much as traditional liberal or Enlightenment perspectives have.

3. Joseph Smith, *History of the Church*, 4:588.

4. Bushman, "Faithful History," 16.

5. This sense of the essay was confirmed in conversation with Bushman, June 18, 2016.

6. George Cotkin, "A Conversation about Morals and History," *Journal of the History of Ideas* 69/3 (July 2008): 494, citing Neil Jumonville, Lewis Perry, and John Higham, http://www.jstor.org/. See George Cotkin, *Morality's Muddy Waters: Ethical Quandaries in Modern America* (Philadelphia: University of Pennsylvania Press, 2010).

7. H. L. Mencken, *Prejudices: First Series* (London: Jonathan Cape, 1921), 198.

8. A convenient introduction is Linda Trinkaus Zagzebski, *Virtues of the Mind: An Inquiry into the Nature of Virtue and the Ethical Foundations of Knowledge* (Cambridge: Cambridge University Press, 1996).

9. Quoted in Bruce Wallace, *The Search for the Gene* (Ithaca, NY: Cornell University Press, 1992), 176.

10. Quoted in Claudia Wallis, Mary Johnson, and Dorothy Ferenbaugh, "Honoring a Modern Mendel," *Time*, October 24, 1983, 43–44. See Wallace, *Search for the Gene*, 176.

11. Barbara McClintock, quoted in Evelyn Fox Keller, *A Feeling for the Organism: The Life and Work of Barbara McClintock* (New York: Henry Holt, 1983), 199–200.

12. Barbara McClintock, "The Significance of Responses of the Genome to Challenge" (Nobel Lecture, Karolinska Institutet, Stockholm, December 8, 1983).

13. Quoted in Keller, *Feeling for the Organism*, 128.

14. Quoted in Keller, *Feeling for the Organism*, 198.

15. Thanks to classicist Mark Damon of Utah State University for provocative and clarifying conversation on the matter.

16. The first nine books of the *Confessions* are autobiographical, while Book X serves as a philosophy and psychology of autobiographical method by probing the nature of memory, and Book XI complements this by probing the elusive character of time itself. The final three chapters are explicitly theological in narrating the eternal story of God, explicitly and implicitly related to the story of the individual soul as explored in what came earlier in the book. However, Augustine's intrigue with time spans his corpus. See Robert E. Meagher's penetrating analysis in Samuel L. Macey, ed., *The Encyclopedia of Time* (New York: Garland, 1994), 48–49.

17. John Smith, "The True Method of Attaining Divine Knowledge," as excerpted in *the Methodist Magazine* 8 (April 1825), 121–22, 124, 126, http://www.fullerconsideration.com/images/methodist magazin1825meth.pdf. The essay is one of Smith's *Select Discourses* (Repressed Publishing, reprint edition [2016] of the original 1660 edition). Thanks to Terryl Givens for pointing me to Smith's essay.

THE POETICS OF PREJUDICE

TERRYL L. GIVENS

Latter-day Saints frequently invoke the ideal of joining faith to scholarship. My thesis is that they are inevitably and ineradicably interwoven already—for all persons, and not just believing Latter-day Saints. I want to explicate and justify their integration by building on a claim made by the philosopher Hans-Georg Gadamer, a claim that positions prejudice (*Vorurteil*) at the heart of intellectual inquiry. It's a long quote from his *Philosophical Hermeneutics*, but worth considering in its entirety:

> It can be shown that the concept of prejudice did not originally have the meaning we have attached to it. Prejudices are not necessarily unjustified and erroneous, so that they inevitably distort the truth. In fact, the historicity of our existence entails that prejudices, in the literal sense of the word, constitute the initial directedness of our whole ability to experience.

> Prejudices are biases of our openness to the world. They are simply conditions whereby we experience something— whereby what we encounter says something to us. . . . But how do we know the guest whom we admit is one who has something *new* to say to us? Is not our expectation and our readiness to hear the new also necessarily determined by the old that has already taken possession of us?[1]

I want to look at two inspired segments of Gadamer's "poetics of prejudice" in more detail and consider their applicability to scholarship and faith. First I will discuss his conception of the "initial directedness of our whole ability to experience." Then I will turn to what Gadamer refers to as the "biases of our openness to the world" and "our expectation and our readiness to hear the new."

The Initial Directedness of Our Whole Ability to Experience; the Conditions of Experience

I take Gadamer's word *prejudice* (*Vorurteil*) to mean the hypothesis with which we launch ourselves into the project of life. Max Scheler expresses the principle beautifully but rigorously as a philosopher of cognition: "How do we know reality as something independently existent? . . . There is no specific sensation (hard, firm, etc.) that gives us the impression of reality. . . . What gives us reality is the *experienced impression of resistance* against the lowest and most primitive levels of our psychic life."[2] Or stated more simply by way of analogy, we can no more find and secure meaning in the absence of prejudice than we could find the traction to run or the breath to sing in the vacuum of space.

Just as this sensation of resistance—not just tactile but cognitive—is our proof of a world outside the mind, so is the tension between our intellectual inclination and the resistance that it provokes from alien voices the only antidote to blind certainty, smugness, and solipsism. Prejudice, predisposition, or a ground of judgment is the provocation that invites challenge and rebuttal in any discursive community. We are no blank slate, and any attempt to emulate one is both self-deceptive and dangerous. The illusion of a neutral ground from which intellectual inquiry proceeds is a relic of Enlightenment optimism. We don't need to be postmoderns to recognize that, as Nietzsche observed wryly, only "the animal lives unhistorically."[3] Not only are we situated in history and in culture, but our history and our culture are always ineradicably situated in us.

Nonetheless, the illusion persists when it serves our purposes, and its invisibility can confound our best efforts at consensus or even progress in intellectual matters. To illustrate, let me take as one case in point Alasdair MacIntyre's diagnosis of the conceptual chaos that reigns in our contemporary culture's conversations about morality. He points out, for instance, that moral discourse was "once at home in, and intelligible in terms of, a context of practical beliefs and of supporting habits of thought, feeling, and action, a context that has [long] been lost." The essence of all prior presuppositions underlying moral discourse was a teleological scheme in which "there is a fundamental contrast between man-as-he-happens-to-be and man-as-he-could-be-if-he-realized-his-essential-nature. Ethics is the science which is to enable men to understand how they make the transition from the former state to the latter. Ethics therefore in this view presupposes some account of potentiality and act, some account of the essence of man as a rational animal and above all some account of the human *telos*"—or end toward which we strive.[4]

23

Contrast these Aristotelian and Thomistic presuppositions (so conformable with a Mormon anthropology) with those evident in a recent critique by Judith L. Poxon, who protests that "an[y] idealized image that would function as a goal for becoming cannot help but retain a normativity that dominates the process of subjectification."[5] That's a mouthful, but her point is simple: ideals are oppressive. Or as I heard a student protest at a conference where I shared the table with Richard Bushman, "But to impose standards is to be elitist and exclusionary!" My point here is that in debates about moral questions especially, we cannot even begin a conversation without always already espousing a human teleology or condemning all human teleology as normatizing and thus oppressive. Arguments about so many moral dilemmas in our current climate will never be genuinely productive until participants can recognize that first premises have already been staked out, though they are generally unarticulated.

Mormons enter the many worlds of discourse with a fairly large set of theological positions—or prejudices—that pertain not just to human teleology but also to human origins, divine ontology, and everything in between. But the conspicuousness of Mormon theological eccentricities and our all-pervading tendency to conflate the heavenly and the earthly, to integrate the spiritual and the intellectual, have made LDS scholars, I believe, unduly self-conscious about the prejudices we bring to the academic table. (Some are too little self-conscious! That is another discussion.) That is why, I believe, LDS scholars are often guilty of "provincial anti-provincialism." The expression is Gene England's[6]—but I fear it remains a peculiarly Mormon affliction. It can manifest itself as a prompt readiness to play on an uneven playing field so that we don't look like whiners. It can manifest itself as a refusal to ask questions that are especially meaningful to us. It can manifest itself as forgetfulness that we inherit disciplines but also have the power to shape them. It can manifest as a phobia that leads us to bracket our heritage or inherited wisdom or core beliefs, instead of letting them be the prejudices that shape the starting point of our investigations and researches. As Charles Taylor comments, "Experience is that wherein our previous sense of reality is undone, refuted, and shows itself needing to be reconstituted," whereas "the aim of science is . . . to take us beyond experience." But we are not scientists. We are engaged in a humanistic enterprise. Again quoting Taylor (who is here reading Gadamer): "Bracketing out human meanings from human science means understanding nothing at all."[7]

Some of the most prominent scholars in religious studies certainly manifest no such insecurities and deference to faded Enlightenment bogeymen. Marie Griffith has used the expression "critical empathy" to acknowledge the limitations, and the complementary strength, of both insider and outsider perspectives. As she writes, "The lived worlds of human experience, after all, are not identical to people's descriptions of these worlds."[8] This is usually interpreted to mean listening respectfully to the insider perspective (empathy) while critiquing it from the outside (criticism). But I believe it can work in reverse. Faithful scholars can listen respectfully to the outside perspective while critiquing it from the inside (as when Mormons must credit as reasonable the [non-Mormon] academic consensus that the Book of Mormon is a nineteenth-century work or seek for naturalistic explanations of Smith's prophetic output).

Robert Orsi begins his work *Between Heaven and Earth* by situating his study in the midst of his own engagement with dying relatives, prayers to saints, and angelic presences; Bart Ehrman begins one of his more popular books by taking us through a deeply personal and subjective account of his deconversion experience from evangelical Christianity. Meanwhile Raymond Brown begins his magisterial work on the New Testament by telling us he is a believing Catholic. Clifford Geertz has coined the term *I-witnessing*, referring to the trend, in one critic's eyes, of scholars "flaunting their subjectivity and thereby acknowledging that any pretense of objectivity is naïve, if not deceitful."[9] Yet Mormons frequently seem to buy into the notion that some kind of feigned objectivity, sprinkled with liberal doses of self-directed cynicism, is the price of admission to the club.

Let me give two examples from outside the humanities of where we find scholars in the hard sciences operating from first premises that are easily deconstructed into faith-based premises—some with greater fidelity to Gadamer's exhortation than others. First is the atheist cosmologist Martin Rees. In his engagement with the much-discussed and -debated anthropic principle ("the Goldilocks Effect," or observation that a hundred cosmic and cosmological coincidences converge to make life possible), Rees reviews six cosmological parameters in particular that together constitute the necessary conditions for the formation of stars and planets, as well as the evolution and subsistence of life (N, Ω, D, Q, ε, and λ).[10] All six of these numeral values—from the mass of the universe to the ratio of gravity to nuclear forces—are defined with exquisite precision (some carried 120 places after a decimal point), and in each case even the smallest deviation from the observed value would be catastrophic for potential life.

Rees concedes that the mathematical probability of such cosmic fine-tuning is near enough to zero that, given the limited prehistory of our universe, the chances of a coincidental convergence of such parameters is effectively zero. Determined to account, in nonreligious terms, for the fact that we are, obviously, palpable proof of such a virtually impossible convergence, he finds refuge in the hypothesis of the multiverse. If an infinite number of universes exist, he reasons (along with numerous scientific colleagues), then a virtual impossibility becomes a statistical inevitability (Ω, λ, etc., "could take different values in each universe").[11] So we posit a literally infinite plurality of universes, and in the midst of this plethora we are delighted but not dumbfounded to find that we exist as an instance of winning an almost but not fully impossible cosmic lottery. The only problem—which he is honest enough to concede—is that a multiverse is a nontestable hypothesis. He has had to depart from the realm of science in order to preserve what is clearly an original predisposition against God theories. As to whether the convergence of astronomically improbable fine-tuning is, in his words, "coincidence" or "the providence of a benign Creator, . . . it is neither. An infinity of other universes may well exist where the numbers are different."[12] Here a renowned scientist finds no shame in making an original prejudice—the absolutely-no-design-behind-creation thesis—the basis for resorting to an *effectively* religious explanation to avoid the alternative of a *conventionally* religious explanation.

A second example of a prejudice operating in a more fruitful way (fruitful in the sense of generating a testable and subsequently proven theory) is from the work of the theoretical physicists Hermann Weyl, Paul Dirac, and Frank Wilczec. Their brilliant colleague Freeman Dyson relates their shared prejudice:

Wilczek believes that the basic laws of nature must be *beautiful,* and therefore a theory that is *beautiful* has a good chance of being true. . . . [Wilczek] points to several famous examples from the history of physics, when theories designed to be beautiful turned out to be true. The best-known examples are the Dirac wave equation for the electron and the Einstein theory of general relativity for gravity. If the grand unified theory turns out to be true, it will be another example of beauty lighting the way to truth. . . .

. . . Hermann Weyl, who was one of the main architects of the relativity and quantum revolutions, said to me once, "I always try to combine the true with the beautiful, but when I have to choose one or the other, I usually choose the beautiful." . . .

. . . Dirac arranged "what had seemed an unlikely marriage—between quantum mechanics and Einstein's theory of relativity—in the form of an exquisitely beautiful equation to describe the electron. Soon afterwards, with no experimental clues to prompt him, he used his equation to predict the existence of antimatter. . . . The success of this prediction is, by wide agreement, one of [the] most outstanding triumphs of theoretical physics."[13]

We cannot operate without our prejudices. We can only make of them assets or liabilities, and that depends largely on the second of Gadamer's formulae.

Biases of Our Openness to the World; Our Expectation and Our Readiness to Hear the New

Our conception of space and time represents the representation of possibilities! —Max Scheler[14]

If the illusion of an Enlightenment ideal of impersonal objectivity with its value-neutral groundwork and purity from any contamination by commitments to a human anthropology is the Charybdis of faithful scholarship, tenacious *adherence* to prejudice is the Scylla. Gadamer's poetics of prejudice emphasizes the "before judgment" as the basis of *openness, readiness.* This is what Gadamer has to say about such openness, or "epistemological humility," in his *Philosophical Hermeneutics*: "No assertion is possible that cannot be understood as an answer to a question. . . . But . . . any experience of life can confirm the fact that there is such a thing as methodological sterility, that is, the application of a method to something not really worth knowing, to something that has not been made an object of investigation on the basis of a *genuine question*."[15]

So what is a "genuine question"? Gadamer elaborates on the marvelous phrase in *Truth and Method*; it is where one's "own prejudice is properly brought into play by being put *at risk*."[16]

A genuine question is a question we ask at personal risk. This is one of those intersections where pure religion and intellectual integrity powerfully align. Openness to risk may in fact prove a useful differentiator between apologetics so-called and a more religious studies–oriented scholarship. *Apologetics*, like *cult*, may be a term that has been too deformed in contemporary discourse to be a useful designation. Its semiotic value is too encumbered with pejorative connotations that overlie its distinguished history. And like *cult*, it has been wielded as a cudgel to discredit and dismiss, under the guise of applying some kind of objective rhetorical label. Since all academic activities involve formal argumentation in defense of a position, we are all apologists of a sort. So let me say instead that Gadamer's "genuine question," which exposes the interrogator to genuine risk, should be a hallmark of any work done in the field of religious studies, by a secularist or by a committed believer. And in its absence we may find the kind of work that deserves the label of "apologetic" in the pejorative sense.

Paul Johnson recognized the problem of genuineness and risk as they pertain to Christian scholarship, and of course the point is even starker with Mormonism. Johnson notes that Christianity

> is essentially a historical religion. It bases its claims on the historical facts it asserts. If these are demolished, it is nothing. Can a Christian, then, examine the truth of these facts with the same objectivity he would display towards any other phenomenon? Can he be expected to dig the grave of his own faith if that is the way his investigations seem to point? In the past, very few Christian scholars have had the courage or the confidence to place the unhampered pursuit of truth before any other consideration. Almost all have drawn the line somewhere. . . .
>
> . . . A Christian with faith has nothing to fear from the facts; a Christian historian who draws the line limiting the field of enquiry at any point whatsoever, is admitting the limits of his faith.[17]

Founding a religion in the age of printing, as Fawn Brodie noted, complicated Joseph's program—and ours—enormously. This is because we are now like the proverbial lawyer, having to ask questions we do not always know the answer to, but recognizing the answers are usually part of the historical record if we dig deep enough. This kind of faithful scholarship *invites—it does not run from—vulnerability.* Not all investigations of LDS scholars may redound successfully. Research into the Mountain

Meadows Massacre and priesthood doctrine revealed more difficulties than resolution. But without exposing themselves to losing battles in the short run, Latter-day Saints cannot merit credibility with Saints or with scholars.

Paul Ricoeur finds this kind of risk goes to the heart of Christian discipleship. "The philosophical progression from religion to faith through atheism involves a purification of man's desire for protection and a purification of man's fear of punishment." "In the book of Job," he finds, "unadulterated faith in God is . . . described as a tragic faith beyond any assurance of protection."[18] If intellectual work is to be, as Latter-day Saints profess, a type of worship, then it must exhibit not just effort and rigor, it must manifest the highest form of faith, which is that trust and confidence that lays one open to disappointment. It must be the faith that constitutes vulnerability. Asking questions without presuming to know the answers is the purest kind of both scholarship and discipleship—but it does not come easy to self-assured scholars or timorous disciples. It is a quality of the childlike. "There is an earned innocence," says one of Marilynne Robinson's characters, "which is as much to be honored as the innocence of children."[19]

Notes

1. Hans-Georg Gadamer, *Philosophical Hermeneutics*, trans. and ed. David E. Linge (Berkeley: University of California Press, 1977), 9, emphasis in original.

2. Max Scheler, *The Human Place in the Cosmos* (Evanston, IL: Northwestern University Press, 2008), 38, emphasis in original.

3. Friedrich Nietzsche, *On the Advantage and Disadvantage of History for Life* (Indianapolis: Hackett, 1980), 61.

4. Alasdair MacIntyre, *After Virtue: A Study in Moral Theory*, 3rd ed. (Notre Dame, IN: University of Notre Dame Press, 2007), ix, 52.

5. Morny Joy, Kathleen O'Grady, and Judith L. Poxon, *Religion in French Feminist Thought* (London: Routledge, 2003), 45.

6. Eugene England, "Provincial Anti-provincialism," *The Student Review* 4 (December 13, 1989): 8.

7. Charles Taylor, "Gadamer and the Human Sciences," in *The Cambridge Companion to Gadamer*, ed. Robert J. Dostal (Cambridge: Cambridge University Press, 2002), 128, 132.

8. R. Marie Griffith, *God's Daughters* (Berkeley: University of California Press, 2000), 12.

9. John Horgan, *The Undiscovered Mind: How the Human Brain Defies Replication, Medication, and Explanation* (New York: Simon and Schuster, 2000), 1.

10. Martin Rees, *Just Six Numbers: Deep Forces That Shape the Universe* (New York: Basic Books, 2000). See pp. 2–4 for a summary of the six numbers.

11. Rees, *Just Six Numbers*, 169.

12. Rees, *Just Six Numbers*, 4.

13. Freeman Dyson, *Dreams of Earth and Sky* (New York: New York Review Books, 2015), 117 (emphasis added), 192, 158 (quoting Graham Farmelo).

14. Scheler, *Human Place*, 32.

15. Gadamer, *Philosophical Hermeneutics*, 11.

16. Hans-Georg Gadamer, *Truth and Method* (London: Bloomsbury, 1989), 310.

17. Paul Johnson, *A History of Christianity* (New York: Touchstone, 1995), vii.

18. Alasdair MacIntyre and Paul Ricoeur, *The Religious Significance of Atheism* (New York: Columbia University Press, 1970), 88, 82.
19. Marilynne Robinson, *Gilead* (New York: Picador, 2006), 30.

TRUTH, COMMUNITY, AND PROPHETIC AUTHORITY

MAURO PROPERZI

Five years ago I was honored by the invitation to speak at a colloquium in honor of our friend and colleague Richard Bushman. I am honored today to have been invited again and already look forward to his ninetieth birthday colloquium in five years. I, like many of you, consider Richard a mentor who has often shown us the way in navigating the challenging interaction of scholarship and faith, or of Mormonism and the academy. Indeed, the marriage of Mormon faith and academic scholarship is not always happy and mutually satisfying. A tension is inherent in this relationship, and Richard knows this quite well since he certainly felt the pulls of the two ends of the spectrum of his *Rough Stone Rolling*'s readership. Still, the interaction is worth pursuing because this tension can be fruitful, especially for Mormon intellectuals. If nothing else, the way we experience it, or come to terms with it, can tell us much about ourselves, including where we are and where we may be going in our identity.

I'd like to reflect on a few aspects of this tension and argue that its permanent resolution is not necessarily ideal for Mormon intellectuals. This is not to say that a level of peace and stability in approaching issues of faith and scholarship is unreachable or undesirable. Coherence and honesty, which provide both emotional and intellectual stability, can consistently ground our voice in these discussions. Yet there may be times when Tertullian's famous quip about the disconnect between Christianity and Greek philosophy—"What does Athens have to do with Jerusalem?"—will apply to our attempts to integrate Mormonism and the academy. Perhaps faith versus scholarship is the paradox that encapsulates all the other Mormon paradoxes proposed by Terryl Givens.[1] As such, it is worth our focus and analysis. In this context my desire is to speak about three interconnected dimensions that directly affect and complicate any attempt to integrate faith and scholarship: truth, community, and prophetic authority.

I begin with a conversation I once had with Richard. In the early days of my employment at BYU, I met with him for lunch and asked him for advice. His response to me as a new religion teacher was brief and to the point: "Teach the truth." On another occasion, at a session of the Faith and Knowledge Conference, Richard responded to a question with a comment that may appear to contradict, or at least qualify, his focus on the centrality of truth. He claimed to be (are you ready for this?) a "postmodern." As you know, many have tried to define postmodernism, and ultimately there are as many definitions as there are postmoderns; but there is one commonality to them all, namely, skepticism toward claims of absolute or universal truths, or to put it in a slogan, "down with metanarratives!" I do not want to project my own thoughts and intentions onto Richard, so you can ask him directly whether he would still make that claim and what he means by it. I can only offer my own reflections on what I see as an uneasy coexistence: the resolute pursuit of truth, even universal truth, on the one hand, and critical thinking and con-textualization of its findings, even skepticism, on the other.

Philosophy, religion, science, and knowledge are human modes of discourse with external referents that are colored by the inherent characteristics of humanity. So the complex-ity and tension are all in the human being and in his or her limitations to experience truth in ways that are not in some way self-referential. While this may sound obvious to some and ut-terly false to those who do not value religion or divine revelation as referents of truth, this limitation is a reminder of an equality of sorts between science and religion. The point is that the same tendencies, the same dogmatism, the same cynicism toward whatever is perceived as threatening a central perspective that makes up our identity may be found in both, clothed in religious or scientific language depending on the occasion. Thus, in af-firming truth as both universal and contextual, I also affirm the necessity of the human filter—in perceiving, using, and applying truth—to both positive and negative ends. Let me explain.

When we speak about the human, we cannot limit ourselves to psychology but clearly need to include sociology. Knowledge, as a human pursuit, is always socially contextualized. It is a re-sult of the language and categories we employ to describe it, as well as the result of the methods and assumptions we use to explore it. They all emerge from a social context that cannot be fully transcended. In other words, the acquisition of infor-mation that is necessary for the formation and recognition of truth is usually connected to meaning-making communities that provide and interpret information in ways that are usually self-reinforcing. Furthermore, we each belong simultaneously to several of these epistemic communities. It is one of the characteristics of modern societies to accommodate belonging to several such communities; hence, our social epistemology becomes inherently complex as the values, goals, assumptions, and data of these various communities interact within thinking individuals, at times smoothly, but often strenuously. The interaction between Mormonism as a religious community of faith and the academy as an intellectual community of knowledge is only one such interaction, which in turn overlaps with other cultural, political, and affective communities. These communities shape the truths that lie at the core of our identities.[2]

It follows that, as a key defining characteristic of individuals, groups, and societies, truth often functions as a means to an end and not as an end in itself. The question remains on whether the ends pursued are good or bad. Postmodern critiques hold absolutist or universalist views of truth to be naive because they fail to recognize this self-referential dimension of knowledge. Some of these critiques also emphasize the negative dimension of non-self-referential truth-making agendas by seeing their purpose as the exercise of power for its own sake, in good Nietzschean fashion. I cannot fully reject these perspectives because they do describe dimensions of reality that are before our eyes, both in individuals and in communities. If we are truly honest, we even find them in ourselves. My LDS theological anthropology in some way supports this descriptive recognition by affirming that humans, in their natural state, are enemies to God. Thus, it is to be expected that the ego-centered, fallen individual will manifest the tendency to negative power, or "unrighteous dominion," as Latter-day Saints would put it, even in the pursuit, possession, and communication of truth (Doctrine and Covenants 121:39). Yet, this same theological anthropology teaches us that we are dynamic rather than static beings, that our roots and destiny are greater than empty self-focus, and that we can transcend or "put off" this natural man by following the "enticings of the Holy Spirit" (Mosiah 3:19). In short, the postmodern critique may have value in a descriptive sense, but not in a proscriptive one.

The sanctifying development of the individual involves both the inside and the outside, the power of God and the agency of man employed in following these transformative corrections. Although ultimately personal, this is a process that happens in and through community, with groups emerging both as facilitators and as obstacles of this very development. But individuals and communities are not to be viewed as separate categories of being, at least in the context of the highly relational theology of Mormonism. In an eternal sense the individual and his family constitute each other, or to put it differently, there is no individual without community and no community without individuals. The ultimate ideal is captured in a Godhead whose divine oneness describes a perfect relationship between beings who interact with mankind as a divine community. Mormons pray to the Father in the name of Christ through the power of the Holy Ghost, and the Father extends his love to humankind through the Son's atonement and the sanctifying, connecting power of the Spirit. This unity in action, purpose, and will is central not only to the Godhead's interaction with humankind but also to the identity of each of its divine components. Yet, for us mortals the picture is not as idyllic: relationships are often far from ideal, communities exist in hierarchies of importance, and conflicts between individuals and communities or between different communities are common. Still, the dynamic tension between individual and community is central to eternal progression, including the realm of truth acquisition, which is not only assertion of propositional statements but also expression of embodied realities.

Then, religion appears as somewhat different epistemically from the social sciences or the humanities, not in relation to its practitioners but to its object of study. Indeed, the certainty associated with God's perfection would be misplaced if applied to humanity. While humans can continue to be uncertain about their own perceptive filters of God, the God who has been chosen as an object of faith is firm, unchanging, and certain in his existence and in his characteristics. Hence, churches are an interesting mix of humanity and divinity: comprised of divine beginnings and ends rooted in certainty on the one hand, and of human filtering rooted in uncertainty and fallibility on the other. Thus, in religion, certainty and uncertainty are always in tension with each other, particularly in this secular age, and notwithstanding institutional religion's historical emphasis on certainty and on the exclusivity of truth over competing perspectives. This is also true of Mormonism and of the epistemic community associated with it.

The epistemology that emerges from the Mormon milieu is characterized by at least two interrelated paradoxes: the individual versus the community on the one hand and divine certainty versus human uncertainty on the other. Given that individuals and communities are central subjects and instruments in the pursuit of truth (even though both are subject to corruptions and deviations from the ideal spiritual trajectory that leads to truth), what can be said about the distinctiveness of Mormon epistemology? Relatedly, what does the Mormon epistemic community have to offer to shore up its members from the dangers of both self-focused conscience and group dynamics gone awry?

Let me propose at least one answer, although there may be many: the prophetic authority claimed by the Prophet Joseph Smith and his successors. Visions, new scriptures, a restored church, saving ordinances, and priesthood authority, to name only a few examples, made Mormonism a religion that dared to claim prophetic possession of a new, purer, direct line of communication with God. The radical claim of being an authoritative epistemic community that had bridged the gap between the sacred and the banal through divine intervention was exclusive in focus and, to many, offensive in its implications. These epistemic claims were and continue to be central to the emergence, survival, and international growth of the faith. Mormonism boldly proclaims that God has spoken again to a prophet in modern times and that a preferred channel of communication between heaven and earth has been established through the restoration of Christ's church and his priesthood authority. And although no church prophet who has succeeded Smith has ever been considered equal to him in terms of revelatory production or prophetic charisma, the LDS Church has continued to teach that prophetic authority—namely, the right to function as God's primary mouthpiece on the earth—is invested in its living prophet. Prophetic expressions have changed in their content, context, and expression, but the same expectation exists now as it existed then: if there is anything that the Lord wants his church to know, practice, or change, the primary channel of communication will be God's prophet as assisted by the other fourteen men, "prophets, seers, and revelators," who constitute the First Presidency and the Quorum of the Twelve Apostles.

At the same time, recognition of prophetic authority within Mormonism does not invariably lead to prophetic infallibility, fideism, blind obedience, or tribal mentality. Mormons are not asked to follow their leaders blindly or to place all responsibility for sacred knowledge upon their prophets and apostles. They are taught that theirs are souls on a path of eternal progression, where personal acquisition of knowledge, through assistance of and sensitivity to the power and influence of the Spirit, is crucial to such development. Hence, individual study and agency, character growth, conscientious obedience, and working things out in one's mind and heart are inherently personal processes that must accompany any institutional guidance from church authorities. For a fully engaged Mormon, thoughtless following of any authority, whether secular, spiritual, or academic, is never a real option. Still, prophetic pronouncements provide parameters that call for both respect and attention.

What, then, if truth, community, and prophetic authority come to clash with each other? A useful organizing principle in addressing these tensions may be the concept of "conscience formation," which is prevalent in Catholic moral theology. According to this view, conscience is the internal compass of individual decision making where reason, God, knowledge, community, values, and desires intersect and interact. As such, it represents the ultimate subjective norm of human behavior. At the same time, conscience is not immune to error, is in need of constant development or formation, and calls for personal responsibility in bringing about its progress. From the church's perspective, a well-formed conscience will be rooted in scripture, church teaching, and the inspiration of the Spirit, thus becoming more fully moral than if built exclusively on principles of reason. Conscience formation employs reason assisted by experience, as well as personal reflection in interaction with loving relationships, with prudence functioning as the virtue that links all these components into a holy process of acquiring God's truth. Education and training are to be centered on objective moral truth, though a truth that needs to be properly applied in the person's reality of daily life.[3] While Mormons would use somewhat different terms to describe this reality and its associated dynamics, the substance of the message would largely be the same.

The late Catholic theologian and cardinal Avery Dulles wrote perceptively about conscience and its relation to authority. He reiterated the centrality of conscience to individual judgment while also adding that conscience "is not autonomous [because] it cannot speak responsibly unless it has been properly educated."[4] People will obviously differ when identifying the sources that lead to a "proper education" of conscience, but most would agree that conscience has as much to do with the nature and origin of the information that is being processed as it does with the processing of the same. Indeed, information does not usually enter individual consciences as neutral to begin with, since it is generally already colored by its source, associations, relationships to existing desires and values, and so on. In other words, processing and receptivity are inherently interconnected and mutually reinforcing, hence the need to choose one's epistemic authorities carefully. Dulles continues:

> The relationship between authority and personal judgment may be described as dialectical. That is to say, the two are neither identical nor separable. Our personal convictions about what is right and wrong are at least partially shaped by what the community and its leaders have taught us, and on the basis of those convictions we determine whether to

follow the community's authorities in a given instance. To
the extent that we have been successfully socialized into the
community, our free and spontaneous judgments about right
and wrong tend to coincide with the rules and expectations of
the community.[5]

This is true not only of religious communities but also of political,
cultural, or family communities, and certainly of academic ones.

What, then, are the boundaries of the Mormon epistemic
community, and what do the boundaries mean for LDS intellectuals and the formation of their consciences? Michael Otterson,
a prior managing director of Public Affairs for the LDS Church,
recently reminded us that these boundaries are broad and the
tent is large, while also emphasizing that there are clear doctrinal boundaries, covenants, commandments, and divine claims
that are stable, nonnegotiable, and foundational to the meaning
of the word *Mormon*.[6] Within this context, prophetic authority
plays a significant role in setting and reinforcing boundaries or
in opening them up to adjustment and change. Mormon intellectuals can play a part in the defense of these boundaries,
in their conceptualization, and in the evolution of their ad-
justments as they operate within the framework provided by
prophetic authority. LDS scholars may even provide a key im-
petus to such changes, as Richard's experience seems to indicate.
As a historian of Mormonism, Richard challenged the cultural
practice, often institutionalized in LDS educational curricula, of
presenting Joseph Smith only though the lenses of hagiography.
Partly as a result of his endeavors, we now live in an era of un-
precedented church openness about the Joseph Smith of history.
Such openness does not inherently challenge the firm doctrinal
boundary of Smith's prophetic calling, but it paints a more nuanced picture of a man who was both holy and human.

The importance of conscience formation is rooted in our capacity to recognize the sources of our truth claims, the influence of our epistemic communities, our existing hierarchies of loyalty, and the difference between provisional knowledge and foundational truths. This process is inherently challenging and never-ending because those who are both Mormons and academics are to remain open to all truth, to challenge individual and communal tendencies to co-opt or corrupt it, and to keep purifying individual motivations in pursuing it. The tension will continue, but it will be a fruitful one, even a desired one. Yes, clearly both truth and uncertainty are real, or to put it in Gandhi's words, "I think it is wrong to expect certainties in this world, where all else but God that is Truth is an uncertainty. All that appears and happens about and around us is uncertain, transient. But there is a Supreme Being hidden therein as a Certainty, and one would be blessed if one could catch a glimpse of that Certainty and hitch one's wagon to it. The quest for that Truth is the *summum bonum* of life."[7]

Notes

1. Terryl L. Givens, *People of Paradox: A History of Mormon Culture* (New York: Oxford University Press, 2007), 3–64.

2. Eastern Asian religions and philosophies place unique emphasis on the interconnected dimension of personhood. These philosophies of the self lie at the foundation of collectivistic cultures and function as needed correctives to the excessive individualistic emphasis of Western thought.

3. *Catechism of the Catholic Church*, 1776–1802, accessed January 13, 2017, http://www.vatican.va/archive/ccc_css/archive/catechism

/p3s1c1a6.htm. See also Rev. Thomas V. Berg, "What Is Moral Conscience?," *Homiletic and Pastoral Review*, January 1, 2012, http://www.hprweb.com/2012/01/what-is-moral-conscience/.

4. Avery Dulles, *The Reshaping of Catholicism: Current Challenges in the Theology of Church* (San Francisco: Harper & Row, 1988), 93–94.

5. Dulles, *Reshaping of Catholicism*, 94–95.

6. Michael Otterson, "Understanding Church Boundaries: How Big Is the Tent?" (presented at the academic conference "Mormonism and the Art of Boundary Maintenance," Utah Valley University, Orem, UT, April 12, 2016), http://www.mormonnewsroom.org/article/boundary-maintenance-mormonism-address-michael-ottereson.

7. Mahatma Gandhi, *Autobiography: The Story of My Experiments with Truth* (Mineola, NY: Dover, 1983), 223.

2 | ANXIETY AND OBLIGATION IN SCHOLARSHIP

ANXIETY AND OBLIGATION IN THE PRACTICE OF HISTORY

Section Introduction

LAURIE F. MAFFLY-KIPP

Each author in this section worries about the distinctive challenges of linking the *practice* of history with the faith of the scholar and subsequently ponders the issue of personal accountability—to scholarship, to students, and to our subjects. Accountability provides an organizing framework by which these authors judge the historical practices we employ. Each also contributes a particular strand to the story: Melissa Inouye focuses our attention on teaching and the mutual obligations that the student-teacher relationship generates. Kate Holbrook explores the relationship invoked between the living and the dead as historians craft their narratives. David Holland questions the appropriate balance between particularity and universality in the writing of biography. Taken together, these papers offer a number of promising ways to explore what we are doing when we "practice" history, be it in the classroom or in print.

Inouye's essay reflects on the ways that her Mormon identity shapes her teaching. Her goal, as she says, is to provoke students to think broadly and carefully about basic questions of meaning and human value. How she does so is shaped by her Mormon beliefs in a number of ways: her socialization into hierarchical pastoral structures shapes her sense of mutual obligation in the classroom, her expectations for student learning are informed by belief in the eternal value of learning and growth, and practicing Mormonism has made her comfortable with messy contradictions and unresolved tensions in human communities.

I greatly appreciate these thoughtful formulations that can lead to both open-ended exploration and respectful dialogue when all participants accept the premises of this format. My first question is how we get our students to share these assumptions, or how one should translate them, when we work in non-church contexts. What does the sense of mutual obligation mean when one teaches non-Mormon students? Can we—or should we—find another idiom for talking about this dynamic, and what might this look like? If the work is, in part, to help students become who they want to be, how do we encourage them to have this expectation of themselves? Creating the kind of dynamic Inouye describes in her classroom is a real art, and I would love to hear more about how she brings her students along with her.

I am also quite taken with her point that college-age students face "a whirlwind of doors to countless futures that are constantly swinging open and banging shut." This is a terrific insight, and it causes me to wonder whether history can be used to take even fuller advantage of this life phase—can we employ historical narratives to help our students make sense of their own decisions? Or is our job simply to show them the doorways to various possibilities? Another way of putting this might be to ask where the critical faculty and particular insights of historical analysis come into play. What difference does the subject matter make, and why can it achieve the goals Inouye describes better than other subjects might? One of the points that I take from her essay is that history, in particular, offers students new possibilities in their lives at a particularly opportune moment.

Finally, Inouye's celebration of messiness is near and dear to my own style of looking for outliers and contradictions. I wonder how we might put this in conversation with David Holland's focus on persistent discordance in the aims of history itself. Is messiness always a good thing? How does this square with the desire to find absolute meaning (Holland's universal level) in history? I'm struck by Inouye's concluding statement that Mormons are good at living with untidiness and are even better bridge builders or translators—I think this is one strand of the Mormon story, but I also see such a strong centripetal tendency that moves toward standardization, orderliness, and absolute meaning. This may be another kind of contradiction that could be addressed in the classroom.

Community and collective obligation also figure prominently in Kate Holbrook's essay. She encourages us to focus on the work of history, family history especially, as in itself sacramental. It forges a connection between the living and the dead and calls on individuals to fulfill obligations to others by telling their stories. And it also "saves" those who are living by providing hope and companionship. In order to "be saved," the historian must preserve "an accurate and inclusive" range of stories. This is a lovely reflection on accountability in our writing, something that can be easily overlooked. I appreciate the reminder that studying past lives can put us in conversation with people in different eras. In the Mormon context, as Holbrook points out, these discussions "beyond the veil" have a particular theological salience, but I wonder whether this isn't true for many scholars. You never know who you'll be face-to-face with in the afterlife, Mormon or not, and I take this as a more general admonition to not limit our conversations to the community of the living.

Yet there are problems with stories because they are rarely straightforward and rarely decipherable in only one way. And this is where the really vexing work begins. This essay offers a number of ways of pursuing this historical labor of "telling" someone's story, and I would love to pursue precisely what this might entail. Are we to provide an accurate record? To "heal and redeem" our subjects? To tell their story the way they would tell it? Or to represent it using our own standards of justice and judgment? What if theirs is a story we don't like? And to what extent is this kind of storytelling a new creation, as the phrase "making the flesh word" might indicate? There is so much messiness, so much that seems contradictory or confusing, and so much that requires us to choose what is important and what is unimportant as we sift through evidence and accounts. The work of accountability is only a starting point, this essay suggests, for a discussion of truth, representation, and, perhaps, even salvation.

Finally, Holbrook does a lovely job of noting the obligations when doing historical work within and for a community of faith. Does this context, or should this context, change the shape of our accounts? Historians, in general, don't talk enough about whom they are writing for or why they are writing. So it is refreshing and helpful to hear these reflections on why Holbrook is doing this work and what she hopes it will accomplish—for herself, for those departed or voiceless others, or for a religious community.

David Holland turns our attention much more closely to biography. He points to another historical problem that biography presents for us: how to narrate the particularity of a single life without falling into antiquarianism on the one hand or complete universalism on the other. Whereas Holbrook asserts that the telling of the individual life story is valuable, even holy, in and of itself, Holland's work notes that this is not a typical way of thinking about the value of biography in the broader academic world. Religious commitments and disciplinary standards do not always mesh easily, and the believing scholar must find a way to make room for multiple obligations.

Holland's essay describes how Richard Bushman creates space for the personal, the social, and the divine in the life of Joseph Smith. He contrasts Bushman's biography with the uneasiness with which he earlier treated Franklin and Edwards and how he felt easier living with the potential discordance in Smith's account. It seems to me that Richard also wrestled with a different dilemma in writing about Smith, for Joseph Smith was not, for Bushman, the existential equal of Franklin or Edwards. He meant something different. How, then, was the dilemma of historiography and sacrality transformed by his subject matter and his own relationship to it? This is the point that Holbrook's paper, in particular, drives us to—how does our own relationship to our subject sacralize the historian's task? Bushman wasn't just writing about *a* prophet—he was also writing about *his* prophet. How does that difference matter?

Holland eloquently disentangles the strands of historical thinking, the focus on both a particular human being and an impulse to make that person stand for something universal and, in this case, theologically significant for the author. History serves various purposes. Does it matter that Bushman was writing for, at least in part, an LDS audience? Does this make his task different from that of "secular" historians? Surely the answer is yes, and David Holland nicely summarizes the space Bushman's work leaves for multiple possibilities that might speak to a variety of readers.

I conclude by asking, what is particularly Mormon about these ways of teaching or writing? Both Inouye and Holbrook make a strong case that their self-understanding is refracted through the lens of their faith. And Bushman, certainly, articulates those linkages elegantly in his own writings. Yet I wonder how many of these questions and concerns are more universal. Historians struggle constantly with issues of obligation and accountability. I wonder, too, whether we should follow more assiduously the path Holland sets out before us: can we find analogies in other religious traditions that can help Mormons gain purchase on the problems of history, on how we pay attention to insiders and outsider, disparate voices, and the needs of our students? The stakes of history within a faith context may be very different than they are outside it—but there may be overlooked opportunities for common conversation that these essays help us begin to explore.

PROPHETIC BIOGRAPHY

The Universal, the Particular,
and the Almost-Amazing Grace of Context

DAVID HOLLAND

Historians have a dilemma, and few disciplinary genres illustrate our consensual solution to that dilemma quite like biography, and few forms of biography challenge that solution quite like writing the life of a prophet. To explore these theses is both to illuminate the challenges of our craft and to recognize the work of Richard Bushman.

The Biographical Dilemma

From the late eighteenth century, a frequently contested but nonetheless unmistakable trend in Western historiography has pushed toward an emphasis on the distinguishing temporal and geographical particularities of historical phenomena. Echoing the words of one of his early modern subjects (Johann Gottfried Herder, who famously argued for the importance of—

in Herder's German—*Individuell* subjects in historical think-ing), the intellectual historian Friedrich Meinecke described the early effort to substitute "a process of *individualising* ob-servation for a *generalising* view of human forces in history."[1] Thus began an intellectual inclination toward particularization among historians. Indeed, the very phrase to "think historically" has frequently come to mean thinking in terms of particularity. As R. G. Collingwood wrote in the mid-twentieth century, "To think historically is to explore a world consisting of things other than myself, each of them an individual or unique agent, in an individual or unique situation."[2] In this disciplinary devotion to the particular it would seem that biography offers the ultimate expression of our field's aspirations. What genre could possibly be, to use Herder and Meinecke's term, more *Individuell*? When the American Historical Association recently published an essay on "thinking historically," it offered biography—or, as the essay puts it, "stories . . . about individual lives"—as the historical genre best suited for teaching students about the historicists' essential commitment to contingency, the idea that a life is shaped by a distinct causal chain of unpredictable events and the interjec-tions of individual agents rather than by an overarching, ahis-torical telos.[3]

In similar terms, sometimes updated for a postmodern age, a "biographical turn" has won praise in various historical sub-fields ranging from the histories of the Black Atlantic to those of modern American women. Looking for historians to counteract the influence of economists and sociologists and structural-ist scholars of various stripes who write of slavery in terms of universal, ahistorical categories, Joseph Miller "welcome[s] the epistemological implications of putting individuals and their ex-periences back where they belong, at the base of our properly historical inquiry."⁴ As Marilyn Booth and Antoinette Burton have observed in a recent issue of the *Journal of Women's History*, contemporary scholarship tends to credit biography's capacity for getting at "the contingent and the fragmentary . . . and (the historically discrete and specific) processes of selving." From such arguments, biography emerges as the ultimate end of our chronic quest for particularization.⁵

And yet, as Booth and Burton also point out, biography remains suspect within the field. This suspicion comes from countervailing angles of critique. One source of suspicion for biography stems from the fact that historians—for all our talk about particularity—often seem unsatisfied with work that hints of merely antiquarian interest or that too fully buys into the mythical agency of the exceptional subject. That is, we see little value in the particulars if they do not contribute to our understanding of bigger issues. To borrow an alliterative phrase from the scholar of American religion Leigh Schmidt, biography promises portraits, but we really want panoramas. Booth and Burton note that the same apologists for biography who tout its attention to the fragmentary, the specific, and the historically discrete also praise its ability to "do more than simply illuminate individual lives." In his excellent recent essay on biography and Mormon studies, Matt Grow accepts as a matter of course that historiographically respectable biography reaches outward to "broad historical themes" and answers a persistent call to "contextualize" its subjects "within their larger cultural milieu."⁶

So while we laud biography for its ability to particularize, we simultaneously challenge the genre to move beyond the purely particular. Indicative of the historian's double bind, however, we then fear its capacity to move too far in *that* direction. Biography—by its biological structure—has the potential to universalize its subjects. Biography offers an unavoidable reminder that even in a world of modern particularisms, all people are born, all die, all live in between. Thus, from an opposite angle of critique, historians argue that biographers risk invoking their subjects as emblems of universal truths about human existence. "Biographers," the historian of American religion Catherine Brekus writes, "have a tendency to collapse the difference between the past and the present, universalizing their subjects' experiences instead of contextualizing them."[7] In such critiques, the biographical subject threatens to stand in for the universal human. From this perspective, historicism looks to be locked in a sort of Sisyphean effort, with biography at the crest of the hill, a point where something resembling particularistic purity might either go too far or not go far enough, and thus either tumbles down one side into universalizing assumption or down the other into atomized irrelevance. The discipline's attitude toward biography has thus been persistently ambivalent.

Precisely because it so clearly elicits expression of these countervailing concerns that plague the work of historians—the impulse to particularize, the quest for bigger connections—biography has also been especially illustrative of a shared disciplinary solution. Note that both those who fear biography as overly specific and those who fear it as excessively universal call for the same solution, the "contextualization" of the subject. Contextualization, an indistinct effort that can expand or contract as needed, promises to keep the historicizing boulder from falling too far in either direction. It both particularizes and renders the particular relevant. When some scholars tell us to contextualize, they mean for us to focus more narrowly on the distinctive features of a specific set of historical circumstances; when others invoke the term, they mean we need to pull out of an overly narrow view and look at the broader world in which an event transpired. *Context* keeps us somewhere in the middle as we sail between the rocks of particularity and the whirlpool of universalization. Our arguments about biography make especially clear the perceived threats from which contextualization promises to save us and our easy—if often ill-defined—confidence in its power.

The Christian Analogue

This modern struggle with the exceptional subject and the universal claim is not purely a problem of historiography; there has been, for instance, a parallel dilemma in Christian theology. How does a historically particular, exceptional story like the life of Jesus Christ accurately capture the eternal truths of the universal God? Not coincidentally, this theological "scandal of particularity" emerged in Western Christian thought at the same moment when history began to celebrate its ability to particularize. In the eighteenth century, Gotthold Lessing spoke of the scandal of particularity as "the ugly, broad ditch" from which he determined that "accidental truths of history can never be proof of necessary truths of reason."[8] In the nineteenth century, thinkers ranging from Søren Kierkegaard to Theodore Parker confronted the same problem, with Kierkegaard ambivalently posing the question, "Can an eternal happiness be built on historical knowledge?" and Parker unambiguously answering that no, it could not. Parker sought instead a faith of universally intuitable truths that were, in his words, "independent of historical documents."[9]

The effort to address this constant Christian collision between historical particularity and eternal universality continued, of course, into the twentieth century. One of the most elegant answers came from the Catholic theologian Hans Urs von Balthasar, who, along with others, believed that the problem was only solved in the traditional Trinitarian incarnation of Christ, where the universal eternal Father and the particular historical Jesus emerged as one.[10] Something of this solution was mirrored in the work of biblical scholars who drew on long-standing Christian traditions to see in Jesus the pivot point between the particular covenant of Abraham and the universalizing preaching of Paul.[11] Historically human and eternally divine, God of Israel and Lord of all nations, particular and universal, Jesus Christ not only redeemed us from sin but also had, in such renderings, the capacity to deliver us from the great intellectual dilemma of the modern age. In the case of Balthasar's theology of the incarnation, such understandings have proved very valuable to his readers, some of whom use them to protect universal truth against the corrosive influence of modern relativism and some of whom use it to particularize the biblical revelation as a necessarily perspectival approach to truth.[12] Thus in the doctrine of the incarnation, Christ lays himself down as the answer to modernity's characteristic struggle for resolution in the conflicts between universality and individuality.

Here, then, we might perceive a point of comparison between the main thrust of modern historiographical thinking and important strands of Christian incarnational theology. Yet there is a fundamental difference. Context and Christ may both be invoked as solutions to a shared problem, but they do not actually do the same work. The historiographical insistence on context is largely driven by a suspicion about both the exceptional individual and the universal claim; the Christian appeal to the incarnation is shaped by a determination to believe in both.

One seeks to address the dilemma by diminishing its competing terms, the other by sacralizing them.

Prophetic Biography

What is one to do, then, when writing the biography of a prophet—by definition an exceptional individual, a historical person produced by a surrounding context, and a figure who is supposed to be the conduit of eternal and universal truths? Discussions of prophetic parentage illustrate the challenge.

In 1850, when Ralph Waldo Emerson published his collection of revised lectures entitled *Representative Men*, he expressed the critique that Emanuel Swedenborg had failed to escape fully the pull of his particular context; a crack at Swedenborg's identity as the child of a Swedish cleric served Emerson well: "The Lutheran bishop's son, for whom the heavens are opened . . . with all these grandeurs resting upon him, remains the Lutheran bishop's son; his judgments are those of a Swedish polemic, and his vast enlargements are purchased by adamantine limitations." When the famed American Swedenborgian George Bush heard Swedenborg described as "remain[ing] the Lutheran bishop's son," he fully caught Emerson's implication and felt compelled to respond. He refused to let the sage of Concord suggest that Swedenborg taught localized truth; either Swedenborgianism was eternally true, Bush asserted, or it was false "in any part of the universe." Emerson's and Bush's choice of words underscored an assumption: To be from a particular place, to have particular parents, was, in some sense, to be tacitly disqualified from the prophet's presumed obligation to the universe.[13]

An especially striking example of this prophetic impasse appears in Mary Baker Eddy's autobiography, *Retrospection and Introspection*, in which she provides her readers with the historical specifics of her life, including stories of her immediate parents and other ancestors, while repeatedly reminding the reader that such historical specifics are meaningless in the pursuit of eternal truths. "God . . . alone is our origin," she wrote. The "father and mother" of every person "are the one Spirit, and his brethren are all the children of one parent."[14] As Eddy's autobiographical ambivalence suggests, the prophet—the figure who occupies a place in history in order to point a way toward eternity—stands at the intersection of converging forces. The biography of a prophet marks a distinctive collision point of both theological and historiographical conversations about particulars, universals, exceptions, and contexts.

Bushman's Resolve and Resolution

Richard Bushman's scholarly autobiography suggests a long-term resolve to function within that tense zone of convergence. In "The Inner Joseph Smith," an article written for the *Journal of Mormon History* a year after the appearance of *Rough Stone Rolling*, Bushman reflects on an interest in psychohistory that he cultivated early in his career. Tellingly, as a young historian he had been drawn to a rapidly arcing methodology that promised to grant a certain historiographical gravitas to both the psychological idiosyncrasies of unique individuals and the general diagnostic categories in which those particularities might be understood. For such luminaries as Benjamin Franklin and Jonathan Edwards, Bushman explained much by the psychology of their filial ties: Franklin's nursing tensions with an earthly mother and Edwards's oedipal struggles with a Heavenly Father. Universal conditions and particular mental states dominated the stories. But Bushman was never quite satisfied with the results. He worried about reductionism, that his approach had reduced these complex men to their psychoses.

Bushman had sought and—at least by his own assessment—failed to match the work of Erik Erikson, who had successfully made the individual psyches of Luther and Gandhi emblematic of the conditions of their time and place and therefore more explanatory of their tremendous impact on their age. Bushman knew that contextualization offered an important answer, but for some reason he had been unable to match Erikson's comfortable appeal to its powers of deliverance.[15] One wonders if the striking lack of attention to context in Bushman's early biographical articles reflects a certain contrarian resistance (a personal tendency to which he confesses in "The Inner Joseph Smith") toward his discipline's relentless confidence in a contextualization that promised to dull everything both exceptional and universally human about these remarkable subjects. Context, after all, also threatens reduction. Given the predilections of the discipline, contextualization's claims on sufficiency would always be more potent than those of psychology. Bushman may have simply been pulling for the underdog.

Whatever his reasons for conspicuously downplaying contextualization in these early forays into biography, Bushman was disappointed with the results and thought he had put his psychohistorical period behind him. But as his scholarly attention turned toward a prophet, *his* prophet, something else happened. The satisfying mix of psychohistory and contextualization that had eluded him in his analysis of other men increasingly seemed achievable in the life of Joseph Smith. As "The Inner Joseph

Smith" shifts from the early scholarship to reflections on *Rough Stone Rolling*, we catch a glimpse of the mature Bushman's intellectual resolutions, a determination to let cultural context do its work of illumination without fully accepting its invitation to a fair and easy way out of the paradoxes of a prophetic life. It seems he found that contextualization could be more comfortably invoked in a subject for which context would not be allowed to account for everything. Context would come with constraints when studying a prophet whose claims were to be taken seriously. And thus faith became the fulcrum on which psychology and culture found balance.

In *Rough Stone Rolling*, Bushman demonstrates his willingness to train his scholarly attention in multiple directions, into the historical particulars of Smith's childhood home, specifically his psychologically charged relationship with his father, but also pulling back the analysis to consider the ways in which Smith's pursuit of familial security for himself and patriarchal dignity for his father led to revelations that spoke to the psychological needs of an entire generation of disrupted and displaced American families. Thus far, Bushman successfully follows the lead of Erikson in effectively contextualizing individual psychic appetites, thus empowering them to sustain generational analyses. But here again, as it always does, context begins to flex its reductive muscles. Both Joseph Sr. and Joseph Jr. almost become overdetermined products of their age. Yet because of Smith's claims to transcendent truths, and because of Bushman's personal investment in those claims, Bushman will not rest with the free grace of contextual deliverance. "Does it detract from the divinity of a revelation for it to resolve personal and social problems?" Bushman asks.[16] In this simple rhetorical query—which invokes the personal, the social, and the divine—we see the three levels of analysis for which Bushman has created space: a father, many fathers, the Father. To give all three a place in the story of a prophetic figure's life is to accept the good work that context does but to place a limit on its ability to shrink either the exceptional individual or the universal experience. Bushman's faith, rather, set bounds on the explanatory reach of contextualization and thus made it for him a more usable instrument in the quest for the historical Joseph. In the absence of the sacred, when context threatened to account for all, Bushman could not bring himself to introduce very much of it into the stories he told about Franklin and Edwards; but within the life of Joseph Smith he could adopt it with remarkable equanimity and to illuminating effect.

During half a century of scholarly work, Bushman has wrestled with this dilemma of the particular and the universal, exceptional figures and common human experiences. As a committed historian, he has embraced the explanatory potential of contextualization and its ability to historicize the two poles of the biographical dilemma, allowing that commitment to address the deficiencies of his early psychohistorical work. Context thus complemented psychology, but what could restrain it once thus invoked? As a tenacious believer in both exceptional individuals and universal truths, as a believer in prophets, Richard Bushman has refused ultimate satisfaction with contextualization's claims to sufficiency. He has graciously accepted its illuminations but not its absolutions, standing resolutely at that intersection where historiographical and theological anxieties most conspicuously collide. And his peace with that place, as well as his deftness of touch amid its conflicting demands, seemed to reach its peak in his work on a prophet, a figure for whom he could concede up front that after particular parents and cultural contexts were all given their due, a remainder would maddeningly, marvelously, endure.

Notes

1. James Connelly, "Philosophising History: Distinguishing History as a Discipline," in *The Edinburgh Critical History of Nineteenth-Century Philosophy*, ed. Allison Stone (Edinburgh: Edinburgh University Press, 2001), 147–48; Michael Bentley, "Introduction: Approaches to Modernity: Western Historiography since the Enlightenment," in *Companion to Historiography*, ed. Michael Bentley and David Morgan (Abingdon, UK: Routledge, 1997), 410–11; and Allan Megill, "Aesthetic Theory and Historical Consciousness in the Eighteenth Century," *History and Theory* 17 (February 1978): 32–34.

2. For this quotation, as well as a discussion of Collingwood's philosophical particularism, see James Connelly, "Collingwood's Moral Philosophy: Character, Duty, Historical Consciousness," in *The Moral and Political Philosophy of British Idealists*, ed. William Sweet (Exeter, UK: Imprint Academic, 2009), 233–50.

3. Thomas Andrews and Flannery Burke, "What Does It Mean to Think Historically?," *Perspectives on History*, January 2007, https://www.historians.org/.

4. Joseph Miller, "A Historical Appreciation of the Biographical Turn," in *Biography and the Black Atlantic*, ed. Lisa A. Lindsay and John Wood Sweet (Philadelphia: University of Pennsylvania Press, 2013), 19–47.

5. Marilyn Booth and Antoinette Burton, "Editor's Note: Critical Feminist Biography II," *Journal of Women's History* 21 (Winter 2009): 8–12.

6. Matthew J. Grow, "Biography in Mormon Studies," *Journal of Mormon History* 41 (Winter 2015): 184–97; Leigh Eric Schmidt et al., "Forum: Religion and the Biographical Turn," *Religion and American Culture: A Journal of Interpretation* 24 (Winter 2014): 9; and Booth and Burton, "Critical Feminist Biography II," 8–12.

7. Schmidt et al., "Religion and the Biographical Turn," 9.

8. On Lessing, see C. Stephen Evans, *The Historical Christ and the Jesus of Faith* (New York: Oxford University Press, 1996), 42–43.

9. Søren Kierkegaard, *The Essential Kierkegaard*, ed. Howard V. Hong and Edna H. Hong (Princeton: Princeton University Press, 2000), 189; and Theodore Parker, *A Discourse of Matters Pertaining to Religion* (Boston, 1842), 364.

10. Hans Urs von Balthasar, *A Theology of History* (San Francisco: Ignatius, 1994); and Rodney Howsare, *Hans Urs von Balthasar: The Ecumenical Implications of His Theological Style* (London: T&T Clark, 2005), 20–22.

11. See, for instance, Michael F. Bird, *Jesus and the Origins of the Gentile Mission* (London: T&T Clark, 2006).

12. Karen Kilby, *Balthasar: A Very Critical Introduction* (Grand Rapids, MI: Eerdmans, 2012); and Thomas R. Rourke and Rosita A. Rourke, *A Theory of Personalism* (Lanham, MD: Lexington Books, 2005), 166.

13. Ralph Waldo Emerson, *Representative Men*, ed. Wallace E. Williams and Douglas Emory Wilson (Cambridge, MA: Harvard University Press, 1987), 76–77; and George Bush, *Prof. Bush's Reply to Ralph Waldo Emerson on Swedenborg: A Lecture Delivered at the Odeon, Boston, on the Evening of Jan. 16, 1846* (New York, 1846), 19–20.

14. Mary Baker G. Eddy, *Retrospection and Introspection* (Boston: W. G. Nixon, 1891), 7, 27–29.

15. Richard Bushman, "The Inner Joseph Smith," *Journal of Mormon*

History 32/1 (Spring 2006): 65–81; Bushman, "On the Use of Psychology: Conflict and Conciliation in Benjamin Franklin," *History and Theory* 5/3 (1966): 225–40; and Bushman, "Jonathan Edwards and Puritan Consciousness," *Journal for the Scientific Study of Religion* 5 (Fall 1966): 383–96.

16. Bushman, "Inner Joseph Smith," 80.

ABOVE, BEYOND, AND IN BETWEEN

A Teacher's Role

MELISSA WEI-TSING INOUYE

As a scholar of Chinese history, I rarely have Mormon topics come up in my class. Unless, that is, you count the Taiping Rebellion, started in 1851 by a guy who saw God and Jesus Christ and who led rebel armies that contemporary observers sometimes called "Mormonites." And yet, Mormonism shapes how I teach Chinese history.

This happens in three ways. First, Mormonism's hierarchical pastoral structures inform my approach to the student-teacher relationship. Second, Mormonism's doctrines of the eternal value of learning guide my understanding of why and what I teach. Third, living as a Latter-day Saint has made me comfortable with messiness. When I teach Chinese history, I aim to teach it all: good and bad, inspiring and despicable.

The Student-Teacher Relationship

First, in embracing my role as a *teacher* (as opposed to an educational service provider), I follow in the footsteps of my Uncle Dillon and Uncle Charles, also Mormon academics. Dillon Kazayuki Inouye, who passed away in 2008, taught in the Instructional Psychology and Technology Department at BYU. He was famous for his speed-reading classes, in which it was clear that the main objective was not really learning to read fast but absorbing provocative perspectives from books like Søren Kierkegaard's *Works of Love* or Michio Kaku's *Hyperspace*. Charles Shiro Inouye's recent book, *The End of the World, Plan B*, shows heavy Mormon and Buddhist influences and grew out of his conversations with students in an undergraduate seminar at Tufts University.

Here I pay my respects to my uncles not only to name role models but also to establish a fundamental premise about teaching: teaching relationships are hierarchical relationships. In liberal Western discourse we tend to see *hierarchy* as a negative word, but the model of an Asian extended family, in which older generations receive deference and give care, shows how vertical relationships can nurture human flourishing. As children within a Japanese American family, my cousins and I were conditioned to assume that when aunts, uncles, or grandparents had something to give, we had something to receive. This differential creates powerful obligations. To be a teacher, as in the case of being a parent or aunt, is to take responsibility for knowing people and knowing their needs.

Mormonism is a theological and cultural system built on hierarchical relationships. In its early years, this hierarchy unsettled many antebellum Protestants who felt that Mormon prophets, patriarchs, and priests invited unflattering comparison to religions they considered despotic, like Roman Catholicism or Islam. And it is true that hierarchism within Mormon administrative structures can lead to a top-down, my-way-or-the-highway approach to leadership that is limited by the absence of a meaningful range of different perspectives. Nevertheless, in both Confucian and Mormon contexts, the power to influence comes with many strings attached. Stewardship has a deep and multivalent meaning, and one fundamental premise is that authority means work. Within local Latter-day Saint congregations, as within multigenerational Asian families, the deeply personal context of hierarchy softens power differentials and strengthens channels of communication.

A student-teacher relationship is hierarchical but also reciprocal. Students are obligated to listen, to prepare, and to rise to challenges. Teachers are obligated to be worthy of this receptiveness through careful preparation. I vividly remember the first class I ever taught as an adjunct at California State University, Los Angeles. The class in question was a survey of Chinese history from the Shang dynasty (circa 1523–1028 BCE) to around 1800 CE. This is a vast swath of time, all of it distant from the twentieth-century era that I knew best. For the first lecture, I had prepared an outline of the history of the Shang and the Zhou dynasties, writing down what I thought were key points. I planned to lecture from this outline. But when the students took their seats and I began to speak, I realized that I actually knew nothing beyond the column of thin little bullet points. As I watched the students taking notes, in my mind I was screaming: "Don't write that down! It's GARBAGE!" This was a definitive moment in my teaching career, a moment when I realized the weight of my obligations.

A student-teacher relationship involves vulnerability on the part of the students. In the worst-case scenario, such as the fiasco of my first class, this is dangerous because what the teacher has to offer may not be worthy, or may even be wrong or harmful. In the best-case scenario, however, vulnerability is a carefully prepared seedbed that can produce optimal yields. This same conscientious preparation takes place in a Mormon context as we publicly sustain and internally commit to support our leaders at all levels and accept their roles as teachers.

Why is it that children watching LDS general conference are shushed to attention when Thomas S. Monson, the prophet, comes to the pulpit? His talks are not as engaging as Dieter F. Uchtdorf's nor as clearly structured as those of Dallin H. Oaks. President Monson comes across as a kind man who tells stories tinged with a mixture of sentiment and admonition, all in soothing cadence ("hearts were touched; tears were shed"). And yet when everyone sits up and tries very hard to learn something from President Monson, *because he is the prophet*, we very often do remember what he says. This fruitful receptiveness is born of the hierarchical student-teacher relationship.

The other side of this coin, of course, is the problem of gender imbalance in hierarchical influence. Currently, the church's hierarchical structure is directly linked to priesthood ordination. There are no roles within our centralized structure in which women are formally set apart as stewards over the entire membership, global or local, men and women. In other words, no man in the church is religiously obligated to recognize a woman as a spiritual authority from whom he must take counsel. This cannot help but affect how Mormon men think about women and how Mormon women think about themselves.

Despite this imbalance and potential for abuse, my Mormon experience has given me a perspective on the positive potential of hierarchical relationships, which informs my relationship with students. I have learned that good teaching, like other kinds of hierarchy, is a personal obligation.

Scope of Learning in the University Classroom

Second, my expectations for what the students learn in my class are directly influenced by the Mormon paradigm that learning is the very purpose of mortal life and an eternal characteristic. As suggested by the revelation in Mormon scripture that says we are to "seek . . . out of the best books words of wisdom; seek learning, even by study and also by faith" (Doctrine and Covenants 88:118), the realm in which human beings acquire knowledge and skills overlaps with the realm in which we realize our divine nature. Even secular learning, from chemistry to home renovation, expands our capacity and brings us closer to our divine potential.

Hence in my mind I have not succeeded as a professor of Chinese history unless I have helped the students to see the connection between the study of history and vital, ongoing issues in their own lives. Their lives are incredibly busy and pressurized, a whirlwind of doors to countless futures that are constantly swinging open and banging shut. In such an environment it is easy to adopt a strategic mindset, to compartmentalize professional success and moral development, which is one reason why some students plagiarize papers from the Internet. And yet the two processes unfold within a shared space. It is impossible for one not to influence the other. My awareness of this process of ongoing moral formation shapes my framing of Chinese history.

Like all rich and well-documented subjects of historical inquiry, Chinese history throughout the late imperial era and the modern era is full of great paradoxes, conflicts, and contradictions. This relatively recent history is also deeply rooted in centuries and even millennia of politics and culture that can be quite bewildering to students encountering Chinese history for the first time. How do I help these students get a purchase on new dates, names, geography, and situations? The key is to frame the unfolding of historical narratives in terms of basic questions of meaning and value. What makes someone a good person? What ideals were the revolutionaries of 1911 and 1949 trying to bring about, and how did they compromise these same values as they strove to make them a reality in the world? These are not academic questions but human questions. My desire to reach my students through them is not an attempt to teach Mormon doctrine, but Mormonism has a clear influence on my belief in the value of such questions in the university classroom. I believe that as a teacher my role is not merely to fill students' heads with dates and facts but to help them to think broadly and carefully about the diverse ideas, problems, and processes that have helped define human life.

As the semester unfolds, in the questions that I ask the students I try to include a combination of critical historical thinking. What is this text saying? Who is its intended audience? How does it reflect its context? I invite them to consider the human questions of value and meaning. Why did Qiu Jin abandon her family and become a revolutionary? Was she being honest and courageous, or was she being selfish and partisan? If you had been a university student in China in 1966, would you have joined the Red Guards? What would have been the consequences of your choice? I find that the students respond to these questions with spirited and thought-provoking debate. Questions of value and meaning draw them into the historical events and characters and motivate them to engage their skills of critical analysis.

In the final lecture of a course, I always seek to extend the lessons of history into the students' lives. In the final lecture of one class, I told a story from my days as a lowly PhD student researching the True Jesus Church in Nanjing, China. I recounted that while there I was visited by an older academic who, it turned out, was also writing a book on the True Jesus Church. I felt quite protective of my research findings. I decided that it wouldn't be a problem to help him find his way to the chapel. I would definitely help translate for him (he didn't speak Chinese). But I thought that to share my best quotes, my hard-won insights, with this "competitor" would be the professional equivalent of shooting myself in the foot. Who would be impressed by a book that didn't have new, rare, original material? I emailed my adviser for her perspective. Maybe there was some sort of strategic framework, widely known to seasoned academics, to guide how much information I should share and how much I should keep to myself.

My adviser, Henrietta Harrison, is an accomplished scholar and a wonderful person. In her reply, she said, "I think that scholars should be generous with their scholarship just as they are with anything else." This was a revelation. It wasn't necessary to adopt a new set of values in order to succeed professionally. Perhaps graduate school was a relatively late time to learn the lesson that one's values should apply to all aspects of one's life,

"even" the rough-and-tumble of establishing oneself professionally. If only someone had taught this to me as an undergraduate!

One's basic values can and should be applied everywhere.
It doesn't matter whether you're dealing with sharing research
materials or sharing your lunch with someone who's hungry.
Sometimes when we feel unsure of our own abilities we feel
that honesty and generosity are luxuries that we cannot afford. In fact, the simple act of treating others as you would
want to be treated will pay huge dividends and make you better at what you do.

Contradiction and Conflict
in Chinese History and Mormon Experience

Third, I teach the students that history is messy. Modern Chinese
history is full of lofty, inspired ideals and ugly, horrific acts. My
students ask me how I feel about China.

When I was younger, my feelings about China were unam-
biguous. First I loved China for its great expanse, its incredible
continuity over millennia, and of course its street food. Then, after learning more about its modern history, I scorned China for
its strongmen, its corruption, its repressive state. Over the years,
however, my thinking about China has become more complex.

This shift in my thinking has corresponded with a parallel
shift in my own understanding of Mormonism. Actually, the history of the Chinese Communist Party is not so far off from the
recent history of the LDS Church in terms of the problems that
arise when charismatic ideals are harnessed to human organization. This coupling facilitates great locomotive potential but is
also a liability. Charisma can disrupt organization. Organization
can stifle charisma.

Mormon history, too, is full of examples of ordinary people struggling with the extraordinary task of building the perfect society. It was an exhilarating work characterized by consecration and inspiration but also by controversy and some serious sketchiness. Amasa Lyman, one of Brigham Young's fellow apostles, later conceded of early attempts to practice plural marriage, "We obeyed the best we knew how, and, no doubt, made many crooked paths in our ignorance."[1] Over time, Latter-day Saints have struggled to overcome the constraints of prevailing cultural beliefs, political pressures, and what the Book of Mormon calls "the natural man" to realize Zion, the community of the pure in heart. Often we fail.

As I have studied Mormon history and thought hard about the meaning of Mormon community, I have become convinced that the Japanese philosopher Nishida Kitaro was right when he argued that the nature of reality is contradiction. Contradictions, as we encounter them in history, in theology, in word and in deed, signify that something is real. We sometimes feel disillusioned when we discover imperfection or even corruption within grand enterprises that are supposed to transcend mundane human life. But every revolutionary or inspired project must also be a human project, and human beings are as unreliable and disappointing as they are beautiful and worthwhile.

In another final lecture for a modern Chinese history class, I raised this issue of contradictions. I told my students that when I was a Mormon missionary in Tainan, Taiwan, many years ago, in the early mornings I often went running along a road. The road ran past a rice factory—a huge shed full of bags and bags of rice. As you can imagine, all of that rice in such a big, industrial space attracted rats. The road outside the rice factory was splotched with flattened rats that had been run over by passing cars. The hot sun dried them out, so they kept their shapes, down to little wiggly coils of intestine, perfectly flat, looped out on the blacktop.

One morning I was running along the segment outside the rice factory where there was also a Taiwanese breakfast shop. As I ran past, I was smelling these wonderful smells of shrimp dumplings and scallion pancakes, feeling the cool breeze, feeling a nice clean sweaty feeling, feeling completely joyful about where I was and what I was doing at that moment. Simultaneously, I glanced down and saw that my foot was plunging down onto a big, fat, freshly exploded rat. This experience taught me a lesson: Very few things are all good with no bad, or the other way around. Everything is mixed up together.

As a scholar and as a Latter-day Saint, I don't value tidiness in history and self-definition as much as I used to. In my mind the tensions that complicate the collective execution of divine mandates do not signify that the whole project is a bust, but authentically reflect how children of God strive to make difficult choices.

My first encounter with Richard and Claudia Bushman was when, in 2003, I went to visit them at their home in New York City. I asked them what it was like to be Mormon academics at Columbia. Richard responded, "We're interpreters." This notion of interpretation—moving between languages, cultures, and epistemological paradigms—has helped to define my understanding of a scholar's job ever since.

As historians, our job is to learn to inhabit multiple worlds and to translate between them so that we and others can understand the meaning and worth of the lives of our fellow beings. Today's world of conflict, fragmentation, and polarization needs such interpreters. As people accustomed to traversing spaces in

between, Mormon academics can make an important contribution as they train others to think critically, expansively, and
constructively—to build bridges among people in a world that
difference has made dangerous, wondrous, and divine.

Note

1. John G. Turner, *Brigham Young: Pioneer Prophet* (Cambridge,
   MA: Belknap Press of Harvard University Press, 2012), 156.

SAVING HISTORY
The Perquisites and Perils

KATE HOLBROOK

Stories matter, and they matter in complicated ways. The tradition of the Latter-day Saints attributes salvific qualities to history. Often Latter-day Saints think of history's saving qualities in terms of providing accurate records of events and performing temple ordinances, seen as mandatory for salvation, on behalf of the dead. The first of these ordinances was baptism for the dead, which Joseph Smith initially introduced at the funeral of Seymour Brunson in August 1840. Smith had worried about the fate of those who, like his brother Alvin, died without having been baptized. At Brunson's funeral he explained that church members could be baptized by proxy for their dead ancestors, enabling their entrance into heaven.[1] This is one way the living save the dead.

Do the dead also save the living? Reflecting on baptism for the dead in his journal, Joseph Smith wrote, "For we without them, cannot be made perfect; neither can they, without us, be made perfect."[2] Latter-day Saints acknowledge how the dead save the living through scripture. Written by the dead, scripture teaches the gospel of Jesus Christ, how to build a relationship with God, the commandments, and other teachings necessary for salvation. Here I would like to explore nonscriptural saving voices. When we humans study history, we give our ancestors the opportunity to save us as well—by helping us to feel and to know that we are not alone and by kindling our hope for the future. History can inspire us to action, either to acknowledge and provide a chance for healing from past wrongs or to build on past rights. But for the dead to save us, some of us have to preserve and publish an accurate and inclusive range of their stories, and all of us have to read them.

Family History

When Latter-day Saints do family history, they try to uncover the names of deceased ancestors to perform ordinances for them in the temple. This is the way Latter-day Saints typically think about their relationship with the dead in the work of salvation. The efforts are about justice, the hope that every person ever born will have the opportunity to choose salvation, whether in mortality or thereafter.

Mircea Eliade's work may have fallen out of academic fashion, but LDS temples certainly do fit his description of a holy place where time and space collapse.[3] Temples are a vibrant nexus where past and present, living and dead, and the wishes of both come into sacred alignment. Often family history researchers report feeling guided by the dead in their work. A senior missionary at the Church History Library, for example, feels promptings almost daily as she searches for biographical information about the dead who appear in Church Historian's Press book projects. Temple attendees doing work for the dead similarly feel close to the people they are trying to serve. One LDS woman reported explicitly feeling her deceased father's presence while she was in a temple session. She concluded that her father had taught the person on whose behalf she was performing ordinances.[4] Her sister reported, "[She] had felt Daddy's presence so strongly that she was sure the person she was doing the work for had been taught the gospel by her father." The separation between realms of living and dead attenuates through temple work and through historical research.

Power in Story

The family history researcher I mentioned is not working explicitly to identify names for temple work. She works to provide accurate records of past lives, to preserve and share their names and their deeds. People's stories can offer meaning no matter your religious philosophy. In his biopic of Clive Staples Lewis, screenwriter William Nicholson had Lewis assert, "We read to know that we are not alone."

Many recognize truth in Nicholson's assertion. Others' stories can help us as listeners to make sense of our own lives and experiences; they comfort, instruct, and anchor us. We also find significant meaning in having our stories told. Isak Dinesen wrote a particularly beautiful illustration of a man deeply stirred by the writing of his story. Recalling the time when she would read and write documents for her neighbors in Kenya, who could neither read nor write on their own, she described one man in particular. Jogona Kanyagga was involved in a legal

83

dispute that required he submit a written account of his side of the story. Kanyagga told his account to Dinesen, who read it back to him after writing it down. Hearing a written version of his own experience, Dinesen reported, "he swiftly turned to face me, and gave me a great fierce flaming glance, so exuberant with laughter that it changed the old man into a boy. . . . Such a glance did Adam give the Lord when He formed him out of the dust, and breathed into his nostrils the breath of life, and man became a living soul."[5] Kanyagga fashioned and embroidered a small leather pouch to contain the account, and he wore the pouch around his neck. Occasionally on a Sunday morning, he appeared at Dinesen's door and asked her to read it to him again. After recording the reaction of Kanyagga, Dinesen then took the significance of storytelling a step further. She often experimented with biblical characters and verses in her writing. The following lines invert the biblical formulation of the word and the flesh: "Here was something which Jogona Kanyagga had performed, and which would preserve his name for ever: the flesh was made word and dwelt among us full of grace and truth."[6] The New Testament describes Jesus's birth as "the Word became flesh and made his dwelling among us" (John 1:14). Perhaps Dinesen meant to play with that image of birth. Perhaps she meant to say that making the flesh word is a new way of being and that this new way of being exudes grace and truth. Referencing Christ's birth as she does also links words with salvation. Jesus was not complete without flesh, and we humans are not complete when our life stories go untold. Isak Dinesen and I may not do exactly the same kind of work, but this is the work that historians do, to preserve the names and deeds of those who have come before.

History and Justice

Jogona Kanyagga first turned to the written word in pursuit of legal justice. Historians, too, can be preoccupied with justice. Brett Rushforth feels an ethical obligation to the human subjects of his books, "particularly the enslaved," he emphasizes, "whose lives were spent trying to assert and insist on their full humanity in the face of a brutal attempt to commodify them."[7] In the introduction to a book, he explained the this-worldly justice that such depictions might achieve: "If their lives are useful because they illuminate the systems through which they passed, their value is intrinsic."[8] Rushforth thus suggests that stories can emphasize a narrative that the dead tried to tell, can humanize the dead, and can correct against the institutions and patterns that tyrannized the dead while they lived.

Nineteenth-century Latter-day Saints felt keenly a yearning for historical records to bring justice to aggrieved peoples. While incarcerated in Liberty Jail, Joseph Smith wrote a letter to his followers, asking them to record all that had befallen them, including perpetrators' names. He wanted official statements and affidavits. "It is an imperative duty that we owe to God, to angels, with whom we shall be brought to stand, and also to ourselves, to our wives and children, . . . to the widows and fatherless, whose husbands and fathers have been murdered. . . . And also it is an imperative duty that we owe to all the rising generation, and to all the pure in heart" (Doctrine and Covenants 123:7, 9, 11). In 1830, the same year the church was organized, Smith had announced the creation of the position of church historian, who was "to combat false reports and to convert and edify future generations."[9]

Historical records, in other words, had the potential to heal and redeem Latter-day Saints from the effect of patterns that tyrannized them while they lived. Violence against women in Missouri has recently captured public attention, and the most solid evidence for that violence came from the affidavits of the survivors.[10] Some commentators have imagined that knowledge of nineteenth-century Saints overcoming sexual violence might offer healing for victims today. In recent decades, Mormon historians have also made a concerted effort to tell the stories of those whom Mormons have harmed, most notably through exhaustive investigation of the massacre at Mountain Meadows, Utah, in which local Cedar City church leaders were responsible for the deaths of 120 people travelling through Utah during their emigration from Arkansas to California in 1857.[11] Historians, the Paiute Tribal Council, and The Church of Jesus Christ of Latter-day Saints have also contributed to construction of a monument in Circleville, dedicated April 22, 2016, to acknowledge a massacre by Mormon settlers of approximately thirty Paiute men, women, and children 150 years earlier in 1866. Settlers buried the Paiute dead, and no one was ever tried or punished for the crime.[12] Construction of the monument signifies a commitment to remembering the full details of this incident, the loss of those who died, and the culpability of those who killed them. Accurate records uncover a truer understanding of what has happened that can offer healing and redemption to those affected by past crimes.

How We Tell the Stories Matters

Professional historians who are also members of the LDS Church feel an obligation to the dead they study. Such obligation is by no means exclusive to Mormons. There are historians who believe in life after death, those who believe they might meet the

subjects of their work after death, and those who believe in neither yet still feel a connection and responsibility to those whose
stories they tell. Yet one of the great perils that comes from being not only a historian of Mormons but a Mormon historian is
the specter that we might meet, on the other side, someone we
have written about. Historians are not the only ones who face
this scenario. I have witnessed LDS Church leaders' efforts to
honor their institutional predecessors through their words and
through policy. Our representations of those who came before
is one of the ways we seek to honor the dead. Richard Bushman
has remarked on this stewardship for historians: "Someday we
will meet in heaven the people we write about, and when we do,
we will have to look them in the eye and account for ourselves.
Have we told their story as fairly as we know how? Have we
told their story without distorting it in order to serve our own
agendas?"[13]

Recently, I only narrowly avoided a grave error in the way I
portrayed someone from the past. My colleague Jennifer Reeder
and I have compiled a collection of discourses by Mormon
women to be published by The Church Historian's Press.[14] One
of the essays is by Judy Brummer, a woman born and raised in
South Africa who was the first adept Xhosa-speaking LDS missionary. Brummer also produced early translations of portions
of the Book of Mormon into Xhosa. When she arrived on her
mission, she met a man named Goliat Kowa. Kowa had come
across an LDS pamphlet and, based on it, founded a church
among black Africans that consisted of several congregations.
He took Brummer and other missionaries to these congregations and taught his followers that they needed to be rebaptized
because he had not baptized them by the correct priesthood.
This seemed to me a tremendous sacrifice. As is consonant with

the churches Kowa and his followers would have known, church members provided a living for Kowa and his family. I find it astonishing that he so readily introduced members of his church to missionaries of the official Church of Jesus Christ of Latter-day Saints.

The only space I had to devote to Kowa was a brief footnote. I learned in doing research for that footnote that Kowa left the LDS Church not long after the end of Brummer's mission. Turning to mission records, I read the report of an interview (not a transcript) in which Kowa was represented to have said there should be two churches, a white church and a black church, and he was the prophet for the black church. The report disclosed he had struggled with the idea that tithing should go to church headquarters instead of helping to support his family (who scarcely had enough to eat). He purportedly said that he initially contacted President Spencer W. Kimball only because his church needed money, especially money for drums. And the congregations still did not have drums. This story felt a little incomplete to me, and it puzzled me. Why did he work with white church members for several years before voicing his philosophy about a black church? Why would the man who so readily guided hundreds of believers from his church to the Church of Jesus Christ of Latter-day Saints suddenly leave over the issue of drums? Nonetheless, I wrote a brief footnote, which included his defection from the church and his comment about being the black prophet.

A few weeks later, I met with Judy Brummer to make sure one last time that I had the facts right in the introduction I had written for her discourse. Although I felt dissatisfied with the Kowa footnote, in my mind I thought it was complete, and I did not plan to ask her about it. I had consulted the appropriate records. But while I met with Brummer, my troubled feelings about that footnote increased until I felt compelled to read it to her. Though she had completed her mission before the events reported in the footnote had taken place, she told me that there had been a personality conflict between Kowa and the American person keeping the mission record, the same person who had conducted the final interview with Kowa. She said she did not believe the translation between Kowa and his interviewer had been adequate, so the parties likely did not fully understand each other during their meeting. She told me that Kowa was an exceptionally spiritual and humble person. I still do not know what was actually said or intended in that significant interview with Bishop Kowa, just as the interview participants themselves might not. But I feel I have a truer sense of who Kowa was and how to represent him in a footnote; now that I have changed the footnote, my feelings about it are at rest.

This story I have just described is twenty-five times longer than the footnote. The footnote is a few sentences in a book that will be several hundred pages long. I did not approach all of the footnotes with this degree of intense review. This particular footnote mattered because it was a representation of a life that is not otherwise extensively recorded. Despite the fact that I could not discover all of the details relevant to Kowa's later relationship to the church, I felt I was spiritually guided to craft a representation of him that was truer to who he was. I have come to believe that a crucial aspect of our work as historians is to represent people in ways that are fair, meaning we consider the whole person and not just those aspects that help us prove a favorite point. There is holiness and responsibility in the work of telling a person's story.

How We Tell History Impacts
Whose History Gets Told

In this short paper I have tried to describe exactly how and why our telling stories matters. But in truth more is going on here than I am able to define. I want to emphasize that it is not only how we write about the dead but which dead we write about that matters. We need to write about the dead's whole selves, and we need to write about a wide variety of the dead.

I myself have been deeply affected by Mormon records, in particular while working on *The First Fifty Years of Relief Society*.[15] I came to this project late; half of the book had been written and most of the documents chosen. Coming to it at that stage—and still being able to research, write, edit, and spend time with the people whose stories it tells—created in me a profound sense of the potential of Relief Society work; of the strength, resourcefulness, and dedication of my spiritual ancestors; and of the potential for members of Relief Society today to do God's work and make this world better. The book contains records of a range of women: leaders, followers, writers, and doers. I have now seen that the book also appeals to a range of readers. A friend's mother, neither a scholar nor a reader of history, has been staying up late into the night to read this very scholarly, intensely footnoted tome. My mother's neighbor, also not a habitual reader of history, calls it one of the most spiritual books she has ever read. I think they and I are so affected by these stories not only because they are about women and we are women, but because we have not known women's contributions or read their words to nearly the same extent we have men's. My male colleagues have also been deeply moved by reading the book. We need the histories of all our people, female and male, black and white, purple and green. I believe students of Mormon history will find ourselves transformed as the kinds of history we read and write become more diverse in other ways. The more adeptly we cast our nets of research and writing, and the more inclusively, the better we contribute to a history that saves.

Notes

1. Matthew McBride, "Letters on Baptism for the Dead: D&C 127, 128," in *Revelations in Context: The Stories Behind the Sections of the Doctrine and Covenants*, ed. Matthew McBride and James Goldberg (Salt Lake City: Church of Jesus Christ of Latter-day Saints, 2016), 273.
2. Joseph Smith, "Journal, December 1841–December 1842," p. 199, The Joseph Smith Papers, accessed August 25, 2017, http:// www.josephsmithpapers.org/paper-summary/journal-december -1841-december-1842/76.
3. Mircea Eliade, *The Sacred and the Profane: The Nature of Religion*, trans. Willard R. Trask (New York: Harvest Books, 1959).
4. Kathy Torkelson, "The Role of the Dead in Family History," sacrament meeting talk, Yalecrest Second Ward sacrament meeting, Salt Lake City, January 31, 2016.
5. Isak Dinesen, *Out of Africa* (New York: Modern Library, 1937), 125–26.
6. Dinesen, *Out of Africa*, 126.
7. Brett Rushforth, email message to author, February 23, 2016.
8. Brett Rushforth, *Bonds of Alliance: Indigenous and Atlantic Slaveries in New France* (Chapel Hill: University of North Carolina Press, 2012), 13.

9. Howard C. Searle, "Church Historians," in *Encyclopedia of Mormonism*, http://eom.byu.edu/index.php/Historians,_Church.

10. The 1830s-era affidavits have been published in Clark V. Johnson, ed., *Mormon Redress Petitions: Documents of the 1833–1838 Missouri Conflict* (Provo, UT: Religious Studies Center, Brigham Young University, 1992).

11. Ronald W. Walker, Richard E. Turley Jr., and Glen M. Leonard, *Massacre at Mountain Meadows: An American Tragedy* (Oxford, NY: Oxford University Press, 2008).

12. Dennis Romboy, "New Monument to Honor Paiutes Slain in Circleville Massacre," *Deseret News*, April 14, 2016, http://www.deseretnews.com/.

13. Grant Wacker, "Reckoning with History: Richard Bushman, George Marsden, and the Art of Biography," Smith-Pettit lecture at Mormon History Association, Snowbird, Utah, June 11, 2016.

14. Jennifer Reeder and Kate Holbrook, eds., *At the Pulpit: 185 Years of Discourses by Latter-day Saint Women* (Salt Lake City: Church Historian's Press, 2017).

15. Jill Mulvay Derr et al., eds., *The First Fifty Years of Relief Society: Key Documents in Latter-day Saint Women's History* (Salt Lake City: Church Historian's Press, 2016).

3 | REENVISIONING
MORMONISM

REENVISIONING MORMONISM: LOOKING FORWARD AND LOOKING BACK

Section Introduction

ANN TAVES

The papers in this section make a case for reenvisioning Mormonism from distinctly different disciplinary perspectives—history and theology (Green), philosophy (Miller), and literary criticism (Hickman).

In her paper, Deidre Nicole Green draws on history and feminist theology to ask, first, whether LDS women can act as theologians and, second, why they should. She makes the case that LDS women can act as theologians based on the revelation given to Emma Smith in 1830 that empowered her to exhort, Eliza R. Snow's canonized hymn "O My Father," and the collaboration between Mary Ann Sterns Pratt and her husband Parley P. Pratt on the missionary tract *A Voice of Warning* (1837). Building on this analysis, she turns to the LDS Church's 1995 proclamation on the family, noting that, despite its emphasis on men and women as equal partners with complementary roles and natures, women were not involved in drafting the document. She questions their exclusion, arguing that their presumed complementarity would suggest that both women and men have important insights to contribute. More pointedly, she argues that insofar as all knowledge is situated and partial, truth must be discerned communally, thus requiring greater openness to women's participation in the revelatory process.

In appealing to Mormonism's commitment to gender essentialism to explain why women's theological voice needs to be heard, she follows in the footsteps of nineteenth-century evangelical women who used women's nature as mothers as a basis for extending their sphere of activity from the home to mothering in the world. While she makes a strong case for an expanded role for LDS women within the constraints of current teaching, her paper may leave readers with the sense that there are questions that neither history nor theology are in a position to ask. The next paper opens up a surprising avenue for posing and discussing questions that cannot be asked in the present.

As a philosopher, Adam S. Miller argues that the discipline-specific task of philosophy is to "fram[e] *hypothetical* scenarios" that allow philosophers to "probe, in especially pointed ways, regions of Mormon state space that our present situation and our historical trajectory may have left largely untouched." He conceives Mormonism's "state space"—its virtual body—as the body of Christ. Within this virtual space, he argues, the philosopher can "extrapolate fictional scenarios from available Mormon materials . . . , stage these scenarios in clearly defined conceptual sandboxes, and then use these fictions to probe the shape of the Mormon virtual." As an example, he suggests we imagine a meeting of senior church leaders convened in 2095 to discuss the meaning of the proclamation on the family, a document whose meaning, he imagines, has become increasingly obscure over time. Within this fictional framework, Miller can then have his imaginary church leaders discuss fundamental questions: "What is gender? What does it mean to claim that sexual difference is eternal? How can men and women have gendered responsibilities and, yet, act as 'equal partners'? In short, . . . what is sexual difference and what is sexual equality?" His approach, thus, offers an ingenious way to explore questions that may be off-limits in the present.

Jared Hickman offers us a reading of the Book of Mormon against the backdrop of Charles Taylor's understanding of the secular age as emerging out of the encounter of peoples with diverse cosmologies. Born in the secular age, Hickman argues that the Book of Mormon does not simply react to it but takes advantage of it in new and creative ways. He pushes back against the Christianization of Mormonism that the previous papers seem to presuppose and encourages us to explore its "post-Christian secularity." Hickman does so by placing the Book of Mormon within larger literary critical frames—Taylor's immanent frame and secular age, Benjamin's messianic time, and Derrida's messianicity without messianism—and in doing so he asserts the claim that the Book of Mormon can be taken seriously at the heights of literary theory. If his larger aim as a literary critic is to bring the Book of Mormon into these sophisticated hermeneutic playgrounds, he does so, I think, with an evident desire to overcome the polarized ways in which scholars have responded to the Book of Mormon's treatment of time. Rather than replicate old oppositions between the book as modern fabrication and as miraculously retrieved ancient record, he wants to, as stated in an earlier version of his paper, "draw attention to how unabashedly the text bends temporality, how unembarrassedly integral its anachronism is," and to argue that this makes it worth understanding not as some "dirty little secret" but as a central feature of the text.

Hickman does a brilliant job of connecting the Book of Mormon's collapse of space-time with the discussions of temporality and messianism in Benjamin and Derrida, but I question whether he has grounded the collapse of time in the Book of Mormon as fully as he might in relation to the biblical text. The Christian Bible is premised on a typological relationship between the Old and New Testaments, such that Christians read the Septuagint as prefiguring Jesus as the messianic bearer of the New Covenant. Ever since I read Phil Barlow's *Mormons and the Bible*,[1] I've thought of the Book of Mormon as an effort to make these typological prefigurations more literal by having Christ actually appear to the ancient Israelites. Doing so, I would suggest, creates just the sort of temporal wormholes that Hickman discusses.

The three papers thus take up intersecting themes. Green and Miller both offer ways of reenvisioning the proclamation on the family. Green does so in light of women's history and feminist theology, Miller in light of an imagined future. Hickman, in conversation with Miller's earlier work on the Book of Mormon, engages both past and future in his rereading of the Book of Mormon. In addition to conversations about gender roles in the LDS Church and the Book of Mormon, the papers open up conversation about the interplay of past, present, and future—the role of history, theology, and hermeneutics (literary and philosophical)—in moving forward.

Note

1. Philip L. Barlow, *Mormons and the Bible: The Place of the Latter-day Saints in American Religion*, 2nd ed. (New York: Oxford University Press, 2013).

CHRISTO-FICTION, MORMON PHILOSOPHY, AND THE VIRTUAL BODY OF CHRIST

ADAM S. MILLER

> We do not even know what a body is capable of.
> —Baruch Spinoza

As a philosopher, I'm not primarily interested in what Mormonism was or is. Rather, as a philosopher, I want to know what Mormonism can *do*. What can it think, what can it build, what can it feel, what can it ruin, what can it heal?

To understand a thing we have to understand not just its kernel of actuality or even its line of development but its halo of potential. We have to understand the powers that it habitually commands. In short, we have to grasp the character of its agency. With respect to the future of Mormon studies, this is my thesis: the only way to substantially define Mormonism is to grasp the shape of its power to act and be acted upon. To grasp

Mormonism, we have to connect with it as a power rather than as a thing. We have to grasp it as a verb rather than as a noun.

Consider a pianist. What is a pianist? Clearly, it's not enough to just be shown a person who is a pianist. Rather, the pianist can be understood only when we grasp the shape of her power to act. That is, the pianist is grasped as a pianist only in the performance itself. But even here—and this caveat is crucial—any given piano performance will still trace only one possible path through the topology that defines her whole field of action. The pianist's power to act as a pianist isn't exhausted in the performance of any particular piece. It's not even exhausted in the performance of any number of pieces. Her power to play is broader and deeper than any particular piece or any number of pieces, and it is this power that most essentially defines her as a pianist. This same principle follows, I would argue, with practically everything. Things in general ought to be defined most fundamentally as *the power to be what they are*, rather than simply as what they are. And this is true for everything from quarks to people to C++ to petunias to religious traditions like Mormonism and governmental institutions like the Internal Revenue Service. What's at stake in each case is not just a thing's current state, or even its historical vector, but the topology that defines its field of action as an agent.[1]

For the sake of clarity, let's borrow some language from Manuel DeLanda's *Intensive Science and Virtual Philosophy*.[2] As we've described things, there are three elements in play when it comes to defining Mormonism: (1) the *actual*, (2) the *potential*, and (3) what DeLanda, following Gilles Deleuze, refers to as the *virtual*. We can understand (1) what is actual as the *point* in space occupied by a thing in its present state, (2) what is potential as the *line* or vector that traces and projects the specific trajectory of a thing's past development and future actualization, and (3) what is virtual as the *state space* that defines a thing's manifold of possible states and vectors—a manifold that, by definition, can only ever be partially actualized in narrow slices that, compared to that thing's entire field of action, are exceedingly thin.

As a philosopher, then, what I'm interested in is not just Mormonism's actual position (Mormonism as a point in space), or even Mormonism's potential (Mormonism as a specific temporal vector, historical or projected), but this deeper category that shapes them both. I want to know what Mormonism can do. I want to grasp the virtual state space that maps Mormonism's field of action.

It's helpful, as DeLanda himself does, to describe the virtual as a kind of state space. *State space* is a term of art adapted from the world of engineering. In mathematical models of discrete dynamical systems, state space refers to the set of possible values a given system can generate. DeLanda simply says, "State space is a space of possible states," or again, "State spaces may be viewed as a way of specifying possible worlds for a given physical system, or at least, possible histories for it, each trajectory in the phase portrait representing one possible historical sequence of states for a system or process."[3] In this sense, a state space is a static representation of an agent's dynamic range of action.

In order to capture the defining role played by agency or power in shaping who or what a thing is, we need to define agents not simply in terms of the point in space they currently occupy, or even in terms of the particular vector they're currently following, but in terms of the topology of their state space, a topology that determines the character of both their position and their vector. We have to grasp something deeper than the actual product of an action or even the performance of any particular process resulting in that product. We have to grasp the *power* of performance itself as what defines a thing, a power that is, of course, expressed in products and particular processes but that is in no way limited to them. We have to grasp, in short, the virtual.

Consider the example of a bicycle. As DeLanda indicates, in order to grasp the nature of a bicycle, we'll have to do more than understand the pieces that compose the bicycle, or even an assembled bicycle, or even one particular instance of the bicycle's operation. Say, for example, that we have twelve variable elements in the bicycle's field of possible action and thus a twelve-dimensional state space. Any given instance of the bicycle's operation will involve some specific realization of the possible combinations of those twelve elements (e.g., handlebars, wheels, pedals, gears, seat position). At any given moment, we could represent this combination of elements as a *point* in space. More, we could represent the whole series of combinations through which the bicycle has turned—that is, we could represent the bicycle's history—as a *line* moving through this same space. But in order to represent the bicycle's state space—that is, the full scope of its power as a bicycle—we have to consider the set of all possible combinations of all twelve elements. *This* set is what defines the bicycle's state space. And this, of course, is the virtual. This set defines not just the bicycle's application of power in a particular instance but the shape of the bicycle's power *as a power*.

Now, as a starting point, this kind of mechanical example is useful for illustrating what's involved in the virtual. But in order to better grasp what's at stake in Mormonism's state space, we would be better off working with examples that are fundamentally organic rather than reductively mechanical. Say we take, instead of a bicycle, something like the unfolding of an embryo. In this case, a kind of state space is also in play, a state space that shapes the field of action in which the embryo's power unfolds. But, unlike a bicycle, the organic character of the embryo entails feedback loops that allow for the state space itself to change shape in response to the realization of specific trajectories. That is, in complex scenarios that involve reflexivity and recursivity, a given agent's state space will itself be a moving target, a target that moves and changes shape in response to realized vectors. In other words, in cases involving things like life, language, and consciousness, the virtual must itself be explicitly modeled as dynamic. In cases like this, state spaces will, in turn, have their own state spaces.

Things are getting a little complicated now, but I think you've got the basic idea. Let's leave these descriptions here for the moment and return to the question of Mormonism. What *can* Mormonism do? What is the nature of the virtual that simultaneously defines the field in which Mormonism's actual history, present condition, and future trajectory unfold?

Though this kind of question is itself properly philosophical, to generate answers we'll need to mobilize a host of disciplines in response. History, for instance, is clearly pivotal. Mormonism's past trajectory through its state space will be exhibit A in any attempt to map the shape of that space. But Mormonism is a complex assemblage of only partly compatible and often competing subsets of people, ideas, institutions, texts, real estate investments, and so on, and the more data points we can amass in more disciplines—including theology, literature, sociology, anthropology, religious studies, rhetoric, political theory, economics, and biology—the more the organic and reflexive shape of Mormonism's state space will itself come into focus.

But what, then, of Mormon philosophy? What discipline-specific role would philosophy play in Mormon studies? In my admittedly prescriptive view, philosophy's discipline-specific question is the virtual. Philosophy's job is, first of all, to *pose* the question of the virtual and, then, to rally a collaborative and cross-disciplinary investigation of this question. (This, for example, is quite explicitly the kind of work we do in the Mormon Theology Seminar.)[4]

But, more than this, I think that philosophy also bears a discipline-specific responsibility for framing *hypothetical* scenarios that can force the question of the virtual and then probe, in especially pointed ways, regions of Mormon state space that our present situation and our historical trajectory may have left largely untouched. In this way, it is one of Mormon philosophy's primary responsibilities to hypothesize, speculate, and extrapolate about just what it is that Mormonism can do. What is the Mormon virtual? What are Mormonism's distinctive powers? What centers of gravity most profoundly warp the shape of its state space? More than outlining the bounds of a Mormon actuality (either past or present), philosophy must address the shape of Mormon's power—not just for the sake of some unrealized possibilities but because, as with the pianist, we will never understand even what is actual unless we acquire some feel for the shape of the virtual power that performatively gives actuality itself.

As a practical matter, I think this means that much of Mormon philosophy should be frequently and explicitly conducted as a brand of fiction. Mormon philosophy should extrapolate fictional scenarios from available Mormon materials (perhaps especially Mormon scripture), stage these scenarios in clearly defined conceptual sandboxes, and then use these fictions to probe the shape of the Mormon virtual.

On this score, we might see this particular element of Mormon philosophy as being similar, in many respects, to something like hard science fiction. As Steven Shaviro argues in *Discognition*, hard "science fiction is a special kind of literature," one "that operates through *speculation* and *extrapolation*, and that takes place (conceptually if not grammatically) in the future tense."[5] Hard science fiction constructively estranges us from the actuality of what seems obvious in the present moment by displacing us into a skewed but adjacent future. This kind of estrangement from our present actuality is a powerful tool for bringing the virtual into view.

Marilynne Robinson makes a similar point in her collection of essays, *The Givenness of Things*. Think of fiction, she says, "as a small model of the simulacrum of reality that is given to us by sense and perception, and as a way to probe anomalies that emerge in the assumed world when it is under scrutiny."[6] Such anomalies, emerging in our assumed worlds, are evidence that reality is broader and deeper than what is actual, and probing this unfamiliar terrain with "small models" and "simulacra" can help trace the shape of this virtual space. We might think of philosophy, then, as an attempt to "fling some ingenious mock sensorium out into the cosmos so that it can report back what it finds there."[7]

Practicing fiction for the sake of mapping the virtual state space that defines the shape of Mormonism as a power and not just as a thing (even a historical thing), philosophy engages in a version of what the contemporary French philosopher François Laruelle calls "christo-fiction."[8] Christo-fiction is a style of speculative inquiry that actively refuses to identify the entity under investigation with its current actuality (or even its traceable vector) in order to, instead, attend to the shape of the state space that gives both. Suspending the assumption that the actual is sufficient to define a thing, christo-fiction is, in this case, an attempt to view both the actuality and potentiality of Mormonism as the expression of an underlying virtuality that, I would argue, we might properly call *the body of Christ*. As a Mormon philosopher probing the nature of Mormonism's state space, I make this my working hypothesis: the body of Christ is Mormonism's virtual body. Christo-fiction, then, is an apt name for the philosophical work of extrapolating fictional scenarios in rigorously constructed conceptual sandboxes in order to bring this Christic state space more clearly into view.

Before closing, let me offer just one example of a christo-fiction to illustrate how such a fiction might illuminate what Mormonism can do. This example is drawn from an actual (though nascent) project that Rosalynde Welch and I are currently assembling.

In 1995 the Church of Jesus Christ of Latter-day Saints first published its landmark statement "The Family: A Proclamation to the World." Sensing an imminent sea change in the Western world's commonly accepted definitions of marriage, family, and gender, church leaders introduced the proclamation in order to clarify and codify its own theological and political positions on these issues. A novel and striking document, the proclamation declares that men and women are created in the image of heavenly parents, that gender is an essential characteristic of eternal identity, that salvation is inextricably tied to marriage and family life, and that men and women, despite differences in their divinely assigned roles, must work as equal partners.

Consider, then, the following christo-fiction. Imagine that one hundred years has passed. The year is 2095 and the proclamation has now been officially canonized for more than sixty years. In this future church, the proclamation has been enshrined as the cornerstone of a Mormon account of life in Christ. But now, framed by a century of social and political upheaval, the document's original sense has also become increasingly obscure. Commonsense definitions of key terms like *gender*, definitions taken for granted as obvious and incontestable by its original authors, are no longer common or obvious. A whole generation of senior church leaders—all born decades after the proclamation's introduction and educated in a world where the predicted sea change in sexual mores and family structures was a fait accompli—are left to wonder exactly what the church itself means by "gender." What is gender? What does it mean to claim that sexual difference is eternal? How can men and women have gendered responsibilities and, yet, act as "equal partners"? In short, senior leaders are forced to ask, What is sexual difference, and what is sexual equality? Recognizing that answers to such questions must now be actively constructed rather than passively assumed, church leaders decide to draw on Mormonism's long acknowledged (but, as a practical matter, never actually decisive) theological commitment to a radical materialism.

Working within this christo-fictional frame, Welch and I then propose a rigorous philosophical model for a radical materialism and attempt to extrapolate what answers to these kinds of questions might look like. If this scenario unfolded and we worked within these conceptual constraints, what would result? What particular states—that is, what particular paths through the state of space of Christ's virtual body—might Mormonism trace? And, in particular, what might these speculative paths reveal about the shape of the state space that even today, here and now, gives and defines both our Mormon present and our Mormon past?

This is just one example—one that I cannot do more than loosely frame here. But it seems to me that asking these kinds of questions, with these kinds of methods and toward these kinds of ends, will define the future of our work in Mormon philosophy and, ultimately, may help redefine what we think it means to be engaged in Mormon studies in general.

Notes

1. Clearly I'm using the terms *agent* and *agency* here in a very broad sense that refers to a thing's power to act or be acted upon, and this approach does not require consciousness or even sentience for something to be an agent.
2. Manuel DeLanda, *Intensive Science and Virtual Philosophy* (London: Continuum, 2002).
3. DeLanda, *Intensive Science*, 27, 32.
4. See http://www.mormontheologyseminar.org.
5. Steven Shaviro, *Discognition* (London: Repeater, 2016), 8.
6. Marilynne Robinson, *The Givenness of Things: Essays* (New York: Farrar, Straus, and Giroux, 2015), 219.
7. Robinson, *Givenness of Things*, 220.
8. François Laruelle, *Christo-Fiction: The Ruins of Athens and Jerusalem*, trans. Robin Mackay (New York: Columbia University Press, 2015).

BECOMING EQUAL PARTNERS
Latter-day Saint Women as Theologians

DEIDRE NICOLE GREEN

Becoming Equal Partners

"For too long in the Church, the men have been the theologians while the women have been the Christians,"[1] assert Bruce C. Hafen of the Quorum of the Seventy and his wife, Marie Hafen, in a 2007 *Ensign* article. In order to become equal partners, they hold, "each should be both a theologian *and* a Christian."[2] According to the Hafens, women are to teach and interpret doctrine at least within the limits of their own marriages. They illustrate what they mean by women acting as theologians within their marriages: when Neal A. Maxwell wanted to succumb to his battle with cancer, his wife urged him to continue to fight his illness on the grounds that Christ *first* pled with God for his life and *then* submitted to his will. Both the notion of theology and the domestic sphere to which the Hafens circumscribe it are limited, but the call for LDS women to be theologians inspires two questions: first, *can* women's theological influence expand beyond the domestic sphere? and second, *why* should LDS women act as theologians? To answer the first question, I will touch upon some moments in church history, and to answer the second, I will look at LDS perspectives in light of feminist philosophy and theology in order to illuminate possibilities for transformation.

Understanding "Theology"

Theology is generally defined as "language or discourse about God" employed in a "methodical attempt to understand God's divine revelation."[3] Philosopher James Faulconer contends that due to its atheological character, Mormon religious understanding includes "revelation, ordinance, scripture, history, and practice," privileging these over "reason and conception."[4] For Faulconer, "revelation is *the* Latter-day Saint theology."[5] This expansive usage of the term informs my discussion of historical and canonical considerations about LDS women's ability to become men's equal partners as theologians.

Women and Theology in LDS Doctrine and History

Latter-day Saint scripture offers an even stronger sense of women's authority to theologize than that which the Hafens present. In the 1830 revelation given to Emma Smith, now known as Doctrine and Covenants 25, she was promised: "Thou shalt be ordained under his [Joseph's] hand to expound scriptures, and to exhort the church, according as it shall be given thee by my Spirit" (D&C 25:7). Significantly, section 24 gives Joseph Smith and Oliver Cowdery the same instruction,[6] suggesting a parity between Joseph and Emma, as husband and wife, with respect to these particular ecclesiastical functions. At the time, the word *expound* meant "to explain; to lay open the meaning; to clear of obscurity; to interpret; as, to *expound* a text of scripture; to *expound* a law."[7] It included explaining the significance of such things as dreams, visions, and symbols.[8] The appellation of "ex-horter" was given to nineteenth-century Methodist women in order to convey a kind of equality with male preachers, allowing them to be practical counterparts without going so far as to share the title[9] or political equivalence.[10] This revelation extends to Emma the authority to instruct the church,[11] as her calling, like Joseph's, was "unto them" (D&C 25:9). Although the *extent* to which Emma used this authority remains a question, it is at least extended to her in LDS scripture.[12] Others, such as Eliza R. Snow, exemplify how such authority might be used.

Snow presented doctrine to the entire church by authoring a poem now known as the hymn "O My Father."[13] Explicitly employing rational reflection, the poem reasons: "In the heav'ns are parents single? / No, the thought makes reason stare; / Truth is reason—truth eternal / Tells me I've a mother there."[14] Snow articulates the doctrine of a female deity by theologizing in a more traditional mode unaided by revelation, yet it was later endorsed as a revelation to the church.

Although Snow was the first to publicly discuss a maternal deity, whether it was her original teaching is debated. LDS Historian Jill Mulvay Derr points out that there is no mention of Mother in Heaven in the writings or recorded discourses of Joseph Smith,[15] yet Susa Young Gates recorded much later, in 1911, that it was Smith that taught the doctrine to Zina Diantha Huntington Young when her mother died. He promised Zina that when she died she would be reunited not only with her deceased mother but also with her Mother in Heaven. According to Gates's record, Smith asked rhetorically, "How could a Father claim His title unless there were also a Mother to share that parenthood?"[16] The deduction attributed to Smith is reflected in Snow's choice of language: it is a claim to reason, rather than revelation, about God.

Despite the debate over who introduced the doctrine, it remains that the hymn offers a distinct contribution to the LDS theological tradition. Even if Smith taught the doctrine as recorded by Gates, Snow goes beyond positing the *existence* of a Heavenly Mother by ascribing to her an agentic role in judgment. The hymn implores *both* female and male divine beings to grant salvation: "Then, at length, when I've completed / All you sent me forth to do, / With your *mutual* approbation / Let me come and dwell with you."[17] Whether Snow was the originator of the idea or was expanding on Smith's revelation, she clearly expounded LDS thought by working to understand and explain revelation.[18] Moreover, she would have been doing so in conjunction with her husband.

Snow's ability to receive revelation—independent of her husband—was later endorsed by the church's highest authority. Emphasizing Snow's hymn as the product of revelation rather than reason, President Wilford Woodruff spoke about "O My Father" in general conference: "That hymn is a revelation, though it was given unto us by a woman—Sister Snow. There are a great many sisters who have the spirit of revelation. There is no reason why they should not be inspired as well as men."[19] In this assertion, Woodruff makes clear that women can introduce new doctrine to the church.[20] Subsequently, Joseph F. Smith, a counselor in the First Presidency, dissented from this view, declaring in a stake conference that Snow merely put Smith's teachings into verse. He taught that as a woman Snow could not have received the revelation directly but must have learned it from her husband, who held the priesthood.[21] This follows from an idea that Brigham Young had taught previously, namely, that women's ability to access divinely revealed truths was mediated by husbands holding the priesthood.[22] These contradictory statements seek to smooth over the paradoxical tension of promises made to women concerning their access to revelation and men's priesthood authority, constricting the sphere of women's theological authority more than was necessary.

A less ambiguous example of a woman's doctrinal influence carrying beyond her domestic sphere comes from the life of Mary Ann Sterns Pratt, wife of Parley P. Pratt. Her daughter records that while authoring *A Voice of Warning* (1837), the principal missionary tract for most of the nineteenth century and one of the most influential pieces of Mormon theology,[23] Pratt read his reflections aloud to his wife, who then offered suggestions for the text.[24] Her daughter describes both wife and husband as authors of the tract, highlighting that "*they* were writing a book about the gospel."[25] This example of the Pratts' coauthoring a major piece of Mormon theology, like Emma's commission to exhort and expound and Snow's presentation—or formulation—of the concept of Mother in Heaven, demonstrates a potential way for women to act in parity with men as theologians, exercising a collaborative influence that would extend beyond the domestic sphere.[26] Attempts to have women's contributions remain unacknowledged, however, has impeded the realization of this potential.

The Proclamation: Excluding and Essentializing Women

The language about becoming equal partners, which the Hafens use to explain why women should act as theologians, comes from the 1995 document "The Family: A Proclamation to the World." It declares that within the family mothers and fathers are "obligated to help one another as equal partners."[27] Despite its internal claim to parity between women and men,[28] female leaders did not play a role in the formulation of the document in a way that fits a collaborative model.[29] Yet its very assertion of the essential nature of women suggests the importance of women's perspectives and voices in its construction. The proclamation on the family states that gender is "an essential characteristic of individual premortal, mortal, and eternal identity and purpose." Later elaborations assert that gender "in large measure defines who we are, why we are here upon the earth, and what we are to do and become" and that "male and female spirits are different, distinctive, and complementary."[30] In addition to defining gender as essential, the proclamation on the family prescribes corresponding roles. Feminist philosophers and theologians offer insight as to why claims about the essential nature of gender might be read not as a reason to exclude women from theologizing but as a way of understanding why their theologizing proves beneficial for all.

Why Women Need to Do Theology: Insights from Feminist Scholarship

Feminist theology reconfigures language and concepts by drawing from women's experience as a source of authority. That is to say, women's experience is not ancillary to, but rather foundational for, the articulation of theology. Most feminist theologians affirm women's experience as a starting place for theology that influences their understanding and interpretation of God's revelation both past and present.[31] Lifting up women's experience seems fitting of an LDS framework, in which revelation and doctrine often derive from questions that arise from embodied encounters with the world.

Moreover, the combination of LDS beliefs in both gender essentialism and revelation might expand rather than contract women's authority to speak about God. Numerous feminist scholars argue that all knowledge is itself gendered because individual perspectives on the world cannot transcend the sexed body. The limitations of the body entail that all individual knowledge is particular, situated, and therefore partial. The inability to transcend sexed, embodied ways of being in the world, a view reified in the proclamation, underscores the need for women to contribute to their epistemic communities in order to enhance the knowledge base of those communities.

Constructing standards of responsible cognitive practice so that participating is empowering for *all* members of the community requires recognition that any account of what it means to be a knower is provisional.[32] The provisional nature of knowledge resonates with Mormonism given its openness to continuing revelation and suggests that knowledge of religious truth may in some respects require community. Donna Haraway argues that because all knowledge is situated and partial, individual objective knowledge is not possible. From her perspective, knowledge "can never be a relation between one knower and the entire world, for one knower is never located in relation to the entire world."[33] From this we can infer that the full participation of each member in the collective epistemic community in a collective approach would better approximate objective and complete truth. Such a view need not revise the structure of revelation within Mormonism but can inform a more sympathetic approach to persons who have different embodied experiences when one seeks revelation.

Envisioning communal establishment of truth is fitting LDS theology, which understands deity both as embodied female and male and as existing always already in community. It further complements the canonical conjunction to empathize with other members of the ecclesiastical community (Mosiah 18:8–9). Haraway offers a model for a communal approach to knowledge that includes "elaborate specificity and difference and the loving care people might take to learn how to see faithfully from another's point of view."[34] Faithful and empathic attention to various types of embodied experience serves the diverse Latter-day Saint community in its quest both to attend to the needs of each member of the community and to attain a fullness of truth.

Women's Authority and Epistemic Confidence

The work of feminist scholarship shows that structural organization must facilitate women's contribution to a collective body of knowledge. According to feminist scholars, one can meaningfully contribute to the community *only if* one is recognized as epistemically authoritative by that community. Although one can apprehend the knowledge claims of an epistemological community without being acknowledged as a member of it, recognition is required in order to contribute to the production of the community's knowledge claims.[35] For this reason, epistemological communities must be constructed in such a way that they both depend on and foster the flourishing of their members.[36] The foregoing discussion of Latter-day Saint women evinces a sense of this sort of epistemic authority, which was promised to Emma Smith and exemplified in the lives of Eliza R. Snow and Mary Ann Sterns Pratt.

These nineteenth-century examples intimate that LDS women felt confident as women to participate in some aspects of theological discourse that would otherwise remain restricted to an exclusively male domain. Their involvement suggests a potential for women's participation in LDS theology that has not yet been fully realized. Illuminating the necessity of gendered epistemic confidence for women, philosopher of religion Pamela Sue Anderson argues that although women have the capacity for cognitive certainty and credibility, they lack epistemic and ethical confidence as a result of their social situation and standing.[37] She observes that the "I can" necessary for woman's epistemic confidence is "inhibited by the gendered formation of human incarnation."[38] I argue that to exclude women from authoritatively speaking about theology is to undermine their epistemic and ethical confidence in debilitating ways.

Such exclusion limits their participation in the ecclesiastical community and extends further to undermine their confidence in other areas, including their trust in their own personal revelation, their own reason, and their own ability to positively influence others. Observing this problem, former first counselor in the Relief Society General Presidency Chieko N. Okazaki reflects, "Wherever I go, I think that [women] already know their place. . . . When women get the message that their job is to be supportive and just agree" with male leaders, they "become clams."[39] Relatedly, Neylan McBaine asserts that Latter-day

Saints collectively "have to overcome the deep-seated cultural bias" that women's words apply only to women.[40] This shift requires acknowledging women's authority to know. This is because one must have authority in the relevant domain in order for one's words to be able to have real impact on one's community.[41]

To ameliorate this problem of failing to acknowledge women's spiritual and epistemic authority, women and men must know who they are and what authority they possess. Cathy Chamberlain predicts that when women "come to really understand who they are, they will understand their role and what they came here to do."[42] In order to be truly efficacious, this self-understanding must be rooted in LDS doctrine and theology rather than in external sources, thereby facilitating the church's becoming a space where women's voices and ideas are valued as being equal to those of men. Former president of the Quorum of the Twelve Apostles Boyd K. Packer's frequently recited perspective on privileging doctrine over the social sciences in shifting behavior proves relevant on this point: "True doctrine, understood, changes attitudes and behavior."[43] This shift in women's self-understanding will be even more fruitful as women collaborate in delineating their own conception of their natures and roles.

It is likely that the epistemic confidence that emboldens women to define themselves and articulate doctrine will only increase within the church given recent changes in policies regarding women, such as the lowered age requirement for women serving missions.[44] One local leader who instituted a practice of assigning young women to visit teach as preparation for missionary service observes, "There is the opportunity and the responsibility now for everybody to be a preacher and a theologian."[45] Former Church Public Affairs director Michael Otterson anticipated that the insurgence of female missionaries after the lowered age requirement would result in an "injection of really theologically well-trained women."[46] Such theological training is imperative in light of Boyd K. Packer's declaration that the responsibility to maintain "the integrity of the doctrine, the ordinances, the covenants, indeed the future of the Church, rests equally upon women."[47] As women increasingly feel confident in their knowledge of LDS doctrine, appropriate it, and assume the authority both to teach and shape it, they can better fulfill the imperative given to them by Russell M. Nelson, President of the Quorum of the Twelve Apostles, to "speak with the power and authority of God!"[48] In order to maximize this potential, Latter-day Saints must collectively seek to understand what this power and authority entails.

Conclusion

In conclusion, the question of whether women can act as theologians beyond their homes and the question of why they should do so remain contentious ones. In answer to the first question, I have argued that church doctrine and historical practice affirm women's ability to theologize in a broader sphere, at least in conjunction with their husbands. In Joseph Smith's vision of the church, women's authority did not necessarily challenge patriarchal authority but could harmonize with it. In answer to the second question, I have argued that the Latter-day Saint position on the essential nature of gender, which limits embodied experience and therefore knowledge, combined with its commitment to receiving a fullness of truth as a result of continuous revelation, points to the need for women to contribute to the epistemic community.

The church can enhance LDS women's ability to respond positively to the prophetic calls of contemporary leaders by providing a context that engenders confidence in their own authority and ability to know. Circumscribing women's experience and then discounting its significance as a meaningful place from which to construct theology in their own voices undermines women's confidence as epistemic and ethical agents, thereby effectively hindering the progress of the entire LDS community. As women claim their authority to know and speak, they can contribute more fully to the defining of their own natures and roles. Echoing Relief Society General President Linda K. Burton, who anticipates that the church will benefit as "men's vision of the capacity of women becomes more complete,"[49] I hold that there is space within Mormonism for women to claim greater theological authority within the current ecclesiastical structure. To fully develop this potential will require us to reevaluate the very nature of women, and women's self-understanding is a critical component in this. Including women's ability to know and to theologize with authority will allow women—and the church as a whole—to fulfill Joseph Smith's vision for the church and their commission to speak with the power of God and safeguard the integrity of Latter-day Saint doctrine.

Notes

1. Bruce C. Hafen and Marie K. Hafen, "Crossing Thresholds and Becoming Equal Partners," *Ensign*, August 2007, 27.

2. Hafen and Hafen, "Crossing Thresholds," 27.

3. *Westminster Dictionary of Theological Terms*, ed. Donald K. McKim (Louisville, KY: Westminster John Knox Press, 1996), s.v. "theology."

4. James E. Faulconer, "Why a Mormon Won't Drink Coffee but Might Have a Coke: The Atheological Character of The Church of Jesus Christ of Latter-day Saints," *Element* 2 (Fall 2006): 28.

5. James E. Faulconer, "Rethinking Theology: The Shadow of the Apocalypse," in *Faith, Philosophy, Scripture* (Provo, UT: Neal A. Maxwell Institute for Religious Scholarship, 2010), 115.

6. The calling to expound scriptures elevates Emma Smith's role in relation to LDS thought even further given that a contemporaneous revelation directed to Joseph Smith and Oliver Cowdery, first and second elders of the church, respectively, prescribes their ecclesiastical responsibility using the very same language: "And thou shalt continue . . . expounding all scriptures unto the church" (D&C 24:5).

7. Noah Webster, *An American Dictionary of the English Language* (New York: S. Converse, 1828), s.v. "expound."

8. *Oxford English Dictionary*, 2nd ed. (1989), s.v. "expound, v."; online version June 2012 (Oxford University Press, 2012). Earlier version first published in *New English Dictionary* (1894), accessed September 6, 2012, http://www.oed.com/. The OED gives examples of such usage of the word "expound" from 1375 to 1815.

9. Within Methodism, both men and women could be exhorters, which meant that they served in a lay position that assisted the preacher. John Wigger observes that joining Methodism was exciting for women, "expanding the horizons of their world." He notes that within Methodism, women and men were intended to work in tandem and that while women were rarely ever allowed to preach, a small yet significant group served as "gifted exhorters." Wigger

explains that it was a very thin line that separated Methodist exhorters from Methodist preachers, and he speculates, "Methodist
female exhorters undoubtedly used their public speaking opportunities to preach what were, in effect, sermons. In New England
in particular, Methodist female preachers/exhorters were much
like other female preachers among the Baptists, Christians, and
smaller sects during the years 1780–1830." John H. Wigger, *Taking
Heaven by Storm: Methodism and the Rise of Popular Christianity
in America* (Urbana: University of Illinois Press, 1998), 151–52.
The revelation known as Doctrine and Covenants 25 may imply that
Emma was intended to assist Joseph Smith in his role as leader of
the church, but the fact that the same title is given to Joseph Smith
and Oliver Cowdery in Doctrine and Covenants 24 complicates
that reading on my view.

10. Catherine A. Brekus explains the nineteenth-century understand-
    ing of what it meant for women to be called exhorters: "Like
    eighteenth-century Separates and Baptists, they never suggested
    that women were *politically* equal to men, but they still argued
    that women could speak in the informal public of the church."
    Catherine A. Brekus, *Strangers and Pilgrims: Female Preaching in
    America, 1740–1845* (Chapel Hill: University of North Carolina
    Press, 1998), 127.

11. Historian Mark L. Staker emphasizes the hortatory, rather than
    administrative, authority extended to Emma Smith: "Emma's call
    and ordination seemed to be one of gospel instruction, much like
    that of a Methodist class leader, rather than administrative re-
    sponsibility over members. Her promise that she would receive
    the Holy Ghost by the laying on of hands, a promise made the
    month following her confirmation as a member of the Church,
    seemed, however, to fit the promise given to teachers they would
    be 'ordained by the power of the Holy Ghost' (D&C 20:60)." Mark

Lyman Staker, *Hearken, O Ye People: The Historical Setting of Joseph Smith's Ohio Revelations* (Salt Lake City: Kofford Books, 2009), 112.

12. The original text of this revelation reads "thou needest not fear for thy husband shall support thee from the church for unto them is thy calling." The text was later emended to read "for unto them is his calling" ("27th Commandment AD 1830," in *Revelation Book 1*, pp. 34–35, in Michael Hubbard MacKay et al., eds., *Documents, Volume 1: July 1828–June 1831*, vol. 1 of the Documents series of *The Joseph Smith Papers*, ed. Dean C. Jessee et al. [Salt Lake City: Church Historian's Press, 2013], 161–64).

13. The poem first appeared in *Times and Seasons*, November 15, 1845. Jill Mulvay Derr, "The Significance of 'O My Father' in the Personal Journey of Eliza R. Snow," *BYU Studies* 36/1 (1996–97): 86.

14. Derr, "Significance of 'O My Father,'" 96.

15. Derr, "Significance of 'O My Father,'" 98.

16. Derr, "Significance of 'O My Father,'" 99.

17. "O My Father," *Hymns*, no. 292, verse 4, emphasis added.

18. Susa Young Gates, corresponding secretary of the Relief Society Presidency, makes the equality of Heavenly Mother even more explicit when she asserts that "the divine Mother, side by side with the divine Father, [has] the equal sharing of equal rights, privileges and responsibilities." Susa Young Gates, "The Vision Beautiful," *Improvement Era* 23 (April 1920): 542.

19. "Discourse by Wilford Woodruff, October 8, 1893 (in Salt Lake)," *Millennial Star* 56 (April 9, 1894): 229; also in *The Discourses of Wilford Woodruff*, ed. G. Homer Durham (Salt Lake City: Bookcraft, 1969), 61–62; quoted in Derr, "Significance of 'O My Father,'" 98.

20. Such a view is well-grounded in the LDS canon, with such passages as Alma's declaration that God "imparteth his word by angels unto men, yea, not only men but women also" (Alma 32:23).

21. Joseph F. Smith asserts that "God revealed that principle to Joseph Smith; Joseph Smith revealed it to Eliza Snow Smith, his wife; and Eliza Snow was inspired, being a poet, to put it into verse." Joseph F. Smith, "Discourse," *Deseret Evening News*, February 9, 1895. Reported by Arthur Winter from Oneida Stake Conference, Franklin, Idaho, Sunday Afternoon, January 20, 1895. It is important to note that this statement was made during the time of the Manifesto ending polygamy, a time of great strife for the church in its relation to American society and a time when it was critical to establish lines of authority, organization, and solidarity.

22. Brigham Young articulated a view similar to that of Joseph F. Smith, unequivocally declaring women's secondary status and dependence upon their husbands for religious knowledge. "God never in any age of the world endowed woman with knowledge above the man and when a woman has in any instance a message from God to man 'tis because of the Priesthood." Recorded in the journal of Martha Spence Heywood: *Not by Bread Alone: The Journal of Martha Spence Heywood, 1850–56*, ed. Juanita Brooks (Salt Lake City: Utah State Historical Society, 1978), 122; cited in Derr, "Significance of 'O My Father,'" 104.

23. Gregory K. Armstrong, Matthew J. Grow, and Dennis J. Siler assert that although he has received little scholarly attention, Parley P. Pratt profoundly shaped nineteenth-century Mormon thought. They further state that his missionary tract, *A Voice of Warning*, was "the most widely read Latter-day Saint book outside of the scriptures during the first few generations of Mormonism." "Introduction," *Parley P. Pratt and the Making of Mormonism*, eds. Gregory K. Armstrong, Matthew J. Grow, and Dennis J. Siler (Norman, OK: Arthur H. Clark Company, 2011), 11–13. Annie Clark Tanner attests the significance of Pratt's text in her autobiography by positioning it alongside the LDS canon: "Belief in the theologi-

cal doctrine was more emphasized in the Church, at that time [in the 1850s]. . . . We had every encouragement to read the Church publications: *The Voice of Warning; The Pearl of Great Price*; and *Key to Theology*." Annie Clark Tanner, *A Mormon Mother: An Autobiography* (Salt Lake City: Tanner Trust Fund, 1991), 12, 14.

24. Parley P. Pratt, *A Voice of Warning and Instruction to All People, Containing a Declaration of the Faith and Doctrine of the Church of the Latter Day Saints, Commonly Called Mormons* (New York: W. Sandford, 1837).

25. Mary Ann Stearns Winters, "An Autobiographical Sketch of the Life of the Late Mary Ann Stearns Winters, Daughter of Mary Ann Sterns Pratt" (stepdaughter of Parley P. Pratt), 1833–1912, MS 119, reminiscences, n.d., Church History Library, Salt Lake City, emphasis added. Typescript from original in possession of Elizabeth Bennett Winters.

26. I make this point about collaborative efforts made in parity on the grounds that Joseph's and Emma's calls to exhort and expound appear to be equal and on the grounds that Snow and Joseph may have worked together in presenting and revealing the doctrine of Heavenly Mother.

27. "The Family: A Proclamation to the World," https://www.lds.org/topics/family-proclamation?lang=eng&old=true.

28. For more discussion on the collaborative structure of Mormonism, see Fiona Givens, "'The Perfect Union of Man and Woman': Reclamation and Collaboration in Joseph Smith's Theology Making," *Dialogue: A Journal of Mormon Thought* 49 (Spring 2016): 1–26.

29. Chieko N. Okazaki describes the Relief Society General Presidency being called to a meeting at which the proclamation, which was "all finished," was read. The Relief Society General Presidency was consulted as to whether the proclamation should be presented at the general women's session or at the general priesthood session

of general conference. Okazaki recounts her reaction: "It didn't matter to me where it was presented. What I wanted to know was, 'How come we weren't consulted?'" Chieko Nishimura Okazaki, "There Is Always a Struggle," in *Mormon Feminism: Essential Writings*, ed. Joanna Brooks, Rachel Hunt Steenblik, and Hannah Wheelwright (Oxford: Oxford University Press, 2016), 235.

30. David A. Bednar, "Marriage Is Essential to His Eternal Plan," *Ensign*, June 2006, 83.

31. Arnfríður Guðmundsdóttir, *Meeting God on the Cross: Christ, the Cross, and the Feminist Critique* (Oxford: Oxford University Press, 2010), 13.

32. Lorraine Code, *What Can She Know? Feminist Theory and the Construction of Knowledge* (Ithaca, NY: Cornell University Press, 1991), 270.

33. Lucy Tatman, *Knowledge that Matters* (New York: Sheffield Academic Press, 2001), 112.

34. Donna Haraway, "Situated Knowledges: The Science Question in Feminism and the Privilege of Partial Perspective," *Feminist Studies* 14 (Autumn 1988): 583.

35. Lucy Tatman, *Knowledge that Matters*, 129, emphasis added.

36. Code, *What Can She Know?*, 276.

37. Pamela Sue Anderson, "The Lived Body, Gender and Confidence" in *New Topics in Feminist Philosophy of Religion: Contestations and Transcendence Incarnate*, ed. Pamela Sue Anderson (New York: Springer, 2010), 172–73, 175.

38. Anderson, "The Lived Body, Gender and Confidence," 173.

39. Chieko N. Okazaki, "'There Is Always a Struggle': An Interview with Chieko N. Okazaki," *Dialogue* 45 (Spring 2012): 136.

40. Neylan McBaine, *Women at Church: Magnifying LDS Women's Local Impact* (Salt Lake City: Kofford Books, 2014), 151.

41. Rae Langton, "Speech Acts and Unspeakable Acts," *Philosophy*

and Public Affairs 22 (Autumn 1993): 325.

42. Jamshid Ghazi Askar, "Common Myths about Mormon Women: Cathy Chamberlain speaks to the LDS Business Conference," *Deseret News*, April 9, 2011, http://www.deseretnews.com/.

43. Boyd K. Packer, "Little Children," *Ensign*, November 1986.

44. The presence and visibility of LDS female leaders on the BYU Board of Trustees and to three high-level councils—namely, the Priesthood and Family Executive Council, the Missionary Executive Council, and the Temple and Family History Executive Council—is also a step toward increasing women's sense of authority. Yet Peggy Fletcher Stack notes that women remain absent from the church's Correlation Executive Committee, which is responsible for reviewing manuals, hymns, software, and various other materials distributed to the membership of the church. Peggy Fletcher Stack, "At Least One Key Mormon Committee Still Lacks Women," *The Salt Lake Tribune*, August 21, 2015, http://www.sltrib.com/.

45. McBaine, *Women at Church*, 140.

46. Jodi Kantor and Laurie Goodstein, "Missions Signal a Growing Role for Mormon Women," *New York Times*, March 1, 2014, http://www.nytimes.com/.

47. Boyd K. Packer, "The Relief Society," *Ensign*, May 1998.

48. Russell M. Nelson, "A Plea to My Sisters," *Ensign*, November 2015.

49. Kantor and Goodstein, "Missions Signal a Growing Role."

THE PERVERSE CORE
OF MORMONISM

The Book of Mormon, Genetic Secularity,
and Messianic Decoloniality

JARED HICKMAN

My aim is to further my previous work on the Book of Mormon toward exposing what I will call the perverse core of Mormonism.[1] This rubric echoes the Slovenian theorist Slavoj Žižek's recent defense of "the Christian legacy."[2] In a nutshell, Žižek offers a counterintuitive Marxist response to the "Christian and other fundamentalisms" and "New Age spiritualisms" that, by his account, plague contemporary society.[3] Žižek refuses the "obvious answer"—that the Marxist should "ferociously . . . attack these [fundamentalisms and spiritualisms]" and, furthermore, "mercilessly denounce the remainders of the religious legacy within Marxism itself." Instead, he suggests Marxists affirm that "there *is* a direct lineage from Christianity to Marxism; [that] Christianity and Marxism *should* fight on the same side of the barricade against the onslaught of new spiritualisms."[4] Through a series of dialectical turns, Žižek ends up arguing that

Christianity harbors in its "perverse core" what might seem to be its exact opposite—the atheistic materialism of Marx.[5] As he puts it, "When Christ dies, what dies with him is the secret hope discernible in 'Father, why hast thou forsaken me?': the hope that there is a father who has abandoned me. The 'Holy Spirit' is the community deprived of its support in the big Other," which is to say, a human community tasked with the revolutionary transformation of its material conditions.[6] Hence, Žižek finds himself defending Christian orthodoxy because he understands it as an indispensable resource and feeder for the Marxism he prizes.

In a similar fashion to but also as a dialectical extension of Žižek's argument, I will suggest that Mormonism, understood as part of the "onslaught of new spiritualisms" he decries, contains at its perverse core that which might well seem to be its exact opposite: decolonization, including the repudiation of Christian evangelization and the valorization of non-Christian spiritual traditions. If, for Žižek, Christianity leads to Marx, then, for me, Mormonism might be said to lead to Frantz Fanon, the great black Martinican anti-colonial theorist and activist who intervened within a Hegelian-Marxist tradition that had exhibited conceptual and practical difficulty with race as a meaningful category of analysis and reality. Or, more precisely, Mormonism ushers us to Glen Sean Coulthard, the Yellowknives Dene political philosopher who, in his recent *Red Skin, White Masks: Rejecting the Colonial Politics of Recognition*, has brilliantly rewritten Fanon from an unapologetically indigenous perspective, experimentally shifting the center of radical critique from Third to Fourth World.[7] Beneath "the capital relation" that has served as the main concern of "critical theory and left political strategy," Coulthard unearths "the colonial relation"—specifically the dispossession of indigenous lands and resources that he persuasively shows is not a past-tense event, as some Marxist formulations of "primitive accumulation" have implied, but an ongoing process, as evidenced by what is happening now at Standing Rock Sioux Reservation and in so many other places.[8]

The perversity of my argument—that the Book of Mormon, the eponymous scripture of what has become the concertedly conservative institution of the LDS Church, might direct us toward the likes of Coulthard—is no doubt manifest. But just to spell it out: a movement that has played—and, apropos Coulthard, continues to play—a central role in the colonial settlement of the US West (and beyond), variously marginalizing thousands of indigenous peoples in the process, and that has proved loath to condemn outright its theological and practical racism might contain within itself, specifically in the text from which it takes its distinctive name, a tendency or potentiality that would undo that very history and point toward a radically different, unrecognizable future.[9]

On the chance this claim might be made remotely convincing, let me briefly elaborate two interlinked theses in support: (1) Mormonism is genetically secular; and (2) Mormon messianism, as initially articulated in and through the Book of Mormon, should therefore be regarded as post-Christian in consequential ways.[10]

Emergent well after the origin date of Charles Taylor's "secular age" in 1500, Mormonism, I argue, exhibits not only the birthmark, as it were, of "secularity" but perhaps something like a birthright.[11] By *secularity*, I here mean, with Taylor, "the conditions of experience of and search for the spiritual" in a time when "faith, even for the staunchest believer, is one human possibility among others."[12] Taylor's concern is twofold. One concern is to capture "the whole context of understanding in which our moral, spiritual, and religious experience and search takes place" arising—in his deeply, problematically Eurocentric account—from certain key developments within Latin Christendom (e.g., the Protestant Reformation, the rise of humanism) that "fragilized" belief, to use his term.[13] A second concern is to maintain, over and against standard secularization narratives, that forms of belief that might be called "religious" or "spiritual" remain viable and vital within this undeniably transformed and transforming "context of understanding," albeit on inescapably different terms. Today, Taylor concedes, we all find ourselves working from within what he calls an "immanent frame." He distinguishes his qualified secularity against two other, more familiar senses of *secularity*: an institutional innovation—church-state separation—that makes it possible to "engage fully in politics" and civil society "without ever encountering God," and an emergent ideology predicting and often prescribing the inevitable "falling off of religious belief and practice."[14] To my mind, rather than conceive these as two other senses of *secularity*, it seems useful instead to delineate them as secular*isms* in order to underscore the point that although they are undeniably operative within and substantially constitutive of the phenomenological background Taylor calls "secularity," they are not perfectly coextensive with it. In a Venn diagram, these secularisms are bubbles whose circumferences never quite align with that of the bubble of secularity encompassing them.

In this scheme, Mormonism might be seen not only as bearing the marks of secularity but also as marking precisely those possibilities within secularity that outstrip what I have just differentiated as secularisms. Put another way, Mormonism is a limit case, both an extreme example of secularity and a liminal, transgressive phenomenon vis-à-vis those increasingly well-worn phenomenological pathways within secularity that can be encapsulated as secularisms—whether in its narrow, political sense of disestablishment, which denominates something called "religion" in the first place and allots it a specific role in the private domain, or in its broader, ideological sense of a self-consciously non- or even anti-religious worldview. Mormonism, with its theo(demo)cratic ambitions (at one point realized in a sovereign state) and its commonsensical (super)naturalism envisioning the mundane mingling of humans, angels, and gods, has never sat well with either of these secularisms.[15] But to cede Mormonism to an all-too-easy reactionary "religious" rejection of the secular *in toto* would be to miss the opportunity to leverage its genetic secularity in order to fathom secularity as a phenomenological condition in part indexed by these secularisms but also exceeding them. For instance, Mormonism could clinch Grant Shreve's important particularization of an "American secularity" in which fragilization of belief is a function of the pluralization of belief rather than the naturalization of unbelief.[16] Secularity, I am saying, is Mormonism's native element and Mormonism its invaluable key. In sum, Mormonism is both fundamentally secular and non- or post-secularist. It stands for secularity's— dare we say—transcendence of secularism.

Even more strongly, Mormonism might be apprehended not only as born necessarily laboring under the burden of justifying what might be deemed transcendental claims, but also as carrying the possibility of the immanent frame's sufficiency as a source of ultimate value. Indeed, I have come to think that one way to conceptualize what are arguably the most distinctive doctrines of early Mormonism—its materialism and its theosis—is to view them precisely as the radical extension of the immanent frame to encompass even the nominally absolute God of

Christian theism, thereby leaving no transcendental outside. In other words, Mormonism would be precisely what the Christian novelist Marilynne Robinson—seemingly a darling of Mormon intellectuals, to judge by recent events[17]—has deplored in her most recent collection of essays: the "scaling upward to infinity of the properties of . . . [the] quasireality that holds us at a remove from the world's true workings."[18] I find myself, then, rebelling somewhat against what might be called the Christianization of Mormonism. Instead of "lusting after the fleshpots of Christian orthodoxy and . . . turning its back on its own best insights," to borrow Sterling McMurrin's memorable phrase, Mormonism might fully explore and express its post-Christian secularity, for instance, by pursuing McMurrin's thought that Mormonism "out-humanisms" secular humanism and "the standard forms of religious liberalism" in its extravagant "conception of human possibility."[19] What if we were to seize on the contingencies of Mormonism's historical emergence and imagine it not so much as a bona fide Christian religion but more as an envelope-pushing secular phenomenology, an organic mode of navigating our current cosmic reality?

For one, this might make clear the ways the Book of Mormon may be an original contribution to a distinctively modern, post-Judeo-Christian tradition of messianic thought. This strain of messianic thought, associated with philosophers like Jacques Derrida and Walter Benjamin, has recently been historicized by Anna Glazova and Paul North as arising from a confrontation with what might be called the *anti-messianic* thought of *extinction*—with "catastrophe . . . as a noncausal and atelic force" portending irredeemable loss.[20] Modern messianic thought, they write, represents "a last and most desperate attempt to return to the idea of loss as the redeemable" precisely in the face of the "possible loss" of what they call a "messianic model of loss" rooted in traditional Judeo-Christian theological convictions regarding the ultimate deliverance (of portions) of the world from death and depravity.[21] Hence, modern messianic thought's attempted return to a notion of redeemable loss cannot be a simple one—one cannot unthink the thought of extinction. "Once eschatological certainty is depleted or shaken," Glazova and North go on, "the messianic thought asks to be rethought or replaced. Two possibilities readily present themselves: either to understand history as a gradual process of fulfillment without reference to a supernatural order or to posit history as constitutionally lacking a purpose." Both of these possibilities incapacitate hope, they suggest, because they don't allow for any discontinuity of time. Hence, "discontinuity," Glazova and North note, "comes to be the only hope for history," and modern messianic thought is "in effect a species of discontinuity."[22]

Glazova and North rather conventionally trace this tradition to the horrified response of Enlightenment skeptics such as Voltaire to the 1755 Lisbon earthquake, and their collection is suggestively titled "messianic thought outside theology."[23] The implication is that the *modernity* of this messianic thought—messianic thought chastened or haunted by the thought of extinction—consists precisely in its migration "outside theology" to enlightened philosophy, and, further, that any messianic thought *inside* theology is anti-modern and reactionary, in denial about the possibility of extinction, myopic in its transcendental convictions. By contrast, I would trace the anti-messianic thought of extinction with which any modern messianic scheme has to reckon to the belief-beggaring debacle of Native genocide beginning in the fifteenth century and underscore the fact that much of the response to this primal scene of the thought of extinction occurred in theological discourses, including, of course, the Book of Mormon.[24] In my globalist corrective of Glazova and North's account, the anti-messianic thought of extinction is bound up with the historical revelation of planetary finitude in the Americas and the cosmos-shattering conundrum of the existence and then the potential nonexistence of the indigenous peoples of the Americas.[25] In this context, the Book of Mormon can be appreciated as an example of *messianic* thought solicited by but also, as I've suggested, shot through with the contemplation of this particular loss as an irretrievable one. If we take the globe—with a neat literalism—as the immanent frame that produces the phenomenological effects in which Taylor is interested, the fact that the Book of Mormon bids to be scripture by way of being "a history of Indians" begins to make more sense.[26]

Perhaps the most direct way to cash out these claims is to engage Adam Miller's groundbreaking application of Walter Benjamin's version of modern messianism to the Book of Mormon.[27] I will all too briefly walk through Miller's argument and highlight a different turn that might be made at a critical juncture. In 1827 Joseph Smith digs up a material object—the golden plates. This is, in Benjamin's terms, the historian or collector's vital encounter with a forgotten historical object, an object charged with "aura" in part by virtue of what Miller calls the "brute material incongruity" of that object's unexpected "continuing subsistence": "How could this thing still be around? It no longer has a place in this world," to borrow Miller's helpful colloquializing paraphrase.[28] In the case of the Book of Mormon, this point is underscored by the fact that for Smith this historical object—the plates—is obviously linked to a population—the indigenous inhabitants of the Americas—understood by many in his moment to be appointed by the march of history for erasure, whether by death or deracination. This presencing of a repressed past thus troubles what had seemed the inexorable, linear unfolding of history. This is the messianic rupture for Benjamin, and it enables "a retroactive reconfiguration of history" under the aegis of which the present and range of possible futures suddenly look radically different.[29] In the case of the Book of Mormon, a continent whose destiny as the home of a Euro-Christian settler civilization seemed to so many to be *manifest*— that is, self-evidently appointed as such by Providence by virtue of the ongoing accomplishments of the colonial project—is impossibly restored to its displaced and decimated indigenous inhabitants, who are elevated as the primary actors in the building of a new heaven and earth in their homeland.[30]

What the Book of Mormon actually tries to pull off is the enactment of a messianic disruption of the empty homogeneous time of the everyday of settler colonialism—that is, Native attrition and anathematization—through the presentation of itself as a record of ancient American Israelites whose contents will empower modern Native Americans by helping them recognize they are a covenant people with claim upon God. This, it seems to me, is where the logic of a Benjaminian reading of the Book of Mormon would lead. Benjamin, after all, was a historical materialist in the Marxian tradition, someone focused on seizing those rare revolutionary chances in history that would transform human life, someone who, in his "Paralipomena to 'On the Concept of History,'" straightforwardly declared that "Marx secularized the idea of messianic time. And that was a good thing."[31] The decolonization I am arguing the Book of Mormon might be understood to call for seems to me a messianic history of the sort Benjamin might appreciate. But this is not where Miller's Benjamin leads us. Instead, in a manner consistent with the rebranding of the Book of Mormon as "another testament of Jesus Christ," he reverses the priorities on the title page of the Book of Mormon, which, I argue, makes Native renewal rather than Christian evangelization the text's primary purpose. In a kind of tautology, Miller argues that the Book of Mormon's messianicity, in the end, consists in its "own explicit purpose of testifying universally 'that Jesus is the Christ,' the *Messiah*, 'manifesting himself unto all nations.'"[32] This, it seems to me, is plain old messianicity *with* messianism. But, by Benjamin's lights, this cannot be the messianic event in this specific context. For insofar as this project of Christian evangelization in the Americas was part and parcel of a colonial project to "kill the Indian and save the man" (or just to kill the Indian), it more properly belongs to what Benjamin—in Miller's own paraphrase—identifies as that "universal history . . . elaborated from the victor's point of view" that the messianic must interrupt.[33] In other words, the Christianization of Native Americans where they survived and remained was, in Joseph Smith's moment, understood to be part of the business-as-usual of secular history. In what would the messianic rupture consist, then?

Paradoxically, challengingly, the Book of Mormon can be taken to suggest that the messianic event that it itself claims to inaugurate necessitates the contradiction rather than consummation of familiar and traditional notions of Christian messianism. In this reading, the Book of Mormon suggests that its faithful readers will honor and sustain Native peoples without the missionary agenda or ethnocentric paternalism found within secular history. This reading, it seems to me, commits readers to the project of decolonization, an undeniable part of which is the renewal and reinvention of non-Christian Native spiritual practices.

Notes

1. Jared Hickman, "*The Book of Mormon* as Amerindian Apocalypse," *American Literature* 86 (September 2014): 429–61; and "600 B.C.E–1830 C.E.," in *Timelines of American Literature*, ed. Christopher Hager and Cody Marrs (Baltimore: Johns Hopkins University Press, 2018). Thanks to Caleb Spencer, who, after a talk I gave at Claremont Graduate University, raised a provocative question that led me to frame my thoughts—usefully, I hope—in this way.

2. Slavoj Žižek, *The Puppet and the Dwarf: The Perverse Core of Christianity* (Cambridge, MA: MIT Press, 2003).

3. Slavoj Žižek, *The Fragile Absolute: Or, Why Is the Christian Legacy Worth Fighting For?* (New York: Verso Books, 2000), 1.

4. Žižek, *Fragile Absolute*, 1–2.

5. Žižek, *Puppet and the Dwarf*, 6.

6. Žižek, *Puppet and the Dwarf*, 171.

7. Glen Sean Coulthard, *Red Skin, White Masks: Rejecting the Colonial Politics of Recognition* (Minneapolis: University of Minnesota Press, 2014). Coulthard's title is a play on Fanon's seminal 1952 text *Black Skin, White Masks*. Coulthard belongs to a cohort of scholars and activists engaged in what has come to be called "indigenous critical theory." Some other texts in this domain that I've found especially useful are Jodi Byrd, *Transit of Empire: Indigenous Critiques of Colonialism* (Minneapolis: University of Minnesota Press, 2011); Aileen Moreton-Robinson, *The White Possessive: Property, Power, and Indigenous Sovereignty* (Minneapolis: University of Minnesota Press, 2015); and Mark Rifkin, *Settler Common Sense: Queerness and Everyday Colonialism in the American Renaissance* (Minneapolis: University of Minnesota Press, 2014). Also pertinent is Arif Dirlik's claim that the Fourth World, "for all its faults," remains as perhaps our most vital "reminder of possible

alternatives to the existing state of things." Arif Dirlik, "Global-ization, Indigenism, and the Politics of Place," *ARIEL* 34 (January 2003): 25.

8. Coulthard, *Red Skin, White Masks*, especially 1–49, 131–79.

9. For a good indigenous-centered, big-picture account of Mormon settler colonialism, see Ned Blackhawk, *Violence over the Land: Indians and Empires in the Early American West* (Cambridge, MA: Harvard University Press, 2006), especially 226–66; and Jared Farmer, *On Zion's Mount: Mormons, Indians, and the American Landscape* (Cambridge, MA: Harvard University Press, 2008), es-pecially 19–138.

10. For a smattering of thinking about Mormonism's "post-Christian-ity," see Harold Bloom, *The American Religion: The Emergence of the Post-Christian Nation* (New York: Simon and Schuster, 1992), 79–128; A. A. Howsepian, "Are Mormons Theists?," *Religious Stud-ies* 32 (September 1996): 357–70; and Jan Shipps, *Mormonism: The Story of a New Religious Tradition* (Urbana: University of Illinois Press, 1985), ix–x.

11. Charles Taylor, *A Secular Age* (Cambridge, MA: Harvard Univer-sity Press, 2007), 26.

12. Taylor, *Secular Age*, 3.

13. For critiques of Taylor's Eurocentrism, see José Casanova, "A Secular Age: Dawn or Twilight?"; Saba Mahmood, "Can Secular-ism Be Other-Wise?"; and "Editors' Introduction," all in *Variet-ies of Secularism in a Secular Age*, ed. Michael Warner, Jonathan VanAntwerpen, and Craig Calhoun (Cambridge, MA: Harvard University Press, 2010); as well as Vincent P. Pecora, *Secularization and Cultural Criticism: Religion, Nation, and Modernity* (Chicago: University of Chicago Press, 2006), 64–65.

14. Taylor, *Secular Age*, 1–2.

15. On Mormonism's battle with secularism as institutionally embed-

ded in the state and ideologically enforcing certain ontological assumptions, see Kathleen Flake, *The Politics of Religious Identity: The Seating of Senator Reed Smoot, Mormon Apostle* (Chapel Hill: University of North Carolina Press, 2004); J. Spencer Fluhman, *"A Peculiar People": Anti-Mormonism and the Making of Religion in Nineteenth-Century America* (Chapel Hill: University of North Carolina Press, 2012); Terryl L. Givens, *The Viper on the Hearth: Mormons, Myths, and the Construction of Heresy* (New York: Oxford University Press, 1997); J. B. Haws, *The Mormon Image in the American Mind: Fifty Years of Public Perception* (New York: Oxford University Press, 2013); and Brent M. Rogers, *Unpopular Sovereignty: Mormons and the Federal Management of Early Utah Territory* (Lincoln: University of Nebraska Press, 2017).

16. Grant Shreve, "Fragile Belief: Lydia Maria Child's *Hobomok* and the Scene of American Secularity," *American Literature* 86 (December 2014): 655–82.

17. I have in mind the multiple papers on Robinson presented at the 2016 meeting of Mormon Scholars in the Humanities (see http://mormonscholars.net/msh-2016-secularisms/) and Robinson's recent Truman G. Madsen Lecture at BYU, "The Sacred, the Human" (see a report of this lecture at https://humanities.byu.edu /marilynne-robinson-the-sacred-the-human/).

18. Marilynne Robinson, *The Givenness of Things: Essays* (New York: Farrar, Straus and Giroux, 2015), 220.

19. Sterling M. McMurrin, "Comments on the Theological and Philosophical Foundations of Christianity," *Dialogue: A Journal of Mormon Thought* 25 (March 1992): 46; and McMurrin, *The Theological Foundations of the Mormon Religion* (Salt Lake City: University of Utah Press, 1965), 110. The Mormon Transhumanist Association perhaps represents a move in this direction, although, tellingly, it makes a point of advertising (whether with

perfect sincerity or out of practical necessity or some combination of both) that its members are first and foremost "disciples of the Gospel of Jesus Christ"; see https://transfigurism.org/.

20. Anna Glazova and Paul North, "Introduction: Saving Hope, the Wager of Messianism," in *Messianic Thought Outside Theology*, ed. Anna Glazova and Paul North (New York: Fordham University Press, 2014), 6.

21. Glazova and North, "Saving Hope," 4.

22. Glazova and North, "Saving Hope," 7–8.

23. Glazova and North, "Saving Hope," 6.

24. On Native genocide as a temporal marker, even in the geological record, of a new era—call it "modernity" or "the Anthropocene"—demanding new modes of thought and feeling, see Simon L. Lewis and Mark A. Maslin, "Defining the Anthropocene," *Nature* 519 (March 12, 2015): 171–80; and Dana Luciano, "The Inhuman Anthropocene," *Avidly: A Los Angeles Review of Books Channel*, March 22, 2015, http://avidly.lareviewofbooks.org/.

25. On "globality" as a possible substitute for "secularity" as the phenomenological background condition under which we now operate, see Peter Coviello and Jared Hickman, "Introduction: After the Postsecular," *American Literature* 86 (December 2014): 645–54.

26. Richard Lyman Bushman, *Joseph Smith: Rough Stone Rolling* (New York: Alfred A. Knopf, 2005), 94–99; Terryl L. Givens, *By the Hand of Mormon: The American Scripture That Launched a New World Religion* (New York: Oxford University Press, 2002), 89–116; and Dan Vogel, *Indian Origins and the Book of Mormon* (Salt Lake City: Signature Books, 1986).

27. Adam S. Miller, "Messianic History: Walter Benjamin and the Book of Mormon," in *Rube Goldberg Machines: Essays in Mormon Theology* (Salt Lake City: Greg Kofford Books, 2012), 21–35; see also Jillian Sayre, "Books Buried in the Earth: *The Book of Mor-*

mon, Revelation, and the Humic Foundations of the Nation," in *Americanist Approaches to* The Book of Mormon, ed. Elizabeth Fenton and Jared Hickman (New York: Oxford University Press, forthcoming). Miller draws on several of Benjamin's essays and fragments, but most central is "On the Concept of History," in *Selected Writings*, ed. Howard Eiland and Michael W. Jennings (Cambridge, MA: Harvard University Press, 2003), 4:395–97.

28. Miller, "Messianic History," 31.
29. Miller, "Messianic History," 31.
30. See my "Amerindian Apocalypse" (fully cited in note 1 above) for an extended close reading of the Book of Mormon that grounds these claims.
31. Walter Benjamin, "Paralipomena to 'On the Concept of History,'" in *Selected Writings*, ed. Howard Eiland and Michael W. Jennings (Cambridge, MA: Harvard University Press, 2003), 4:401.
32. Miller, "Messianic History," 34.
33. Miller, "Messianic History," 23.

4 | CAN HISTORIANS QUEST AFTER RELIGIOUS TRUTH?

MORMONISM IN THE ACADEMY: SCHOLARSHIP, TEACHING, AND FAITH

Section Introduction

ROBERT A. GOLDBERG

These essays approach the issues of scholarship, teaching, and faith from different angles and perspectives. I will comment on the specifics of each but focus on larger themes: What can we expect of historical analysis? Can historians quest after religious truth?

Matt Bowman's essay assesses the Catholic Church's Second Vatican Council and the LDS Church's Correlation Committee as responses to secularism. Seeking restoration, the two initiatives sought to legitimize ecclesiastical authority and firm up members' commitment. Note that Professor Bowman alerts us to the matter of discordant conversations about the meaning of events. He writes of "a variety of readings" of Vatican II and that it "was endlessly contested." Some interpretations were ideological while others were rooted in gender analysis.

Similarly, correlation in the LDS Church was framed as pro- and anti-feminism.

This is a complex story well told. Rather than being mired in parochialism, Professor Bowman finds distance from his own tribe to draw insights from a different faith tradition. It is imaginative and analytical. Nor does he seek consensus or order. Instead, Matt Bowman is comfortable with divergent voices.

These are the marks of a well-trained historian. Historians are not taught to search the past to uphold truth claims. They sift through history's artifacts—newspapers, diaries, and documents—to discover what men and women did and believed. The historian knows past events only through the eyes, ears, and minds of history's participants. Historians are well aware that these sources carry their creators' opinions and are filtered through specific race, class, gender, and religious identities. Nor does the coloring of the historical data end there. The past's record of ideas and arguments are then sifted through the historian's own identities to be fashioned into interpretations. This merging of observed and observer references German physicist Werner Heisenberg's uncertainty principle. The idea here is that the very process of observing alters the thing or event being observed. The "truth" is elusive and unknowable. It is dependent on time, place, and community.

In his comparative piece, Matt Grow takes us to the Church History Department to consider change over time. His insights are valuable and put this story into clear perspective. Grow discusses evolving dynamics relating to shifts within and beyond the church. Also, he is struck by continuity in mission and agenda. The goal remains: "history that is candid, professional, and true to the sources." What Leonard J. Arrington identified as the "toughest problem" continues: the tension of balancing on two legs, "the leg of faith and the leg of reason." This is the great challenge. Can the Church History Department be credible with professional scholars yet publish works that "build testimonies . . . [and] the Kingdom"?

The History Department produces documentary publications that are vital for two reasons: they provide the raw material for research and counter conspiracy theories of official cover-up. More problematic are interpretive histories. If LDS authorities have extensive oversight, the peer-review process can be difficult to navigate. Are the gauges of honesty and faithfulness compatible?

All of this raises an even broader question: how will the department explain the most troubling events of Mormon history to the faithful? Matt Grow insists that there is now a "broad consensus" in the church that "transparency is essential." Yet, how is transparent history to be revealed so that members are not tested? Grow admits, "Vigorous discussions still occur over how we explain certain controversies." Has the church moved beyond its previous strategy of *inoculating* members by exposing them officially, a bit at a time, to uncomfortable and painful history? The implication of this medical metaphor is that doubt is a disease. Perhaps we need to reconceptualize this. Doubt is not a step away from faith. It is a step away from indoctrination. Only when women and men feel they have been blindsided or intentionally misled is faith questioned.

Also visible in this paper is a strategy that can work to cut through some of these issues. It resembles history writing that comes out of a Jewish tradition. Except with children, Jews rarely talk about parting seas or walls tumbling down. Nor are they defensive when discussing figures who, like Kings Saul and David, were not only complex but also deeply flawed. Narrative Jewish histories are stories of achievement, of struggle, of persecution, of disappointment. There is little attempt to hide from the past. What these accounts reveal is a past that guides the present and future. They also secure identity and intensify community. With such histories, Jews in full knowledge come to understand who they are and what is of deepest meaning.

In "transitioning to a stronger focus on narrative history," the History Department can lead the way in these matters. Histories that consider Latter-day Saints politically, socially, and economically and that maintain professional standards will open up a dialogue with those beyond the Mormon community. They can only add luster to the History Department.

Jana Riess's subject is Richard Bushman. She draws his portrait with passion, and her essay is a model for pedagogical excellence. Bushman is not just a source of information. His listening acts to suspend judgment and show respect. Bushman exemplifies a teaching philosophy that is not simply vertical but has most effect horizontally among peers and in community. Riess also praises Bushman for his openness to the complicated narrative of Mormon history. She concludes by noting Bushman's "wholism," that his sense of faith and community animates his scholarship.

As a community, Jews lavish great praise on their teachers and scholars. In the Talmud it is written: "The real guardians of the state are the teachers."[1] It also records Rabbi Chanina, who once remarked: "I have learned much from my teachers, more from my colleagues, and the most from my students."[2] Riess has convincingly shown that Richard Bushman is a latter-day Rabbi Chanina!

Jana Riess is privileged to have a teacher like Richard Bushman. Richard, in turn, is fortunate to have a student who so eloquently captures the essence of his contribution.

In responding to this piece, I echo earlier points. Religion and history ask different questions and seek different answers. Religion is not rooted in facts and dates. It is about relationship with God. Religion teaches values, how to live a humane life, and service to all. History is about interpretations that are subject to logic and evidence. These interpretations are not truths but are conditioned by circumstances, both personal and societal. We do not impose an obligation on the biologist or chemist or physicist to confirm faith. Nor should we expect the historian to shoulder the burden of religious truth. That is a matter for the theologian and the believer.

Notes

1. Talmud, Hagigah 1:7.
2. Talmud, Ta'anit 7b.

RICHARD BUSHMAN
AND THE FUTURE
OF MORMON TEACHING

JANA RIESS

In the summer of 2015, I was privileged to be part of a Mormon Theology Seminar at Union Theological Seminary in New York City. We participants spent our days dissecting a chapter from the Book of Mormon and our evenings enjoying the city—not a bad way to live! For one of those evenings, we walked around the corner to Richard and Claudia Bushman's apartment for dinner and conversation. Even though they had just arrived back in New York after spending time in Provo, they took it in stride that *of course* they had the energy to shop for and feed and entertain eight more people. So after a delicious dinner, we retired to their living room and talked for a couple more hours. In particular, Richard wanted to go around the room and ask us a question that I hope I'm not embarrassing him by discussing here: he wanted to confer about best practices to communicate with his grandkids. How, he asked, could he show them how much he cared about what they were interested in, even when those interests led them away from the LDS Church? How could he let them know that his love for them extended far beyond whether or how they chose to be Mormon? Since some of our younger seminar participants were the same age as or just a little bit older than Richard's grandchildren, he thought they could offer some insights into shared connection.

I don't remember much about how we responded, but I was struck by the question itself. Here was an elder statesman who sincerely wanted to learn from people one or two generations younger than himself, someone who was eager to put being in *relationship* above being *right*. He basked in the role of the student as much as he did in the role of the teacher.

> This is not an isolated incident. Back in 2007, when Richard was speaking at a forum sponsored by the Ethics and Public Policy Center, he looked out at the roomful of mostly young journalists and apparently was as covetous of their insights into how Mormonism was or was not assimilating into the political mainstream as they were of his. "I was struck by the immense cultural power that resides in all of these young people," he told them. "In fact, I asked . . . if during the second half of the Q&A I might take over the meeting for a while. Instead of you asking impossible questions and me generating imaginary answers to them, I would begin to ask *you* some questions, because I would be very interested in knowing how you situate Mormonism and your estimate of what is happening on the religious scene generally."[1]

Richard Bushman is not just a scholar but a deep listener. And as I think about the future of the LDS Church, I must confess that I believe we should clone him. I want to see more

Richard Bushmans, those who are as committed to listening and learning as they are to imparting knowledge.

Richard's question about communicating with his grand-children suggests three different ways in which I think his approach offers a way forward, a new pedagogy, for the LDS Church today.

Listening

Over the past year, I've been in the early stages of "The Next Mormons" survey, a research project about Mormon young adults. Among the questions I'm raising through a social science component and qualitative interviews are issues such as: Are we Mormons in fact losing more of our young adults than in the past? If so, why do they leave? Is it true they are upset about thorny questions in Mormon history or troubled by contemporary social issues like LGBT equality? Do they feel left out of decision-making? Or do they feel *burned* out, with too many church responsibilities? Are they simply bored?

All of these issues have been suggested as possibilities, but in the aforementioned survey the three most common reasons millennials (young adults ages eighteen to thirty-six) cited for leaving the LDS Church were that they felt judged or misunder-stood, they did not trust church leaders to tell the truth about controversial issues, and they disagreed with the church's position on LGBT issues. The first two reasons, certainly, are related to failures in communication; young adult former Mormons were far more concerned about feeling judged and not being able to trust leaders than they were about specific doctrinal or historical issues such as polygamy, seer stones, or a lack of financial transparency about how tithing money is spent.

How many Mormons are leaving? If the Pew numbers are to be believed, the overall Mormon retention rate declined from 70 percent in 2007[2] to 64 percent in 2014[3]—and, if we are to believe other, earlier studies, the 70 percent figure from 2007 already represented a decline in retention from what it used to be in the 1980s. I would suspect, based on cohort patterns more generally, that when we are able to break down the 2007 and 2014 Pew numbers, we will find that millennials are more likely than members of earlier generations to say they grew up LDS but no longer identify that way as adults.[4] This conclusion is also suggested by Darren Sherkat's longitudinal analysis of Mormons in the General Social Survey, which showed a significant drop in retention among LDS adults born after 1971 compared to earlier cohorts.[5] And internal research presented to top LDS leaders in November 2008 indicates that activity rates among millennials are a growing source of concern for the church's General Authorities. In North America 30 percent of young single adults (YSAs) were active in the church, and only 20 percent internationally.[6]

Throughout that videotaped meeting, church leaders discussed strategies for restructuring YSA wards, keeping better records, sending YSAs on service projects as directed by leaders, and giving Aaronic Priesthood holders more responsibility— all in an effort to stem the rising tide of inactivity. However, at no point in the meeting did the General Authorities discuss feedback from young adults themselves about why they had stopped attending church in large numbers.[7] Nor did they devise any plans for collectively listening to their concerns. If this videotaped discussion is any indication of the leadership's usual approach to young adults, it seems shortsighted. The first thing we as a church should be doing right now is not rescuing millennials, however noble that impulse is. It's not fellowshipping them back into church activity. It's doing what Richard does, either naturally or because he has cultivated it as a spiritual practice: we need to listen. Just listen.

As a church we do so many things so well. One of those is coaching: we set clear objectives for ourselves and others; we communicate those goals; we have certain milestones in place to let us know whether we're achieving those goals, whether it's an Eagle Scout Court of Honor or a mission's baptism rate; and we train people to perform at their highest level of effectiveness. Through lessons, talks, and firesides, we convey our standards and instruct others in how those standards can be realized. We are terrific coaches, but we do not have mechanisms in place to encourage people in our church to simply listen. That's particularly true when it comes to listening to young adults, who have very little institutional voice in the church beyond what leadership roles they may serve in at the local level, particularly in singles wards. Also, never before have we seen such a large generation gap between the LDS membership in the United States and their top leaders, who are collectively older than ever before.[8]

If two-way communication is going to begin, the leaders have to initiate it. Some recent initiatives show that they are trying to help young adults and youth. The recent transparency in matters of LDS history demonstrates a willingness to grapple with more difficult questions. Commitments to include controversial issues in seminary instruction, in what Elder M. Russell Ballard in 2016 called the "Doctrinal Mastery" program, sound promising.[9] What appear to be rare are any formal (or even informal, for that matter) programs to suggest that the LDS Church is listening to the concerns of young adults. By listening I mean not just hearing but also suspending judgment, refraining from giving advice, and learning to ask open-ended questions that don't necessarily have obvious acceptable right answers. Strong listening skills are predicated upon a real openness to questions, a lack of defensiveness, and an absence of fear about where the conversation may head next. All these are qualities I have observed in Richard Bushman.

Truth-Telling

As a historian, Richard has been one to gently but firmly lead the way for greater openness about the most controversial or complicated narratives from LDS history. He has been saying for decades now that we owe it to our young people to tell them the truest versions of these stories that we can access: "We want the story we tell each other to be based on the best possible historical evidence. Any shrinking from that mandate will only lead to more problems down the road. I think the Church is trying to create that kind of comprehensive, accurate narrative. In a few years there won't be any more surprises."[10]

At times it has been fashionable in the study of pedagogy to see the teacher as a truth-telling figure who smashes ignorance and releases intellectual captives from the bondage of their mistaken ideas. And despite the arrogance of such a view, there is probably a part of every teacher that sort of hopes it is true. Without at least a shade of that superhero complex, it can be difficult to stay motivated. But what I see in Richard's example is that he is not interested in playing the superhero. In one interview, he conceded that "contradicting the standard narrative of church history is a delicate matter. People get disturbed and the questioner feels rebuffed. I ran into this problem at Claremont where the graduate students offended Church members with their expert knowledge on the New Testament when it ran against the standard views. I think two things have to be kept in mind. If your secret wish is to be an iconoclast, to break the images, church members will sniff that out. Or if you want to parade superior knowledge as some of the Claremont students did, you will meet resistance. If your wish is to help people understand our history better, you are more likely to be accepted."[11]

I see Richard's approach to teaching as very much in line with what Parker Palmer espouses in *The Courage to Teach*, namely, fostering what Palmer calls a "community of truth." The community of truth challenges the top-down flow of knowledge that has been the dominant model in most institutions, including both the academy and the church. In the traditional model we have long employed, the subject matter becomes an object and the one disseminating information the unquestioned expert; everyone else is in a posture of learning about the object from a distance. In a community of truth, "as in real life, there are no pristine objects of knowledge and no ultimate authorities. In the community of truth, as in real life, truth does not reside primarily in propositions, and education is more than delivering propositions about objects to passive auditors." Instead, all of those we formerly cast as "students" become "knowers" who are also in *relationship* with the subject, giving it "the respect and authority that we normally give only to human beings."[12]

I would not go so far as to say that truth-telling can only occur in Palmer's community model, but I would say that *relationship* with the subject is only possible in that environment. Richard's educational model, both in Mormon studies and when he was my professor at Columbia, incites passion in students because of community. I'm pretty sure that in my five years as a graduate student, Richard and Claudia were the only professors who routinely had students over for dinner. This seems a small thing, doesn't it? And yet it's not. Seminar papers were read and debated outside the classroom—in the home—with Richard and Claudia just as concerned about the kind of community their classes were fostering as they were about how we assimilated the subject matter.

A Holistic Approach

For Richard, scholarship and church and community have never been neatly compartmentalized. He models a wholeness, an integration of his person, that I deeply admire. Mormonism affects his scholarly output despite the fact that others in the academy might see a wide fissure between his LDS beliefs and his capabilities as a historian. "I am asked to give papers and review books and have never felt that my religion prevents me from engaging in all the usual routines of modern academic life," he has said. But, "apparently, the crazy Mormon side of my mind is envisioned as sequestered in some watertight compartment where it cannot infect my rational processes. Beliefs inhabit a realm of feeling and traditional loyalties where we are not called to rational account and where eccentricities and bizarre ideas can be tolerated. Probably my colleagues have peculiar notions of their own that they would not want to defend before a panel of academic critics."[13]

There is a pragmatism to Richard's refusal to separate his faith from his scholarship, what the Greeks would have called *phronesis*, or practical wisdom. What do these truths mean in the living of your life? How do they augment your ability and inclination to bless the lives of others? Richard has been clear that in his teaching and his scholarship he is not interested in the pursuit of knowledge purely for its own sake: "Objectivity is the claim of people who think they are gods now, not of persons worshiping God and striving to be like him, nor of persons who understand the reality of finite human life without God. . . . Even when science has done its work to perfection, it fails to tell us how to live a life."[14]

I appreciate the wholeness of Richard's point of view and feel that it's something many people have lost in the academy. Richard has famously, as Philip Barlow noted when introducing Richard's essay in the pioneering volume *A Thoughtful Faith* more than two decades ago, exemplified the irony of "one of the church's finest intellectuals" arguing for "the final irrelevance of the intellect in matters of faith."[15] I think *irrelevance* is too strong a word. Richard does not see the intellect as unimportant but as a catalyst to the deeper growth that is possible with faith and humility. I'd like to close with Richard's own thoughts on the intersection of faith and scholarship, as told to historian Quincy Newell in correspondence reproduced in Richard's autobiographical work *On the Road with Joseph Smith*. Mormons stick with the Book of Mormon, according to Richard, because "we find God in its pages—or inspiration, or comfort, or scope. That is what religion is about in my opinion, and it is why I believe the Book of Mormon. I can't really evaluate all the scholarship all the time; while I am waiting for it to settle out, I have to go on living. I need some good to hold on to and to lift me up day by day. The Book of Mormon inspires me, and so I hold on. Reason is too frail to base a life on. . . . I think it is far better to go where goodness lies."[16] Parker Palmer would argue that such goodness lies in mutual learning and conversation, among other things. In an era when the LDS Church risks losing young adults who feel alienated and judged, goodness can be expressed by active, intentional listening to their concerns. Richard Bushman embodies such goodness, both as a scholar and as a Latter-day Saint.

Notes

1. "Dr. Richard Bushman at the May 2007 Faith Angle Forum," Ethics and Public Policy Center, Pew Forum on Religion and Public Life, May 14, 2007, http://eppc.org/publications/richard-bushman-at-the-may-2007-faith-angle-forum/.
2. Charles H. Lippy and Eric Tranby, *Religion in Contemporary America* (London: Routledge, 2013), 110. See also the 2007 Pew Religious Landscape Survey at http://www.pewforum.org/2008/02/01 chapter-2-changes-in-americans-religious-affiliation/.
3. 2014 Pew Religious Landscape Study, May 12, 2015, http://www.pewforum.org/2015/05/12/chapter-2-religious-switching-and-intermarriage/.
4. The 2014 Pew Religious Landscape Study suggests that nationwide 35 percent of millennials are "Nones," meaning they do not affiliate with organized religion. In 2007, when Pew asked the same question of the oldest millennials, only 25 percent identified as "Nones," reflecting a rapid rate of growth among the unaffiliated between 2007 and 2014 as younger millennials aged into the study. Michael Lipka, "Millennials Increasingly Are Driving Growth of 'Nones,'" Pew Research Center, May 12, 2015, http://www.pewresearch.org/fact-tank/2015/05/12/millennials-increasingly-are-driving-growth-of-nones/. In 2016 the Public Religion Research Institute found that 39 percent of young adults ages eighteen to twenty-nine were unaffiliated, three times the number

of unaffiliated Americans age sixty-five and older. Betsy Cooper et al., "Exodus: Why Americans Are Leaving Religion—and Why They're Unlikely to Come Back," Public Religion Research Institute, September 22, 2016, https://www.prri.org/research/prri-rns -poll-nones-atheist-leaving-religion/.

5. Darren E. Sherkat, *Changing Faith: The Dynamics and Consequences of Americans' Shifting Religious Identities* (New York: NYU Press, 2014), 62–63.

6. On October 2, 2016, the "Mormon Leaks" YouTube channel posted more than a dozen videos that had been recorded behind closed doors of top LDS leaders between 2007 and 2012. While this author deplores the release of communications that were intended to be private, the videos in question do provide a rare glimpse of the inner deliberations of the LDS Church and as such are of value to scholars. See "In Which They Fret Over the Young Single Adults," YouTube video, from a meeting of LDS leaders taped November 12, 2008, posted by "Mormon Leaks," October 2, 2016, https:// www.youtube.com/watch?v=FBH045ooaY0.

7. Three minutes before the end of the meeting, Sister Julie Beck, then the Relief Society General President (and apparently the only woman present), was given the opportunity to speak. In her brief remarks she referenced what she had learned from young adults themselves about dating and singles wards. There's no parallel in the meeting of the General Authorities discussing having actually spoken to any YSAs about their concerns.

8. Sixty-two percent of US Mormons are under age forty-nine. Only Muslims (81 percent), Orthodox Christians (66 percent), and Buddhists (64 percent) outstrip Mormons in the total percentage of adherents who are a combination of millennials and Generation Xers. Meanwhile, the average age of the LDS apostles crept upward until 2015, when the appointment of three apostles in their

sixties brought the average down but still not close to historical norms. See Peggy Fletcher Stack, "With Average Age of 80, Mormon Church Has Never Had Older Top Leaders," *Salt Lake Tribune*, March 3, 2015, http://www.sltrib.com//home/2245029-155/with-average-age-of-80-mormon.

9. Jana Riess, "Mormon Apostle Urges Teachers to Address Controversial Topics like Polygamy and Seer Stones in Class," Religion News Service, March 3, 2016, http://religionnews.com/.

10. Hawkgrrrl, "9 Pro Tips from Richard Bushman," Wheat & Tares, July 21, 2015, http://www.wheatandtares.org/17915/richard-bushman-on-mormonism/.

11. Hawkgrrrl, "9 ProTips."

12. Parker J. Palmer, *The Courage to Teach: Exploring the Inner Landscape of a Teacher's Life*, 10th anniversary ed. (San Francisco: Jossey-Bass, 2007), 103–5.

13. Richard L. Bushman, "The Social Dimensions of Rationality," in *Expressions of Faith: Testimonies of Latter-day Saint Scholars*, ed. Susan Easton Black (Salt Lake City: Deseret Book, 1996), online at Neal A. Maxwell Institute for Religious Scholarship, http://publications.mi.byu.edu/fullscreen/?pub=1127&index=8.

14. Bushman, "Social Dimensions of Rationality."

15. Richard L. Bushman, "My Belief," in *A Thoughtful Faith: Essays on Belief by Mormon Scholars*, ed. Philip L. Barlow (Centerville, UT: Canon Press, 1986), 17.

16. Richard L. Bushman, *On the Road with Joseph Smith: An Author's Diary* (Salt Lake City: Greg Kofford Books, 2007), 15–16.

THE ROLE OF THE CHURCH HISTORY DEPARTMENT IN MORMON SCHOLARSHIP

A Reflection on the Leonard J. Arrington
Era and the Present

MATTHEW J. GROW

Shortly after I began my graduate studies at the University of Notre Dame, I received an invitation to work for the Joseph Smith Papers, then a part of Brigham Young University and now a part of the Church History Department of the Church of Jesus Christ of Latter-day Saints. The previous year, I had attended a summer seminar program sponsored by BYU's Joseph Fielding Smith Institute for Latter-day Saint History, studying Joseph Smith and the culture of nineteenth-century America under Richard Bushman's guidance. At that time, I envisioned two paths to influencing the understanding of Latter-day Saint history in the academy. In my mind, each path was represented by one of the giants in the field of Mormon history over the past several decades: Richard L. Bushman and Leonard J. Arrington. The Bushman path meant writing on areas outside of Mormon history so that one could later use that broader understanding to deepen insights into the Latter-day Saint past. It also meant working from a university position, most likely outside Utah. The Arrington path, by contrast, emphasized working primarily on Mormon history and doing so from within the institutional church.

These paths were never as distinct as I had envisioned. Bushman, the outsider, was a savvy insider, while Arrington was the insider who often felt on the outside. As a faithful Latter-day Saint, Bushman has used his status as a distinguished scholar to influence Mormon history in insider circles, including his participation in writing a book for Arrington's sixteen-volume sesquicentennial series in the 1970s and 1980s and his crucial role in establishing the Joseph Smith Papers in the 1990s and 2000s. Arrington, who from one perspective was the ultimate insider as the official Church Historian, imagined the Church Historical Department operating much like a semiautonomous academic department and was thus surprised to find that ecclesiastical superiors questioned the propriety of some publications.

As I thought about taking time off from graduate studies to join the Joseph Smith Papers, I decided that I wanted to pursue the Bushman path, not the Arrington path. I declined the offer to work for the Joseph Smith Papers, stayed at Notre Dame, completed my graduate training in US religious history, and landed a job at the University of Southern Indiana.

And then the Arrington path interceded in summer 2010. Reid Neilson, with whom I had become friends during Bushman's summer seminar, was now the managing director of the Church History Department. Reid asked if I would be interested in a job in his department. I told him no, but Reid is a persuasive recruiter who painted a compelling picture of the present dynamics and future possibilities at the department.

Before I returned to Indiana that summer, I had met with Reid; Richard E. Turley Jr., the assistant church historian; and Elder Marlin K. Jensen, the Church Historian. They were admirably patient with me as I wrestled spiritually and intellectually with the decision. What would it mean to abandon the Bushman path for the Arrington path? And what if I ended up not liking the Arrington path or being particularly good at it? The position, after all, would require me to manage roughly forty full-time employees, which was thirty-nine and a half more than I was managing at the University of Southern Indiana's Center for Communal Studies. I worried that I could transition from the Bushman path to the Arrington path but not so easily in the opposite direction.

After several months, accepting the job at the Church History Department felt spiritually right. When I arrived in Salt Lake, Rick Turley told me that not only had I taken the Arrington path but I now occupied Arrington's position. Certainly I did not have his title as Church Historian nor his sterling reputation or credentials. But as director of the Publications Division, I occupied the same place in the organizational chart. Arrington had never managed the Historical Department; rather, he had managed the History Division, a team of researchers charged with publishing Mormon history. Today's Publications Division is the successor to Arrington's History Division.

What is the role of the Arrington path—and, more specifically, of church-sponsored publications—in the study of Mormon history? The Church History Department plays an unusual role in the historical study of a religious tradition. I know of no counterpart of similar scope in Methodist history or American Catholic history or Jewish history. To answer this question, I will reflect on the Arrington era, the so-called

Camelot period with its reputation of wide-open archives and cutting-edge contributions, by using Gregory A. Prince's new biography, *Leonard Arrington and the Writing of Mormon History*.[1] In Prince's estimation, Arrington is clearly in the right as he battles members of the church hierarchy in defense of an honest telling of Mormon history. But Arrington is a flawed hero in Prince's telling; had he been more attuned to the realities of working for the institutional church, had he fought his battles with more savvy and less naïveté, he might have been able to effect more consequential and lasting change.

Fulfilling Arrington's Agenda

As I've read Prince's biography, I've been struck by how much today's Church History Department is still working on Arrington's agenda. In 2016 Church Historian's Press published three books—two volumes of the Joseph Smith Papers, including the minutes of the Council of Fifty, and a documentary history of the Relief Society. Arrington anticipated at least two of these books. When he accepted the position of Church Historian in a meeting with Elder Howard W. Hunter of the Quorum of the Twelve Apostles, he recorded Hunter's comment that the church should not conceal documents, including the minutes of the Council of Fifty: "They are a part of our history, why should we withhold things that are a part of our history?"[2] The history of the Relief Society has its roots in the 1970s when members of Arrington's team—including Jill Mulvay Derr and Carol Cornwall Madsen, two of the coeditors of the recent documentary history—first studied the earliest minutes of the Relief Society.[3]

The documentary impulse that animated Arrington remains crucial to our own agenda. Whereas Arrington envisioned a multivolume documentary series on Brigham Young, a reflection of his interests in the American West, our defining project has considered the church's founding decades through the Joseph Smith Papers, which will include more than two dozen books and a website. Given the centrality of the Joseph Smith era for Latter-day Saint history and identity, the Joseph Smith Papers has exerted a more profound influence on Mormon culture than the Young Papers could have. Arrington's hopes for a larger series of documentary histories was scuttled as a result of controversies surrounding the first volume published.

Arrington also believed in narrative history, as evidenced by the aborted sixteen-volume sesquicentennial history series *Story of the Latter-day Saints*, written by two members of his staff; his own coauthored *The Mormon Experience*; and numerous other historical monographs written under his direction.[4] While we have focused more on documentary than narrative histories at the Church History Department, we are currently transitioning to a stronger focus on narrative history. Arrington also strongly advocated for women's history and for history from the ground up, impulses that we share with him.

We also share Arrington's vision of how an honest and scholarly history can contribute to the good of the church as well as the good of the academy. Many of us who work for the Church History Department were mentored by historians who worked in Arrington's History Division. The last of those historians—Ronald K. Esplin—retired from our department in September 2016. These concrete ties to the Arrington era explain in part our shared agenda. In addition, Arrington articulated a vision (as well as a resulting tension) that we still believe in and experience. He wrote in his journal in August 1972, "On the one hand, I am the *Church* Historian and must seek to build testimonies, spread the Word, build the Kingdom. On the other hand, I am called to be a *historian*, which means that I must earn the respect of professional historians—what I write must be craftsman like [*sic*], credible, and of good quality. This means that I stand on two legs—the leg of faith and the leg of reason." Balancing the two, Arrington admitted, "is our toughest problem." As he phrased it on another occasion, "We are trained to publish for our professional colleagues—being honest, straightforward, fearless, analytical, raising questions." But he also recognized "that Church authorities and Church audience want and have a right to expect faith-promoting history."[5]

Like Arrington, we write to two audiences: an audience of scholars and an audience of general church members. In each of our products, we clearly decide which audience has priority. With the Joseph Smith Papers, we write as scholars to scholars; with articles on the church's website, we write as historians and as fellow believers to church members. For both audiences, we must write history that is candid, professional, and true to the sources. Arrington recognized the importance that the storytelling aspect of history plays in the creation of a religious community. He reflected, "We receive spiritual uplift and enjoyment from the exchange of experiences of faith." I appreciate both Arrington's caution and his search for the divine in history: "We will also not use history as a storehouse from which deceptively simple moral lessons may be drawn at random. . . . Behind the personal decisions and the vast impersonal forces of history we will also see divine purposes at work."[6]

A New Era

While we share many of Arrington's impulses, there are deep differences between Arrington's era and our own because of changes internal and external to the church: a new acceptance of transparency, structural changes in the department, and the internationalization of church membership.

Shifts within Mormon culture mean that we experience a very different climate than did Arrington and his fellow historians. In the 1970s, deep divisions existed within the church's leadership and membership and between different segments of church employees (such as between historians and seminary and institute instructors) over the value of transparency on historical topics. Arrington bore the scars of these battles. Prince argues that these clashes, particularly the opposition of some apostles to Arrington's approach, were the primary reason that Arrington's team was transferred from church headquarters to Brigham Young University in the early 1980s.

By contrast, today's Church History Department is the beneficiary of a broad consensus among church leaders, employees, and members that transparency is essential, that it will ultimately build faith rather than destroy it. Vigorous discussions still occur over how we explain certain controversies. But a consensus has emerged that introducing church members, especially young people, to controversial topics within church settings is preferable to individuals learning about these topics through websites without an official connection to the church. Arrington believed that the church should give Latter-day Saints "exposure to facets of the history of the Church that might be uncomfortable" and taught, "God does not need our lies."[7] I likewise heard Elder Marlin K. Jensen teach that "the Spirit cannot witness to a false history." The Gospel Topics essays on complex historical topics that were produced by the Church History Department with oversight and approval by church leaders (including members of the First Quorum of the Seventy, the Twelve Apostles, and the First Presidency) are evidence of this new climate. Prince documents the acrimonious disputes between some historians and members of the Church Educational System in the 1970s. By contrast, the Gospel Topics essays are being integrated into seminary and institute curricula.

Richard Bushman has helped create this new climate of openness and has in fact celebrated it. In 2011 Bushman labeled the current era of Mormon historical scholarship a "golden age" because of the "conviction that the Church and its history can flourish in the realm of free and independent inquiry." "For decades," Bushman reminisced, "Mormon history was a kind of warfare where friends and enemies of the Church lined up to do battle. . . . Friends could not concede a single mistake on the part of the Church; enemies could not concede a single virtue." Bushman cited several products of the Church History Department—including *Massacre at Mountain Meadows: An American Tragedy* (2011) and the Joseph Smith Papers—as evidence of this new climate of openness.[8]

Structural changes within church administration and within the Church History Department have also created a different climate. Arrington was the only Church Historian who was a professional historian and not an ecclesiastical leader. Since the revival of the position of Church Historian in 2005, the Church Historian has been a senior member of the First Quorum of the Seventy: Elder Jensen and, later, Elder Steven E. Snow. Prince suggests that Arrington was unable to navigate the complex dynamics of church headquarters, including opposition from some members of the Quorum of the Twelve Apostles. A

Church Historian who is a General Authority has helped create an atmosphere of cooperation between historians, church leaders, and church staff in other departments. Arrington worried intensely about ecclesiastical reviews of historical publications, either from apostles or from the Correlation Department, which is charged with ensuring doctrinal accuracy. In my experience, church leaders now have greater trust in publications written at the Church History Department, and historians have a greater appreciation for working with church leaders and the Correlation Department. This trust and appreciation reflect both the consensus of how to approach difficult historical topics and a change at church headquarters as the church has come to value professionals in areas from public affairs to website design to history. I don't recognize many of Arrington's struggles in my own experience at church headquarters. Arrington lamented, "One cannot raise questions with ecclesiastical superiors."[9] My own experience is that ecclesiastical leaders expect that we bring our best ideas, raise questions, and appropriately challenge their own thinking.

The internationalization of church membership has also changed how we write history, particularly when we are writing for church members. When Arrington, who had a deep interest in international Mormon history, became Church Historian, Latter-day Saint congregations in much of the developing world were still in their infancy. The dramatic growth in Latin America was just beginning, and the growth in Africa was in the future. The "average" church member looks much different today than in the 1970s in terms of geography, demographics, and level of education. Today the Church History Department has volunteer historians (including Richard and Claudia Bushman) around the world who gather material, conduct oral interviews, and write histories for websites and church magazines. Today's department must plan for substantial translation resources when we wish to reach church members.

A final difference between Arrington's time and our own is the size and composition of the Publications Division. With the exception of Davis Bitton and James Allen, who had joint appointments with the History Division and their universities, Arrington primarily hired historians who were beginning graduate programs or whose graduate training was in the future. We have been fortunate to hire many individuals with PhDs in history. Their graduate training and wide-ranging dissertations mean that they have embraced a key element of the Bushman path—writing on areas outside Mormon history—before joining the Arrington path. Our operation is much larger than Arrington's. Part of that increase in size relates to the formation of the Church Historian's Press, established in 2008. Arrington had one editor on his staff; we have many who help guide our publications from initial research to typesetting and printing. These changes in professional training, number of staff members, and editorial competence have expanded what the Church History Department has been able to accomplish.

The Future

What is the role of the Church History Department in future Mormon scholarship? In the Doctrine and Covenants, the Church Historian is charged with "writing . . . for the good of the church, and for the rising generations" (D&C 69:8). We see in this a scriptural mandate that history should be written at the institutional level and that accurate and authoritative publications from the Church History Department should play a role in both academic scholarship and public understanding of Mormon history. In planning for the future, we have asked, What can we do better from the Church History Department than can be done anywhere else?

In the future, we hope to advance these objectives:

1. Highlight the department's archival collections
2. Provide an authoritative voice on church history
3. Exercise leadership by focusing resources on topics that have been relatively neglected, such as women's history and the international church

After I decided to take the Arrington path rather than the Bushman path, I read Arrington's autobiography, *Adventures of a Church Historian*.[10] While my time at church headquarters has also felt like an adventure, it has been less tumultuous than Arrington's. We are the beneficiaries of Arrington's vision and the work of many others, including Richard Bushman, who have contributed to the cultural change in which an honest and faithful appraisal of Mormon history is embraced rather than discouraged. Like Arrington, I and other historians at the Church History Department have responsibilities both to "build testimonies, spread the Word, build the Kingdom" and to produce history that earns "the respect of professional historians." If we strike the right balance, the Arrington path will continue to play a vibrant role in the writing of Mormon history during this golden age of Mormon history.

Notes

1. Gregory A. Prince, *Leonard Arrington and the Writing of Mormon History* (Salt Lake City: University of Utah Press, 2016).
2. Prince, *Arrington*, 161.
3. Jill Mulvay Derr et al., eds., *The First Fifty Years of Relief Society: Key Documents in Latter-day Saint Women's History* (Salt Lake City: Church Historian's Press, 2016).
4. Leonard J. Arrington, *Adventures of a Church Historian* (Urbana: University of Illinois Press, 1998), 122–57, 165–68.
5. Prince, *Arrington*, 162, 263.
6. Leonard J. Arrington, "Clothe These Bones: The Reconciliation of Faith and History," in *Reflections of a Mormon Historian: Leonard J. Arrington on the New Mormon History*, ed. Reid L. Neilson and Ronald W. Walker (Norman, OK: Arthur H. Clark, 2006), 155–68.
7. Prince, *Arrington*, 177.
8. Richard L. Bushman, "After the Golden Age," *Journal of Mormon History* 38 (Summer 2012): 227–28.
9. Prince, *Arrington*, 263.
10. See note 4 herein.

THE SECOND VATICAN COUNCIL AND MORMON CORRELATION FROM THE PULPIT AND THE PEW

MATTHEW BOWMAN

In 1963, Students for a Democratic Society issued a statement called *America and the New Era* warning that America was mired in "a politics of adjustment." The nation was dominated by the "Establishment," a "mediating, rationalizing, and managerial" elite that "views its problems as technical and administrative, rather than in ideological or moral terms."[1] But this rationalism offered liberation as well as captivity. SDS promised that, thanks to science, working people would soon enter politics in greater numbers and the Cold War's tension would diminish.[2] The document spoke about historical change in secular language, which is to say it credited progress to forces outside those they deemed to be religious: reason, science, democracy.[3]

This way of thinking about history and modernity was commonplace in the mid-twentieth century. But other Americans had a more fraught relationship with secular ideas about history.

Mormons and American Catholics were members of traditions that sought to resist secular narratives of social change. "There is no such thing as an accurate, objective history of the Church without consideration of the spiritual powers that attend this work," claimed the Mormon apostle Boyd K. Packer in 1981. Far earlier, at the Fifth Lateran Council in 1512, Cardinal Egidio da Viterbo offered a similar axiom repeated in Catholic circles into the twentieth century: "Man must be changed by religion, not religion by man."[4] Both traditions have faced challenges engaging a particular aspect of modernity that can be described using an axiom of the New Left as shorthand: confidence that historical change derives from human effort. Put another way, the Mormon and Catholic traditions have struggled with what Grant Wacker has called "historical consciousness"—acknowledgment that ideas, particularly religious ideas, are conditioned by the age in which they occur.[5] Christians in the West from Roman Catholics to Mormons have grappled with the notion. There are, I suspect, few Latter-day Saint scholars who have not paused for a moment above their keyboard, grappling—perhaps not with historical consciousness itself, for hardly any would deny its power as an explanatory mechanism—with how their interpretations might be received by those convinced that history works differently.

For reasons of chronology if nothing else, many scholars of Mormonism locate its origins in the evangelical ferment of the Second Great Awakening. But doing so places Mormonism in a certain historiographical narrative about American Christianity. In the two or three generations after independence, so the story goes, American Christians absorbed the sensibilities of Revolutionary and Jacksonian America and hence embraced a democratic culture. They discarded Calvinist gloominess in favor of an enthusiastic, Arminian optimism. They rejected theological debates in favor of relentless ethicism. Placing Mormonism in this narrative conditions us to emphasize certain of its aspects and, hence, perhaps overlook others.[6]

Indeed, the further into Mormonism's twentieth century we get, the less useful this evangelical model appears. By 1960, 10 percent of LDS Church membership lived outside the United States.[7] Similarly, Mormons from Joseph Smith forward constructed a church hierarchy far more powerful than the Protestant ministers the Smith family knew. By the twentieth century, the church's leadership apparatus was so unwieldy that several church presidents in a row sought to wrestle it into order, an effort culminating in the correlation program.[8] It is in this era that Mormons grappled with historical consciousness in earnest.

Jon Butler's 1991 essay "Historiographical Heresy: Catholicism as a Model for American Religious History" makes the case that certain features of American Catholicism—heterogeneity, material culture, institution—are often neglected in the historiography of American religion in favor of traditional Protestant themes like conversion and liberty.[9] This point particularly resonates, I think, because both American Catholicism and Mormonism have found that the issue of historical consciousness takes on a particular sharpness within a tradition that claims its institution has origins outside history. A juxtaposition of Mormon correlation with the American Catholic response to Vatican II will, I hope, shed new light on how these forms of Christianity have adapted to an American public sphere increasingly dominated by secular ways of talking about history.

In the 1960s both traditions mounted a major reinvention. The Second Vatican Council, which was held from 1962 to

1965, altered the liturgy to emphasize collegiality and lay participation, downplayed a monarchical interpretation of Catholic hierarchy, and took steps toward a Catholic concept of religious freedom. The Mormon program commonly called "correlation" or "priesthood correlation" was a bureaucratic reorganization inaugurated in 1960 and concluded roughly a decade later. While Vatican II emphasized decentralization and institutional authority, in part because the Catholic Church was gigantic and cosmopolitan, correlation, implemented in a much smaller church, emphasized institutional authority and the power of the male priestly hierarchy.[10]

And yet there are also similarities. On the face of it, both programs appear to assimilate modern values, downplaying monarchical authority as did Vatican II, or at the very least, like correlation, implementing corporate, modern methods of organization. Indeed, leaders in both traditions appeared to concede the point. Pope John XXIII spoke of "aggiornamento," an Italian word referring to bringing in of the new or engaging with the times.[11] Similarly, the Mormon apostle Boyd K. Packer observed that "there was a certainty at the beginning of the Correlation that we were moving into some major social changes."[12] And yet, advocates for both traditions also invoked the rhetoric of restoration, claiming the church was returning to its original identity.[13] In both cases this language rippled through the tradition in unexpected ways. Restorationism did not have a single definition, but rather enabled a variety of ways of engaging with modern ways of thinking about history. This essay evaluates the ways in which members of both churches used competing definitions of restoration to offer a variety of ways of thinking about their religious pasts.

Many Catholic leaders who supported Vatican II embraced "ressourcement," a term derived from the French *Nouvelle Theologie* movement emphasizing that a return to the early church, to patristics and the Bible, would invigorate the church's engagement with the modern age. Thus John XXIII, upon opening the Council, called for "faithful and perfect conformity to the authentic doctrine."[14] More, after the Council the language of ressourcement became a tool to enforce a particular interpretation of what the Council meant. Soon after his election, Pope Benedict XVI argued that Vatican II should be interpreted with a "hermeneutic of reform" that emphasized continuity rather than transformation.[15] This interpretation is popular among those annoyed with interpretations emphasizing how the council sought "modernization." The theologians Matthew Lamb and Matthew Levering, for instance, express impatience with interpretations of the Council as "a liberal or progressive accommodation to modernity that aimed to overcome Catholicism's traditional conservative resistance to modernity."[16]

But some American Catholics disagreed. For instance, some American Catholic women read Vatican II as a mandate of engagement with a pluralist society and reform predicated on the scientific and professional methods that the New Left embraced. The sisters in the Congregation of the Immaculate Heart of Mary in Los Angeles were educators. Two years after the Council, Mary Humiliata Caspary, the reverend mother of the order, announced reforms designed to "reflect a new understanding of the contemporary world's need" and "the growing importance our society attaches to the services of professionally trained women." Sisters could now adapt their clothing styles to fit the world around them and pursue training and vocations outside the order's traditional emphasis on education and healing. According to Caspary, they were simply following the spirit of "the Vatican II Ecumenical Council."[17]

While Catholics like Caspary viewed the Council as a way to reconcile modernity with their traditional mandate, others found that idea horrifying. The New York visionary Veronica Lueken was sure that Vatican II had surrendered to a techno-cratic and bureaucratic modernity. Instead Lueken offered herself as representative of spiritual authority that defied the modernizing Council. In September 1969 Lueken delivered to Pope Paul VI a message she claimed to have received in a vi-sion: "The word of God is eternal and must not be altered or changed. Restore all changes to the original word of God. Have men follow the rules with a love of God, not change the rules for the love of man."[18] The meaning of Vatican II was endlessly contested, and its restorationist appeal to a genuine ancient Catholicism opened the doorway to a variety of readings of its intent, which reflected the differing needs, emphases, and inter-ests of Catholics in America.

In contrast, Mormonism from the beginning had linked no-tions of restoration to ecclesiastical authority. While Catholics worried about the relationship between the pope and the bishops and the Roman and local leadership, leaders of Mormon priest-hood worried that the powerful auxiliaries of the church, which they perceived to be focused on modern values like expertise and efficiency, were stifling the traditional, religious authority of priesthood. The apostle Harold B. Lee chaired a committee with the formidable name of the All-Church Coordinating Council, the central force of the correlation movement. In 1965 he stated that his goal was "to get the priesthood fully defined and work out the scope of its program . . . [to] bring the priesthood back to where it should be, according to revelations, and then determine the relationship of the auxiliaries to the priesthood."[19] In practice this led to the centralization of authority in the male priesthood hierarchy, which weakened the authority of the primarily female-led auxiliaries.[20]

The disjuncture between the anxiety that drove correlation and its product seems striking. On the face of it, correlation appeared eminently bureaucratic. Lee commissioned an array of new committees, regularized lines of authority, instituted reporting procedures, and produced standardized manuals of instruction for church programs.[21] But Mormon leaders read the centralization of priestly authority as a restorationist gesture, invoking the Mormon past rather than the present. The apostle Marion G. Romney claimed that these reforms meant the church was "moving the way the Lord presented it to Joseph Smith before the Church was organized."[22] This process strengthened the church by restoring its original order. Bruce R. McConkie wrote, "If attempts are made to transmit the power of the gospel through auxiliary circuits or fringe committees appointed for specific purposes, the Lord's people are denied the blessings that a perfect organization perfectly operated would bring."[23] The BYU religion professor Hyrum Andrus asked perhaps most grandly about the biblical prophet Enoch, who "walked with God" in Genesis 5:24: "Do you know the reason why the City of Enoch was translated? It was because they had the correlation program of the priesthood."[24]

For some Mormons, the defiant anti-modernism of this rhetoric was compelling, and for some women it could serve as a source of authority against a largely male world of training and expertise. Barbara Smith, who served as general president of the church's Relief Society between 1975 and 1984, argued that correlation was successful precisely because it spurned those modes of authority. Smith observed in 1977 that her position on one of Lee's committees put her at loggerheads with "these men in the Church who had their doctorates . . . and I could see that sometimes their academic training led them to put material and information in ways that would not be helpful to the members of the Church." Smith thus found in correlation authority to override academic training, despite her embrace of complementarian gender roles and, hence, the church's male hierarchy.[25]

But other Mormon women embraced a very different notion of restorationism, which they believed would weaken the male authority of correlation. In 1992 the Mormon scholar Maxine Hanks published a thick edited collection titled *Women and Authority: Re-emerging Mormon Feminism.* Throughout, Hanks and her authors are inspired by, as she puts it, both "larger feminist waves" as well as the "150th anniversary of the Relief Society (the women's organization of the LDS church)." Hanks clothed feminism in the language of restoration, writing "feminism has always existed in Mormonism."[26] Scholars like Hanks, Linda King Newell, and other contributors to *Women and Authority* argued that the Mormon past required a larger place for women in their church. For Newell the lesson was clear. "A broader, more inclusive understanding of priesthood could . . . mean a reexamination of the LDS policy of ordaining women to priesthood offices or it could simply mean making changes in the *General Handbook of Instruction* which has stripped women of these opportunities."[27]

Both *Lumen Gentium,* one of the constitutions the Second Vatican Council issued, and Harold B. Lee, the main driving force behind correlation, invoked Paul's metaphor in Corinthians to describe their respective churches as the body of Christ. *Lumen Gentium* insists that the passage teaches that the church and its people are a mystical whole. When Lee mused on Corinthians, he drew a far different lesson. "As you think about those scriptures," he said, "they were given to impress the need for constant and continued consultations and correlations of the various subdivisions."[28] Vatican II uses restorationism to distance Catholicism from bureaucracy and institution; Lee seeks to baptize them. Both the Mormon apostle and the bishops who supported *Lumen Gentium* appealed to the religious past to define what their respective religious tradition should be like, and yet neither could return to that past in pure and uncomplicated ways. Indeed, neither really wanted to, because restorationism is less a quest for historical purity than it is a strategy of legitimacy. Thus, both programs sought to appeal to the past as a means to grapple with the modern values secular reformers embraced, and in neither case was it an unqualified success. In each case other voices variously pleased, distressed, or dissatisfied with the language and programs of the institution also seized upon the rhetorical strategy they saw Lee and the Council invoking, and the uses to which they put the past illustrate the endless malleability the language of restoration offers to institutional religious traditions.

Notes

1. Students for a Democratic Society, *America and the New Era (Chicago: Students for a Democratic Society, 1963)*, 6–7. See also Todd Gitlin, *The Sixties* (New York: Bantam Books, 1993), 196–97.
2. *America and the New Era*, 1.

3. Charles Taylor, *A Secular Age* (Cambridge, MA: Harvard University Press, 2007), 1–3.

4. Boyd K. Packer, "The Mantle Is Far, Far Greater than the Intellect," *BYU Studies* 21 (Summer 1981): 259–78; da Viterbo is discussed and cited in John C. Olin, *Catholic Reform: From Cardinal Ximenes to the Council of Trent* (New York: Fordham University Press, 1990), 35–36.

5. Grant Wacker, *Augustus H. Strong and the Dilemma of Historical Consciousness* (Macon, GA: Mercer University Press, 1985), 9–19.

6. For works in this school of thought, see Whitney Cross, *The Burned-Over District: The Social and Intellectual History of Enthusiastic Religion in Western New York, 1800–1850* (Ithaca, NY: Cornell University Press, 1950); Nathan O. Hatch, *The Democratization of American Christianity* (New Haven, CT: Yale University Press, 1989), 113–22; and Gordon Wood, "Evangelical America and Early Mormonism," *New York History* 61 (October 1980): 361.

7. James B. Allen and Glen Leonard, *The Story of the Latter-day Saints* (Salt Lake City: Deseret Book, 1976), 564.

8. Gregory Prince and William Robert Wright, *David O. McKay and the Rise of Modern Mormonism* (Salt Lake City: University of Utah, 2005), 139–59; and Armand Mauss, *The Angel and the Beehive: The Mormon Struggle with Assimilation* (Urbana: University of Illinois Press, 1994). I have adapted some of the previous paragraph from my "Toward a Catholic History of Mormonism," *Journal of Mormon History* 41 (January 2015): 198–216.

9. Jon Butler, "Historiographical Heresy: Catholicism as a Model for American Religious History," in *Belief in History: Innovative Approaches to European and American Religion*, ed. Thomas Kselman (South Bend: University of Notre Dame Press, 1991), 287–88.

10. Adrian Hastings, ed., Modern Catholicism: Vatican II and After (New York: Oxford University Press, 1990); John O'Malley, What

Happened at Vatican II (Cambridge, MA: Harvard University Press, 2010); and Matthew Lamb and Matthew Levering, Vatican II: Renewal within Tradition (New York: Oxford University Press, 2008).

11. Vincent Yzermans, *A New Pentecost: Vatican Council II: Session 1* (Westminster: Newman, 1963), 116–18.

12. Cited in Peter Wiley, "The Lee Revolution and the Rise of Correlation," *Sunstone* 10/1 (1984): 20.

13. Mircea Eliade, *Myth and Reality* (New York: Harper and Row, 1963), 5–6; and Richard T. Hughes and Leonard C. Allen, *Illusions of Innocence: Protestant Primitivism in America, 1630–1875* (Urbana: University of Illinois Press, 1988). Massimo Faggoli, *Vatican II: The Battle for Meaning* (New York: Paulist Press, 2012), argues that restoration was the central theme by which Vatican II explained itself.

14. Yzermans, *New Pentecost*, 118.

15. Quoted and discussed in Martin Rhonheimer, "Benedict XVI's 'Hermeneutic of Reform' and Religious Freedom," *Nova et Vetera* 9 (Fall 2011): 1029–54.

16. Lamb and Levering, *Vatican II*, 3, 4.

17. Dan Thrapp, "Order of Nuns Here Plans to Modernize Dress, Ideas," *Los Angeles Times*, October 18, 1967, B1, 8. See also Mark Massa, *The American Catholic Revolution: How the Sixties Changed the Church Forever* (New York: Oxford University Press, 2014), 75–103; and Colleen McDannell, *The Spirit of Vatican II* (New York: Basic Books, 2011), 130–37.

18. Joseph Laycock, *The Seer of Bayside: Veronica Lueken and the Struggle to Define Catholicism* (New York: Oxford University Press, 2014), 56–60, 109–14; and Michael Cuneo, *The Smoke of Satan: Conservative and Traditionalist Dissent in Contemporary American Catholicism* (Baltimore: Johns Hopkins Press, 1999), 121–79.

19. "Correlation Chronology as reflected in the minutes of Correlation Executive Committee Meetings," 3, Church History Library, Church of Jesus Christ of Latter-day Saints, Salt Lake City, Utah.

20. Marie Cornwall, "The Institutional Role of Mormon Women," in *Contemporary Mormonism: Social Science Perspectives*, ed. Marie Cornwall, Tim Heaton, and Lawrence Young (Urbana: University of Illinois Press, 1994), 239–64; and Tina Hatch, "'Changing Times Bring Changing Conditions': Relief Society, 1960 to the Present," *Dialogue: A Journal of Mormon Thought* 37 (Fall 2004): 65–94.

21. Kendall O. Price and Kent Lloyd, "New Approaches to Church Executive Leadership: Behavioral Science Perspectives," *Dialogue* 2 (Winter 1967): 41–49.

22. *Deseret News*, December 11, 1971, 3, cited in Jerry Rose, "The Correlation Program of the Church of Jesus Christ of Latter-day Saints during the Twentieth Century" (master's thesis, Brigham Young University, 1973), 2, https://scholarsarchive.byu.edu.

23. Bruce R. McConkie, *The Ten Commandments of Priesthood Correlation* (Salt Lake City: Deseret Book, 1976), 10.

24. Hyrum Andrus, *Priesthood Correlation: The Lord's Battle Plan* (Provo, UT: BYU Fourth Stake, 1972), 3. In Mormon scripture, in the Book of Moses, chapter 7, Enoch builds a city that is taken to heaven.

25. Barbara B. Smith, interview with Jesse Embry, Salt Lake City, 1977, OH 311, Church History Library.

26. Maxine Hanks, ed., preface to *Women and Authority: Re-emerging Mormon Feminism* (Salt Lake City: Signature Books, 1992), viii–xi.

27. Linda King Newell, "The Historical Relationship of Mormon Women and Priesthood," in Hanks, *Women and Authority*, 44.

28. Harold B. Lee, "New Plan of Coordination Explained," in *Conference Report*, October 1961, 78–79.

5 | SCHOLARSHIP IN ITS PUREST AND BEST FORM?

MORMONISM IN THE ACADEMY AND IN THE SECULAR STUDY OF RELIGION

Section Introduction

RICHARD D. BROWN

In commenting on the learned and insightful observations of Professors Grant Underwood and Brian Birch,[1] it is appropriate for me, a historian of early American social and political history, to explain that my familiarity with religious studies, and Mormonism in particular, is at most rudimentary. The remarks that follow come from an interested, though not especially well-informed, observer.

Grant Underwood's discussion on Mormonism in the academy provides a clear and persuasive overview of the challenges Mormon scholars have faced in engaging the broad, non-Mormon academic world. Because of the Latter-day Saints' comparatively recent origins, and their condemnation by some as a non-Christian cult or an irrational pseudo-religion, LDS scholars have faced challenges to the legitimacy of their work that academics belonging to older faiths—or no faith—have not confronted. This is particularly true of the academic study of religion. Underwood cites church president Spencer Kimball's insight that LDS scholars must be "bilingual," capable of mastering the "language of scholarship" as well as "the language of spiritual things." To this outsider, Underwood and Kimball's understanding of the relationship of scholarship and faith applies equally to members of all faiths and to all scholars of religion. Indeed, if this secular person can speak metaphorically, then surely Neal A. Maxwell's observation that "academic scholarship is a form of worship"[2] possesses a similarly broad application. Although some in academe doubt there is such a thing as truth, in my view scholarship in its purest and best form, like religion, seeks to discover and reveal truth. Certainly, scholarly understandings of truth are mutable, but belief in a search for truth is common to both scholarship and religion.

Underwood embraces "the Marsden settlement," the idea that "Christian historians should leave the theologizing to the theologians" and avoid "pinpointing God's particular interventions." This would appear a wise strategy when a religious historian, Mormon or other, seeks to be "bilingual." One might also add that historians, religious or not, properly operate in at least three different modes: descriptive, analytical, and interpretive. One of Richard Bushman's particular skills when writing of Joseph Smith and Mormon history in his academic works is his capacity to emphasize the descriptive and analytical while leaving key interpretive questions to the judgment of his readers. Some have argued this is a weakness, but actually this is one key to his "bilingual" success.

Where I part company with Bushman and Underwood, however, is where Underwood approvingly quotes Bushman urging scholars and students to change themselves, as Bushman says he changed, "until I could see the world as God sees it. . . . I had to be more godly." Here Underwood and Bushman eschew bilingualism. No secular scholar, and many religious scholars, would ever imagine possessing the capacity to see the world "as God sees it," and few would confidently profess becoming "more godly."

Here, perhaps, Brian Birch's careful and insightful analysis of LDS scholarship in relation to the broad field of religious studies is especially helpful because of Birch's rigorous attention to distinctions between theology, religious studies, and apologetics. Birch recognizes that joining the pluralistic approach he advocates to apologetics—as the Maxwell Institute intends—will be challenging. He notes the concern of at least one BYU professor who warns that the institute may be "succumbing to a secular paradigm." Birch argues that both apologetic and pluralistic methods are legitimate; but if they are to live happily together under one roof, scholars using these different approaches will need to exercise mutual forbearance and self-restraint. They must restrain claims to "seeing the world as God sees it" and to possessing increased godliness.

As to the entire corpus of academic inquiry, I see nothing distinctive to Mormon religion that would be an impediment to the search for truth. In mathematics, physics, engineering, and the natural sciences, or applied fields such as business or medicine, LDS teachings need not compromise scholarship any more than do the contents of other religions. Biblical and Book of Mormon literalism, which deny the findings of geology and biological evolution, can handicap the scholarship of all the Abrahamic faiths.

Some might suspect that LDS teachings handicap scholarship in the "human sciences"—anthropology, psychology, sociology. But that would only be when the scholar rejected "bi-lingualism" and chose to impose Mormon teachings on scholarly observations. As in the natural sciences, the first task of the human scientist is observation—data collection—and description. Arguably, a Mormon might improperly filter those observations according to the teachings of faith, but so might a Buddhist, a Catholic, a Jew, a Hindu, a Muslim, or anyone among the many varieties of Protestants. The scholar strives for objectivity, and while the achievement of objectivity may never be total or entirely pure, the issue of objectivity is not distinct for Mormons.

As Underwood and Birch have explained, there remain several areas of academic inquiry where concern about "Mormon bias" may be legitimate: history, philosophy, and religion. As to Richard Bushman, whose "presumption" I questioned above, there is no scholar whose work or integrity I admire more. I know no one who tries harder, or more successfully, to investigate historical sources and to "listen" to them carefully and conscientiously. That is why he is a master scholar. Nevertheless, as alluded to earlier, some scholars have criticized his Joseph Smith studies because he is not critical of Smith and the origins of Mormonism. Why do I, a secular scholar, reject this line of criticism? Though trained to be skeptical, I cannot find fault with Bushman's treatment, because it is scrupulously informed by and descriptive of the sources. Nor does Bushman shy away from recounting contemporary critics of Smith and his followers. He does not assert that Smith was an authentic voice; he invites his readers to judge whether Smith was or was not a genuine prophet.

Let me illustrate with an analogy based on teaching the history of New England's "Great Awakening." For years my students and I read the Reverend Jonathan Edwards's account of the revival he witnessed in Northampton, Massachusetts, and surrounding parishes. Edwards was one of the great learned and sophisticated intellects of his era. Many believe he had the best mind in colonial Anglo-America. Moreover, he was an observer-participant at the epicenter of the religious awakening, and as it was happening he described events in detail. His was precisely the kind of eyewitness account that historians hunger after and seldom possess. What better source could there be into how and why the awakening occurred? And how did Edwards explain the phenomena he witnessed so closely? He explained it as an outpouring of the Spirit of God. So we must ponder: was the awakening an outpouring of the Spirit of God? My personal "antisupernatural" belief system makes me reject Edwards's explanation, yet who am I to rebut a brilliant, conscientious eyewitness observer? I will not rebut Edwards. I can doubt him, I can hypothesize alternative explanations of the awakening, but it is a fact that I do not know why it happened. For me to dismiss the testimony of Edwards would be both arrogant and parochial.

The same, I believe, is true of Bushman's account of Joseph Smith's prophesying and the golden plates. I am skeptical, but I am not prepared to dismiss it any more than I would dismiss the stories of the Old and New Testaments. What we must all admire in Richard Bushman's recounting of early Mormon history is his readiness to expose his readers to the sources, to describe them faithfully, and to allow readers to draw their own conclusions. Here we see a rare scholarly humility. Other scholars, non-Mormons, have often felt compelled to dismiss Joseph Smith as a fraud. They have allowed their own religious beliefs to dictate their interpretation. From my own personal perspective, one might as well declare Buddha, Jesus, Moses, and Muhammad frauds—together with everyone else across history who dealt in the supernatural. Some scholars have made the choice to dismiss the supernatural, or that fraction of the supernatural with which they disagree. But that choice does not enlarge our understanding of history or of humankind. It is not a choice that Underwood, Birch, or the Maxwell Institute would embrace.

If I understand correctly, there is at least one aspect of traditional LDS understandings of the Book of Mormon that does not stand the test of academic scholarship—that is the idea that the Native Americans were descendants of the ten lost tribes of Israel. But if Christian, Jewish, and Muslim scholars do not have to defend the historical accuracy of the Old and New Testaments, then Mormon scholars are not compelled to do the same for the Book of Mormon. These religious texts were not established according to the canons of academic scholarship. Indeed, were it not for the long history of America's Christian majority dismissing the LDS Church as an illegitimate cult, unworthy of respect, there would be no question of the legitimacy of the scholarship of Mormons. In this century the standards Mormon scholars must meet are in no fundamental way different from the standards that scholars of other faiths, and no faith, must meet.

Notes

1. Patrick Q. Mason was unable to present his essay at the June 2016 colloquium. Accordingly, this introduction does not take Mason's work into account.
2. Neal A. Maxwell, "The Disciple-Scholar," in *On Becoming a Disciple-Scholar*, ed. Henry B. Eyring (Salt Lake City: Bookcraft, 1995), 7.

ON BEING EPISTEMICALLY VULNERABLE

Mormonism and the Secular Study of Religion

BRIAN D. BIRCH

On a March evening in 1955, Sterling McMurrin presented a paper at the University of Utah's Great Issues Forum entitled "Religion and the Denial of History." The occasion was a debate between McMurrin and Hugh Nibley on the potential conflict between the claims of faith and the claims of history. Among his more provocative claims, McMurrin asserted that religion undergoes its most severe testing when it is "studied and discussed seriously by rational and informed persons with open minds and honest intentions."[1]

As I reread this essay in recent months, I imagined Richard Bushman sitting in the Orson Spencer Hall auditorium that spring evening ruminating over his response to McMurrin. By all accounts, Richard meets the conditions specified above. Here is a person who is rational, informed, intellectually generous, and impeccably honest, and yet who comes to very different conclusions about the implications of history for lived religious experience. As the author of the seminal essay "Faithful History," Bushman cautions his reader that "scriptural principles will guide us toward more powerful works of history only when those principles are fully and naturally incorporated into our ways of thinking; so that when we look at the world we see it in these categories without lying to ourselves or neglecting any of the evidence."[2]

The ways in which religious beliefs are tested by evidence and shaped by spirituality have been an abiding fascination of mine. A handful of questions predominate as I continue to wrestle with how Latter-day Saints engage with questions of faith, reason, and the principles of empirical investigation.

1. How much secular knowledge can Mormonism embrace without eroding the claims of the faith?
2. How vulnerable can Mormonism be relative to critical inquiry into its history, theology, and culture?
3. How does Mormonism navigate the distinction between the empirical and the spiritual?
4. How much disagreement is present within the LDS community regarding the role of academic scholarship in understanding Mormonism?
5. What metaphors, scriptures, and narratives have been employed in thinking about the relationship between secular scholarship and the LDS gospel?
6. What has been the effect of these narratives in shaping the educational culture of the Latter-day Saints?

These are, of course, prodigious questions that require careful and sustained attention. For the purposes of this colloquium,

I will focus attention on a few features that are informed by my own fields, namely, the philosophy of religion and theological studies. I have no pretensions toward settling any of these issues. My aim, rather, is to help *clarify* some issues at stake, to help map the terrain a bit, and to briefly point in a direction I believe Mormon studies should go.

To our good fortune, there is no better time to be exploring these questions together as we experience the dramatic growth of Mormon studies. The explosion of publications, the development of institutional programs, and the ecclesiastical support for academic engagement have been both exciting and rewarding. We also know that these developments have not come without their share of struggles, tensions, and misunderstandings. These obstacles and challenges have been informed by considerations present within American academic culture and how these relate to (or bypass) the sensibilities of Mormon thought and practice.

For example, Mormonism has not had any substantial stake in the debates at the AAR regarding the role of theological education (as compared to other Christian denominations). Among the distinctive features of the Latter-day Saints is the perpetuation of a lay clergy without regard for professional studies in theology, ministry, or religious education. The absence of divinity schools (and related academic programs) has contributed to an environment in which LDS clergy and institutional educators have largely been removed from the dynamics of both theological and religious studies.

Despite this fact, there are a number of key issues in the academy that have, I believe, profound implications for the study of Mormonism. For example, a prime debate in religious studies has been the extent to which theology serves as a protective strategy in the face of critical scrutiny. Scholars such as

Donald Wiebe and Russell McCutcheon have spent the better part of their careers arguing that theology can have no substantive role in understanding religious phenomena. For them, there exists a "tremendous gulf" between "scholars of religion, on the one hand, and theologians, on the other."[3]

Religious Experience

Examples of what they find objectionable can be readily found in Christian apologetic discourse—particularly as it relates to religious experience. The evangelical philosopher William Lane Craig provides a dramatic illustration in his discussion of Christian epistemology: "I shall argue that the inner witness of the Holy Spirit gives us an immediate and veridical assurance of the truth of our Christian faith" such that "rational argument and evidence may properly *confirm* but not *defeat* that assurance."[4]

For the sake of this presentation, I will call this the *immunity principle*—that is, the idea that certain religious beliefs are immune or insusceptible to revision or abandonment. This unidirectional approach to Christian belief has long been an object of tension in religious studies—in part because the ultimate appeal to religious experience is said to subvert the legitimacy of academic inquiry. Because reason and evidence are *subsumed* by religious concepts and narratives, critics maintain that the entire enterprise is hopelessly compromised.

One can easily recognize the resonance between Craig's account and that of many Latter-day Saints. Despite historical tensions between the two traditions, Mormonism and evangelical Christianity share a particularly strong reliance on individual religious experience in shaping their approach to the proprieties of human knowledge. In both cases specifically, religious experience is frequently said to function as a secure footing to withstand the storms of secular scholarship. For Protestants, this "self-authenticating" nature of religious experience plays an important role in the theology of the magisterial reformers—most notably John Calvin.

> If we desire to provide in the best way for our consciences—
> that they may not be perpetually beset by the instability of
> doubt or vacillation, and that they may not also boggle at
> the smallest quibbles—we ought to seek our conviction in a
> higher place than human reasons, judgments, or conjectures,
> that is, in the secret testimony of the Spirit.[5]

Martin Luther, for his part, drew a distinction between the *magisterial* use of reason, which is employed to stand in judgment of the Christian gospel to determine its truth or falsity, and the *ministerial* use of reason, which serves the gospel and defers to the teachings of the Holy Spirit.

Among Latter-day Saints, reason is said to play a similarly deferential role. In his discussion of reason and revelation, Dallin Oaks maintains that "study and reason are a means to an end, and the end is the revelation of God."[6] Harold B. Lee puts the matter more directly: "The revelations of God are the standards by which we measure all learning, and if anything squares not with the revelations, then we may be certain it is not truth."[7] Individual religious experience serves in these cases to *confirm* the content of revelation as taught by the church.

Returning to Craig, it is worth noting that, in his consideration of rival religious experiences, he explicitly rules out the legitimacy of Latter-day Saint accounts.

Why should I think that when a Mormon claims to experience a "burning in the bosom" he is having an experience qualitatively indistinguishable from the witness of the Holy Spirit that I enjoy? Why should I think that the cognitive mechanism that enables me to form the belief that I am a child of God is the same mechanism that produced the psychological experience he *mistakenly* identifies as the witness of the Spirit?[8]

Of course, from the perspective of Latter-day Saints, Craig is the one who has mistakenly identified his experience and who lacks the *genuine* witness of the Holy Spirit. What is vital for our purposes, however, lies not in their status as rival claimants—that is an argument for another day—but rather in their shared approach to their experiences, namely, to invoke them as the final court of appeal in relation to the findings of scholarship.

Apologetics, Pluralism, and the Virtues of Openness

These considerations lead to a second set of points regarding questions of academic capaciousness. I have argued elsewhere in favor of a kind of "methodological pluralism" in approaching Mormon studies—the primary purpose of which was to identify the conditions under which apologetic scholarship may contribute in *academically* productive ways to this subfield.[9] I took up this issue with the aim of proposing a constructive way forward in the debates between the apologetics community and scholars advocating the development of critical methodologies in the academic study of Mormonism. The relevance of these issues is evident in the fracas surrounding the change of leadership and direction at Brigham Young University's Neal A.

Maxwell Institute for Religious Scholarship. As the traditional epicenter of Mormon apologetics, the Maxwell Institute has expanded its reach to engage more deeply with the religious studies community.

Though apologetic work will remain a part of the institute's new direction, it will not dominate to the exclusion of other methodological approaches. The creation of the new *Mormon Studies Review* is a substantial investment in this new direction. The institute's new director, Spencer Fluhman, has stated that the *Review* "aspires to provide a forum where the shape of these conversations can be made apparent, where underlying assumptions can be assessed, and where comparative possibilities can be explored."[10] These changes are significant for many reasons, not the least of which because it allows for a degree of reciprocity and vulnerability heretofore not seen among LDS educational institutions. If "underlying assumptions can be assessed," how far may this assessment reach into the faith claims of the Latter-day Saints? How will the institutional dynamics of authoritative discourse inform the conversation? To what extent will this inclusiveness be seen as an erosive force to traditional faith?

One of the more fascinating features of these debates has been the accusation that the Maxwell Institute is opening the door to a creeping secularism—that the quest for academic legitimacy has led to an unhealthy compromise of spiritual values. Among the most vociferous has been BYU political science professor Ralph Hancock, who openly worries that Brigham Young University is "succumbing to a secular paradigm" and thus losing the distinctiveness of its institutional mission. "There comes a point where the secular framework . . . can no longer be translated into the community's authoritative religious idiom. When this happens, faith is left speechless, defenseless, resourceless."[11]

This point leads us back to questions of a pluralist approach to Mormon studies.

On the one hand, my inclusive approach would actively invite secular and other critical "frameworks" to engage with apologetic, fideistic, and confessional approaches. Of course, translation into a community's idiom may or may not be possible given a diversity of methodologies. I would argue, however, that translation is neither necessary nor realistic in maintaining a healthy academic culture among the Latter-day Saints. Though vigilance is a virtue in retaining the religious vitality and distinctiveness of Mormonism, there is considerable danger in the isolationism that comes with assuming a monolithic Mormon idiom—authoritative or otherwise. There is a form of "speechlessness" in this situation as well.

From another direction, the pluralist position has been criticized for its alleged failure to maintain an appropriate division of labor between apologetics and religious studies. Because apologetics seeks to defend the Christian *faith*, it is said to be oriented toward different objects and ends. This is a widespread approach among historians and social scientists that allows for a tidy compartmentalization of the empirical and the spiritual—it is also a close relative to methodologies that call for the "bracketing" of religious truth claims.[12]

Though I can appreciate the advantages of this approach, it also opens the door to confusion and mischief. Some forms of apologetics are explicit in making rival *empirical* claims that are, in principle, testable and thus subject to the same kind of scrutiny that any other empirical claim invites. Others are more self-consciously nonempirical and lend themselves to different forms of appraisal.[13] Thus, there are occasions that require drilling beneath the surface grammar of apologetic accounts in order to clarify what kinds of claims are being advanced and the proper method for assessing them. A pluralistic approach also requires caution and introspection when attempts are made to either (a) *imperialize* rival accounts within one's home categories or (b) *alienate* alternative methodologies as irrelevant.

Engaging with, and learning from, one's critics is an essential part of the academic enterprise. So to the extent that apologetics is truly an academic endeavor, it is, in my mind, obligated to be in active conversation with rival paradigms and theories. Of course, the same principles hold for critical appraisals of Mormonism. To the extent this occurs, it is at once both painful and therapeutic—painful because it lays bare inaccurate histories, bad arguments, anachronistic evidence, and destructive narratives; therapeutic because it has the potential to create live possibilities for those who are rightfully dubious of some traditional narratives.

My idealized intellectual community is one in which rival paradigms productively engage one another in terms of *the very ways in which* they imperialize one another and what this means for their respective projects. If one person's datum is another person's axiom, should not this be the subject of probing discussion rather than grounds for dismissal? I say this not in the interest of mere peacemaking, but rather to insist that quality scholarship demands that we take our critics seriously. It is an unfortunate fact that the history of Mormon apologetics has been spotted with episodes in which the best virtues of scholarship and collegiality were lacking. It is also unfortunate that the culture of Mormon apologetics has not been a more inclusive and reciprocal endeavor. But it did not *need* to go in this direction, and there is no necessity for its continued direction.

Fortunately, there are positive and hopeful signs that the enterprise is becoming more dialogical and rigorous.

Beyond apologetics, I am hopeful that Mormon studies will become a model interdisciplinary field. To be realized, this would involve much more than the mere presence of different disciplines. It would involve genuine *interdisciplinarity* such that scholars from a variety of outlooks actively engage one another to explore how their diverse experiences and methodologies bear on one other. It would also be aggressively inclusive and exercise good faith in all directions. Of course, I do not mean to imply that this has not happened, or that it has not happened well—it certainly has and I am grateful for it. But there is much more that can be done to realize Joseph Smith's response to ideological diversity, namely, to lift humankind up "in their own way."[14]

Notes

1. Sterling M. McMurrin, "Religion and the Denial of History" (Great Issues Forum, University of Utah, Salt Lake City, March 23, 1955). A portion of the paper was published in *Sunstone* 82 (March/April 1982) and was revised and reprinted in Sterling M. McMurrin, *Religion, Reason, and Truth: Historical Essays in the Philosophy of Religion* (Salt Lake City: University of Utah Press, 1982), 133–44.
2. Richard L. Bushman, "Faithful History," *Dialogue: A Journal of Mormon Thought* 4 (Winter 1969): 25. The essay was reprinted alongside other related works by Bushman in his *Believing History: Latter-day Saint Essays*, ed. Reid L. Neilson and Jed Woodworth (New York: Columbia University Press, 2007).
3. Russell T. McCutcheon, "The Study of Religion as an Anthropol-

ogy of Credibility," in *Religious Studies, Theology, and the University: Conflicting Maps, Changing Terrain*, ed. Lindell E. Cady and Delwin Brown (Albany: State University of New York Press, 2002), 15. See also Russell T. McCutcheon, *Manufacturing Religion: The Discourse on Sui Generis Religion and the Politics of Nostalgia* (New York: Oxford University Press, 1997); and Donald Wiebe, *The Politics of Religious Studies: The Continuing Conflict with Theology in the Academy* (New York: Palgrave MacMillan, 1999).

4. William Lane Craig, "Classical Apologetics," in *Five Views on Apologetics*, ed. Steven B. Cowan (Grand Rapids, MI: Zondervan, 2000), 28, emphasis added. See also William Lane Craig, *Reasonable Faith: Christian Truth and Apologetics* (Wheaton, IL: Crossway Books, 1984). Though Craig's writings on the subject are less nuanced than other accounts, his candor and directness are effective in identifying the key issues at hand. For more rigorous treatments, see, for example, Keith Yandell, "Self-Authenticating Religious Experience," *Sophia* 16 (October 1977): 8–18; Caroline Franks Davis, *The Evidential Force of Religious Experience* (Oxford: Clarendon Press, 1989); Alvin Plantinga, *Warranted Christian Belief* (New York: Oxford University Press, 2000), especially part 3; and William J. Abraham, "The Epistemological Significance of the Inner Witness of the Holy Spirit," *Faith and Philosophy* 7 (October 1990): 434–50.

5. John Calvin, *Institutes of the Christian Religion* (1559), trans. F. L. Battles (London: SCM Press, 1961), I.7.4.

6. Dallin H. Oaks, *The Lord's Way* (Salt Lake City: Deseret Book, 1991), 65.

7. Harold B. Lee, *Stand Ye in Holy Places* (Salt Lake City: Deseret Book, 1974), 143.

8. Craig, "Classical Apologetics," 36, emphasis added.

9. Brian D. Birch, "In Defense of Methodological Pluralism:

Theology, Apologetics, and the Critical Study of Mormonism," *Mormon Studies Review* 1 (2014): 53–62. See also Birch, "'Faith Seeking Understanding': Mormon Atheology and the Challenge of Fideism," in *Mormonism at the Crossroads of Philosophy and Theology* (Salt Lake City: Greg Kofford Books, 2012), 47–68; and Birch, "Theological Method and the Question of Truth: A Postliberal Approach to Mormon Doctrine and Practice," in *Discourses in Mormon Theology: Philosophical and Theological Possibilities*, ed. James M. McLachlan and Loyd Ericson (Salt Lake City: Greg Kofford Books, 2007), 103–31.

10. J. Spencer Fluhman, "Friendship: An Editor's Introduction," *Mormon Studies Review* 1 (2014): 3.

11. Ralph Hancock, "Keeping Faith in Provo: Warning of the Dangers of Secularism for Brigham Young University," *First Things* (March 2014), https://www.firstthings.com/article/2014/03/keeping-faith-in-provo. See also Hancock, "Who's Afraid of Secularism?," *Meridian Magazine*, March 3, 2015, http://ldsmag.com/whos-afraid-of-secularism/; and Hancock, "To Whom Shall We Go? From 'Apologetics' to 'Mormon Studies,'" *Meridian Magazine*, December 21, 2014, http://ldsmag.com/to-whom-shall-we-go-from-apologetics-to-mormon-studies/.

12. See, for example, Stephen Prothero, "Belief Unbracketed: A Case for the Religion Scholar to Reveal More of Where He or She Is Coming From," *Harvard Divinity Bulletin* 32 (Winter/Spring 2004): 10–11; and Robert A. Orsi, "A 'Bit of Judgment,'" *Harvard Divinity Bulletin* 32 (Summer 2004): 15–16. Similar compartmentalization occurs in the science and religion literature (e.g., the concept of "nonoverlapping magisteria"). See Stephen J. Gould, *Rocks of Ages: Science and Religion in the Fullness of Life* (New York: Ballantine Books, 1999); and Gould, "Nonoverlapping Magisteria," *Natural History* 106 (February 1997): 16–22, 60–62.

13. See, for example, C. Stephen Evans, *The Historical Christ and the Jesus of Faith* (New York: Oxford University Press, 1996); and Van A. Harvey, *The Historian and the Believer: The Morality of Historical Knowledge and Christian Belief* (New York: MacMillan, 1966).

14. Smith preached a sermon in July 1843 in which he is reported to have said, "If I esteem mankind to be in error, shall I bear them down? No. I will lift them up, and in their own way too if I cannot persuade them my way is better; and I will not seek to compel any man to believe as I do, only by the force of reasoning; for truth will cut its own way" (*History of the Church*, 5:499).

"MORMONISM IN THE ACADEMY"
Reflections on Its Meaning

GRANT UNDERWOOD

This paper seeks to address three basic questions suggested by the title of our colloquium. Is there a place for *Mormons* in the academy? Is there a place for the *study* of Mormonism in the academy? And is there a place for *Mormon values and beliefs* to inform work done in the academy?

The first question—whether Mormon scholars have a place in the academy—is easily answered yes today. In ever-growing numbers, particularly over the past half century, distinguished scholars who happen to be Latter-day Saints can be found in almost every academic discipline. Indeed, a recent study sponsored by the Institute for Jewish and Community Research found that Mormons were "overrepresented" in academia.[1] Happily, the days of blatant discrimination against highly trained, exceptionally talented scholars from historically marginalized sectors of society on grounds of religion, race, or gender have largely passed. With few exceptions, Mormons today who learn and play by the rules of the academy have the same opportunities as any other scholars in their fields.

Playing by the rules may not be difficult for the devout Christian when one's field is mathematics or mechanical engineering. What about the realm of religious scholarship? Here one of the cardinal rules of the academy is to recognize that its methods do not provide the tools necessary to determine the reality or presence of the supernatural. This means that ultimate truth claims must be set aside or "bracketed out" of the academic study of religion. The goal, explains Stephen Stein, "is not to declare one or another religious group to be 'true' and all others 'false,' but rather to understand the ways these religious communities have functioned in the lives of their members and the roles they have played in the story of our nation."[2] The academic study of religion is about investigation, not indoctrination; analysis, not catechesis. Its objective is to probe, not propagate, particular religions. When I describe to my LDS students the academic ground rules for the study of religion, it at first seems to them that such an approach asks that they abandon the testimony-bearing part of their identity. Then we discuss a statement by Margaret Miles in her 1999 presidential address to the American Academy of Religion: "Believing strongly in the divine revelation of one's own religion," she declared, "one can still recognize that its beliefs and practices emerged in history as human efforts to give form and substance to that revelation. As human products, religious beliefs, practices, and institutions are always in need of critical scrutiny. Their *effects*, not merely their intentions, must be acknowledged and examined."[3]

Lest this seem like a high-level cop-out, I remind my students that no less a figure than LDS Church president Spencer Kimball had this to say to Mormon scholars: "[Your] dual concerns with the secular and the spiritual require you to be 'bilingual.' As LDS scholars you must speak with authority and excellence to your professional colleagues in the language of scholarship, and you must also be literate in the language of spiritual things. We must be more bilingual."[4] LDS apostle Neal A. Maxwell, after whom the institute hosting this conference is named, put it this way: "For a disciple of Jesus Christ, academic scholarship is a form of worship. [That gets my students' attention.] It is actually another dimension of consecration. Hence one who seeks to be a disciple-scholar will take both scholarship and discipleship seriously."[5]

In the decades since President Kimball made his remarks, mastery of the language of scholarship has become ever more apparent among Mormon scholars of religion and religious history. Consequently, to the second question—whether the *study* of Mormonism has a place in the academy—a number of twenty-first-century markers provide a clear yes. First and foremost is the proliferation of books and articles about Mormons and Mormonism that have been published by top-tier university presses and journals. Second is the recognition by national scholarly institutions that the academic study of Mormonism is both possible and desirable. In 2005, largely on the strength of Richard Bushman's academic track record, the National Endowment for the Humanities for the first time accepted a Mormon topic for one of its annual Summer Seminars for College and University Teachers. Two years later, the American Academy of Religion approved inclusion of a Mormon Studies Group in its expansive family of thematically focused units. Almost concurrently, the first endowed chairs in Mormon studies appeared at non-Mormon universities.[6] These milestone acknowledgments signal that enough academically acceptable work on Mormonism has been produced, especially in the last half century, that the study of Mormonism is now a viable, vibrant, and full-fledged part of the academy.

The third question—whether Mormon beliefs and values can successfully inform scholarly work in the academy without violating its procedural protocols—is more complicated. With regard to the discipline of history, the question parallels a discussion that has been taking place at least since 1948 when, at the annual meeting of the American Historical Association, Yale historian Kenneth Scott Latourette delivered his famous presidential address, "The Christian Understanding of History."[7] Is there, or should there be, a distinctively Mormon understanding of, or approach to, history? At the very outset, we are confronted by the challenge of identifying that which might distinctively be called "Mormon." Years ago Perry Miller remarked that what one finds in seventeenth-century New England is one-tenth Puritanism and nine-tenths a culture common to all English people. Yet "their attitudes towards all sorts of things," he wrote, "are pounced upon and exhibited as peculiarities of their sect, when as a matter of fact they were normal attitudes of the time."[8] Much the same can be said of Mormonism. So what is that "one-tenth" that truly is uniquely Mormon? The situation is further complicated by the fact that Mormonism is not a monolith. A somewhat different pattern of Mormon values and beliefs is discernible across time, space, and socioeconomic situation. Gender, race, and cultural background also all inform one's inflection of Mormonism. Given the size and complexity of the Mormon community today, sweeping generalizations about what constitutes Mormon values or beliefs are to be eschewed.

Multivocality makes application of the Mormon label contested terrain.

A multivalent, multifarious Mormonism may be part of the reason why the question of how to do Mormon history excites little theoretical discussion today. When I was a young graduate student and fledgling member of the Mormon History Association, however, it was a hot topic and seemed to be a manageable one. Conferences of the Mormon History Association were much smaller then, and I can vividly remember cramming into the hotel room of Leonard Arrington or Jan Shipps or Tom Alexander after the day's sessions had concluded to get down to the real business of debating the proper nature of Mormon historiography. More essays were published in the 1980s on how to do Mormon history than in any decade before or since. Believing Mormon historians wrestled with the tension between the methodological imperatives of the academy and the tendency of many church members to "see in every hour and in every moment of the existence of the Church, from its beginning until now, the overruling, almighty hand of God."[9] The tension was heightened when influential apostle Boyd K. Packer, while addressing teachers of LDS youth, cautioned Mormon scholars elsewhere about "writ[ing] history as they were taught in graduate school, rather than as Mormons."[10] What exactly he meant by that has been vigorously debated. In the end, encouraged by President Kimball's call to bilingualism, Mormon historians focused on demonstrating their mastery of "the language of scholarship."

To this day, both because of how religion is studied in the academy and because of the improbability of attaining a God's-eye view of the past in any case, most Mormon historians embrace what others have called the "Marsden settlement."[11]

Along with his many other historical interests, George Marsden spent the final quarter of the twentieth century exploring what writing history "as a Christian" might entail. This culminated in his influential 1997 discussion *The Outrageous Idea of Christian Scholarship*.[12] Previously, Marsden had written, "Since God's work appears to us in historical circumstances, the actions of the Holy Spirit in the church are always intertwined with culturally conditioned factors." Therefore, and this is the "Marsden settlement," the historian should "refrain from explicit judgments on what is properly Christian while he concentrates on observable cultural forces. By identifying these forces, he provides material which individuals of various theological persuasions may use to help distinguish God's genuine work from practices that have no greater authority than the customs or ways of thinking of a particular time and place."[13] In other words, just as Christian historians should leave the theologizing to the theologians, Mormon historians leave pinpointing God's particular interventions in history to those they regard as apostles and prophets. Indeed, for the ten years I worked as a volume editor for the LDS Church's Joseph Smith Papers, we were explicitly told *not* to make theological judgments, let alone attempt to identify God's actions.

None of this, of course, says anything about the ultimate reality of God or the possibility of divine intervention in human history. It simply acknowledges the limitations of finite human beings in trying to discern the Infinite. Some have suggested, however, that leaving God out of history is like trying to describe a football game where half the players are invisible.[14] I would change the analogy by saying that all the historical players *are* visible, but the divine coach is not. Depending on one's theology, God may be calling some, many, or all of the plays—

think of this as revelation or providence—and, unbeknownst to observers, he may also be slipping performance enhancers—grace—to the players. But this is not visible to ordinary human observers. Only when the game of life is over and the Coach discloses his actions will the full picture emerge. Meanwhile, without denying the possibility of divinity or its involvements, most historians, like play-by-play sports broadcasters, focus on what is visibly happening on the field.

Recently, however, some Christian scholars have argued that the Marsden settlement does not go far enough.[15] Among the ways in which they seek to broaden the conversation is the idea that history writing more overtly informed by Christian perspectives could contribute to the moral and spiritual advancement of humankind. Yet there are obvious liabilities with "preaching through history" even when it is not explicitly Christian. John Patrick Diggins's *On Hallowed Ground* presents Abraham Lincoln's political philosophy as a panacea for current American woes, but Gordon Wood rejects such an instrumentalist approach to history as "perilous" to the discipline. "Diggins," writes Wood, "thinks of himself as an intellectual historian, but in fact he is not a historian at all. He is a cultural critic who uses history" to preach to modern America.[16] Historian David Hollinger notes the resistance of some "mainstream" historians to studying religion. "My chief instruments for overcoming this perception," he writes, "have been works of religious history that do not carry the marks of religious apologetics and can be easily incorporated into the episteme of modern scholarship."[17] Hollinger holds up Jane Shaw's *Miracles in Enlightenment England* as a paragon of proper religious history.[18] In Hollinger's assessment, "Shaw practices the traditional historian's virtue of empathic identification with historical subjects, enabling her reader to recognize how vivid the evidence for divine interven-tion in the form of miracles appeared to many persons in early modern England." Yet, he continues, "one can read Shaw's book with deep appreciation without being required to believe that a supernatural power actually caused the experiences to which so many English Christians testified."[19] Much the same can be said, and has been said, about Richard Bushman's treatment of Joseph Smith and early Mormons.[20]

Here, then, in my view is the sweet spot for historians of religion: to re-present religious experience in ways that seem plausible, even compelling, without making claims of normativ-ity or ultimate "truthfulness." For this reason, many of us who are believing historians do not see great promise in attempting to more overtly infuse distinctive Mormon beliefs or claims to divine intervention into the histories we write. "Such works," observed Bushman years ago, "always seem stilted, forced, and artificial."[21] Consequently, he reflected some years later, "I de-cided that the answer was not to force myself into an orthodox program of history-writing." The proper way for Mormon be-liefs and values to inform scholarly work in the academy, he concluded, is subtly and internally: "I had to change myself until I could see the world as God sees it. To write godly history I had to be more godly."[22] Historians seeking the sweet spot of doing religious history that is both credible and compelling to believer and unbeliever alike can find in the work of Richard Bushman an outstanding model to be emulated.

Notes

1. Gary A. Tobin and Aryeh K. Weinberg, *Profiles of the American University, Volume 2: Religious Beliefs and Behavior of College Faculty* (San Francisco: Institute for Jewish and Community Research, 2007), 20.

2. Stephen J. Stein, *Communities of Dissent: A History of Alternative Religions in America* (New York: Oxford University Press, 2000), 11.

3. Margaret R. Miles, "Becoming Answerable for What We See," *Journal of the American Academy of Religion* 68 (September 2000), 473.

4. Spencer W. Kimball, "Second Century Address," *BYU Studies* 16 (Summer 1976): 466.

5. Neal A. Maxwell, "The Disciple-Scholar," in *On Becoming a Disciple-Scholar*, ed. Henry B. Eyring (Salt Lake City: Bookcraft, 1995), 7.

6. Utah State University established the Leonard J. Arrington Chair of Mormon History and Culture in 2007. The same year Claremont Graduate University in California inaugurated the Howard W. Hunter Chair of Mormon Studies.

7. Kenneth Scott Latourette, "The Christian Understanding of History," *American Historical Review* 54 (January 1949): 259–76.

8. Perry Miller and Thomas H. Johnson, eds., *The Puritans*, rev. ed. (New York: Harper & Row, 1963), 1:7.

9. Joseph F. Smith, *Conference Report*, April 1904, 2.

10. Boyd K. Packer, "The Mantle Is Far, Far Greater Than the Intellect," *BYU Studies* 21 (Summer 1981): 259–78.

11. John Fea, Jay Green, and Eric Miller, eds., *Confessing History: Explorations in Christian Faith and the Historian's Vocation* (Notre Dame: University of Notre Dame Press, 2010), 4.

12. George M. Marsden, *The Outrageous Idea of Christian Scholarship* (New York: Oxford University Press, 1997). Of particular relevance is his third chapter—"Christian Scholarship and the Rules of the

Academic Game." Of related interest is Bruce Kuklick and D. G. Hart, eds., *Religious Advocacy and American History* (Grand Rapids, MI: Eerdmans, 1997).

13. George M. Marsden, *Fundamentalism and American Culture* (New York: Oxford University Press, 1980), 230.

14. Marsden, *Outrageous Idea of Christian Scholarship*, 95.

15. In addition to Fea, Green, and Miller, *Confessing History*, see Douglas Jacobsen and Rhonda Hustedt Jacobsen, *Scholarship and Christian Faith: Enlarging the Conversation* (New York: Oxford University Press, 2004).

16. Quoted in William Katerberg, "The 'Objectivity Question' and the Historian's Vocation," in Fea, Green, and Miller, *Confessing History*, 106.

17. David A. Hollinger, "The Wrong Question! Please Change the Subject!," *Fides et Historia* 43 (Summer/Fall 2011): 35.

18. Jane Shaw, *Miracles in Enlightenment England* (New Haven, CT: Yale University Press, 2006).

19. Hollinger, "Wrong Question," 35.

20. Richard L. Bushman, *Joseph Smith and the Beginnings of Mormonism* (Urbana: University of Illinois Press, 1984); and Bushman, *Joseph Smith: Rough Stone Rolling* (New York: Alfred A. Knopf, 2005).

21. Richard L. Bushman, "Faithful History," *Dialogue: A Journal of Mormon Thought* 4 (Winter 1969): 25.

22. Richard L. Bushman, "Would Joseph Smith Attend the New York Stake Arts Festival?," *Dialogue* 35 (Fall 2002): 219.

A MODERN RELIGION

PATRICK Q. MASON

That Mormonism is "the American religion" has become something of a truism. Leo Tolstoy probably never actually made
the claim that others have attributed to him, but literary critic
Harold Bloom certainly did: he held up Mormonism (or at
least an earlier, precorporate version of it) as the paradigmatic
example of "the American religion."[1] Influential works by historians such as Nathan Hatch, Jon Butler, Laurence Moore, and
William Hutchison have also offered Mormonism as a major
component of understanding American religion, certainly in its
nineteenth-century varieties.[2] Once relegated to a virtual footnote in mainstream historiography, now Mormonism plays an
essential and often leading role in the ensemble cast of American
religions in high-level treatments by historians, social scientists, religious studies scholars, and even playwrights.

The list of Mormonism's many apparent Americanisms is not short. To name just a few: the geographical location of the religion's historical foundations and its still-dominant (if no longer technically majority) population; its sacralization of the American landscape and Constitution; the nationality and world-view of the vast majority of the LDS Church's senior leadership, past and present; and the church's global export of readily identifiable American religious forms, style, and content.[3]

Perhaps, however, we have focused too much on the particularity of Mormonism's *American* origins and still-early history. When I recently asked a Polish-Romanian Latter-day Saint whether she considered her religion to be American, she brushed off the question by responding simply, "It had to start somewhere."[4] Without minimizing the deep, obvious, and abiding Americanness of Mormonism, especially in its predominant LDS form, it may be worth considering how that Americanism is less a defining category itself than a variation on a theme. In other words, perhaps we have confused the discrete manifestation of the phenomenon with the phenomenon itself, somewhat like saying that Notre Dame football *is* football. What I am suggesting is that Mormonism may be understood less fruitfully as an American religion than as an American variety of modern religion. If we want to be audacious, we might even say that Mormonism is *the* modern religion—not in an exclusivist or triumphalist way, but in the sense that in Mormonism we see a paradigmatic encapsulation of religion born, raised, and still maturing in our modern age.[5]

A reconsideration of this sort does not require the adoption of a new set of lenses so much as the removal of our usual American filter. This is true because America is itself the quintessential modern nation—again, speaking descriptively and not exceptionally. In viewing history or religion through an American lens, then, we are always understanding our subjects modernly. If we lay aside for a moment the American filter we have grown so accustomed to viewing Mormonism through, what we see is that Mormonism is modern not just temporally but also, importantly, epistemically and ontologically. Talal Asad has defined modernity as "a *project*—or rather, a series of interlinked projects . . . [aiming] at institutionalizing a number of (sometimes conflicting, often evolving) principles: constitutionalism, moral autonomy, democracy, human rights, civil equality, industry, consumerism, freedom of the market—and secularism."[6] To Asad's list we could add other characteristics such as nationalism, a scientific worldview, mass social organization and mobilization, economic specialization, and faith in human progress. Underpinning the entire "modern moral order," in Charles Taylor's term, is an emphasis on individuals and human freedom, as opposed to the human person being primarily constituted in relation to a larger hierarchical social whole.[7]

Born in a modern age, Mormonism's ethos and spirit have been thoroughly modern. It thinks, acts, and feels modern. To put it negatively, the religion did not come with premodern baggage to discard or repack. Mormonism never had a prehistorical, predemocratic, prescientific worldview; unlike religions of more ancient origin, it did not have to figure out how to put premodern wine into modern wineskins. This is one reason—though rarely stated—why Mormonism often seems such an odd fit alongside older religions, which rightly view it as not only a troublesome upstart but indeed a genuine categorical anomaly. Of course, Mormonism is neither sui generis nor alone in its inherent modernity. Much of the same can be said for many emergent forms of traditional religions—evangelical, Adventist,

Pentecostal, and liberal Christianity; Reform and Conservative Judaism; the Ahmadiyya and Gülen (or *Hizmet*) communities in Islam; or various global fundamentalisms.[8] Similar patterns hold true in other new religious expressions, such as Bahaism and Scientology. Interpreting Mormonism as a modern religion, rather than as a more specialized category of American religion, thus enables greater comparative perspective, but it also yields greater insight into both Mormonism and our understanding of "multiple modernities."[9]

Moving from the abstract to the concrete, what—beyond its obvious and contingent temporality—makes Mormonism a modern religion?

First, and I would suggest most importantly, Mormon theology, like the dominant traditions of modern Western thought and social organization, is anthropocentric rather than theocentric. This will undoubtedly seem to be a strange and even provocative statement to many. After all, Mormonism's very first article of faith affirms a foundational faith in the Christian Godhead—not the sovereign and inviolable Self. In all the restoration churches' names, Jesus Christ gets lead billing over the Saints. (This is true even of the Community of Christ, where the community is listed first but is constituted in its relationship to Christ.) Ask any practicing Mormon, and he or she will reflexively say that of course Mormonism is God-oriented, like any good religion is.

But Joseph Smith's revelations and prophetic statements—the sine qua non of Mormonism—accomplished the delicate balancing act of keeping God permanently enthroned in his heaven while decentering him as the ground of all being and thus the universe's absolute sovereign. Sterling McMurrin's brilliant 1965 treatise, *The Theological Foundations of the Mormon*

Religion, opens by stating that in Mormonism "God is not the totality of original being and he is not the ultimate source or the creator of all being." Contra the traditional Christian conception of an absolute God, Mormon theology posits that "God is a being among beings rather than *being* as such or the ground of being, and that he is therefore finite rather than absolute." McMurrin concedes that Mormon discourse, on both an official and grassroots level, is "replete with the vocabulary of absolutism," but he interprets this as both an understandable personal response—many people are unwilling "to worship anything less than ultimate and absolute power"—as well as a lack of conviction among Mormon theologians who should know better.[10] Terryl Givens agrees with McMurrin, noting that "out of fear of misunderstanding," Mormons typically "avoid the language of finitism" despite its being at the core of their theology.[11] In the quest for respectability in conversation with traditional Abrahamic believers, and in the context of a general religious culture that simply assumes the construct of an absolutist God, Mormons have often failed to recognize the strength of their position and have sold short their remarkably distinctive theology.

Rightly prior to the discussion of God in his overview of Mormon theology, *Wrestling the Angel,* Givens outlines Mormon notions of "eternalism" ("the belief that the content of the universe is uncreated and unending"), "monism" ("the ontological sameness of matter and spirit"), and "laws physical and spiritual" (existing independently of God and which he is subject to).[12] Joseph Smith's rejection of creation ex nihilo, and his corresponding teaching that all matter—including human intelligence—is uncreated, provides the foundation for a radical departure from traditional Abrahamic theologies, one that reads the existence and purposes of the cosmos in relation to the exaltation of human persons. Citing the lynchpin scripture of the Mormon plan of salvation, Moses 1:39—"For behold, this is my work and my glory—to bring to pass the immortality and eternal life of man"—McMurrin astutely observes "that God's goodness is described not in reference to an arbitrary absolute will but rather as the divine will directing itself to a valued end, where the human soul is the end."[13] Taylor notes that in modernity "political society is seen as an instrument for something pre-political," namely, the human.[14] In Mormonism the plan of salvation is an instrument for something pretheological, namely, the human.

Not only is the human soul the *end* of Mormon theology, it is also the *beginning*. "Man was also in the beginning with God," taught one of Joseph Smith's most profound revelations. "Intelligence, or the light of truth, was not created or made, neither indeed can be" (Doctrine and Covenants 93:29). Thus, the core of our being is "uncreated, underived, and unbegun"—neither contingent nor created. "In Mormon doctrine," McMurrin affirms, "the individual has necessary being. He exists *necessarily*. That is, he could not *not* exist. . . . Whatever the predicament of man, it does not arise from an essential insecurity in his being. However finite and involved with finitude, the existence of man is not precarious or in doubt, because his existence is given as a central and irreducible fact of reality."[15] Regardless of what one thinks of the Book of Abraham's authenticity or astronomy, its anthropology is nothing short of breathtaking. Virtually the entire theological history of Christianity could be written starting with John 1:1—"In the beginning was the Word, and the Word was with God, and the Word was God." In similar fashion, the core of Mormon theology is encapsulated in Abraham 3:18—

"they existed before, they shall have no end, they shall exist after, for they are . . . eternal."

With eternity as its backdrop, Mormonism is a religion of human progress and perfectability that could meaningfully converse with modern philosophies and ideologies from transcendentalism to liberalism to Marxism. It optimistically orients toward the realization, not annihilation, of human identity and capacity—both in terms of the individual (exaltation) and society (Zion). Of course, these end-states are achieved paradoxically only by passing, like Jesus, through a process of *kenosis*, or the "self-emptying" of one's natural will and the taking up of the divine will (again, both individually and collectively). Yet as we also see with the Kantian categorical imperative, a high anthropology should also lead to a deep humanistic ethic. C. S. Lewis beautifully wrote that "next to the Blessed Sacrament itself, your neighbor is the holiest object presented to your senses."[16] Without the assumption of transubstantiation or another form of Divine Presence in the host, Mormonism revises Lewis's formulation so as to affirm—seemingly in line with Jesus's parable of the good Samaritan and other teachings—that, in fact, there is absolutely nothing in this world that is holier than one's neighbor. This is true not simply because one's neighbor is created in the image of God, but rather because she existed with God from the eternities and will continue to do so forever and ever, potentially as a god herself. That a human—an eternal intelligence and god-in-embryo—would ever be subordinate to or unwillingly sacrificed for a mere idea, ideology, or doctrine is horrendous from the standpoint of a Mormon ethic. Ontology thus precedes ethics and should act as a constant check and critique of various inhumanities.

The coeternality of God and humanity conditions a second characteristic of Mormonism's inherent modernity—namely, a historical consciousness. Richard Bushman, Jan Shipps, and other scholars have repeatedly and convincingly demonstrated the permeability of Mormon history and theology. There was never a moment when Mormonism was not historical, in the sense of being present in this world and utterly implicated in contingent human choices. Naturally, modern scholars will say that about all religions (and every other social construction), but that is not necessarily the understanding of the religions themselves. For instance, most Muslims believe that the Qur'an is uncreated. That is not an option for Mormon scripture, which is self-consciously a product of human narrators—to the point that some have interpreted the Book of Mormon in particular as prototypically (post)modern.[17] Indeed, human subjectivity is established with literally the book's very first word. We should not be surprised that the scripture that begins with "I, Nephi," has arguably enjoyed its greatest influence in the age of the iPhone.

Mormonism has always been self-consciously historical and textual, beginning with historians' favorite divine command, given to the church on the first day of its corporate existence: "Behold, there shall be a record kept among you" (D&C 21:1). In the premodern world the Word was made flesh, but in the modern age of mass literacy the word was made text. Joseph Smith's first calling was as a translator—a producer of texts. Following in that pattern though without the same charisma and originality, the fire from heaven brought down by modern LDS prophets looks less like Elijah's dramatic show of force than Hamlet's "words, words, words."[18] Furthermore, the historical turn that both allowed for and consummated so much of modern thought was unnecessary in Mormonism, which was born in linear, progressive—that is to say, secular—time. Even Mormon dispensational thought is only a pale shout-out to pre-modern cyclical temporal notions, as this final dispensation will end with the bang of millennial culmination—a la Marx and so many other secular modern fantasies—rather than the whimper of denouement, decay, and yet another go-around.

Another sign of Mormonism's inherent modernity is that it natively adopted the twin impulses of modern political life, namely, the democratic and the authoritarian. Intoxicated on the mythic pageant of individual freedom, American popular discourse (if not reality) has too often ignored how frequently democracy and authoritarianism are compatible, even mutually reinforcing, rather than contradictory. One of the recurring debates in the historiography of American religion over the past quarter century is whether the narrative is best told through the prism of democratization, freedom, and individualization or of authority, coercion, and hierarchy.[19] The answer, of course, is that both interpretive lenses are compelling. This is also the case in Mormon history (and historiography). Indeed, what is true of Mormonism is true of virtually every other modern form of social organization, and vice versa. Whether in American democracy, Soviet communism, or Mormon ecclesiology and culture, all people are equal—it's just that some people are more equal. The modern paradox of freedom and authority plays out in seemingly endless ways. Liberty and surveillance are two sides of the same coin, as any citizen in the post-9/11 world, reader of Foucault, or student or faculty member at Brigham Young University will attest.

The list of features speaking to Mormonism's inherent modernity—and not merely its Americanness—could proliferate far beyond this essay's available space. One immediately thinks, for instance, of the market logic that prevails within the Mormon imaginary, displayed most prominently in the religion's approach to evangelization; Mormon missionaries have traditionally fared poorly where the logic of a religious market has not yet been established (usually via European colonization). We might consider the Weberian processes of rationalization, professionalization, and disenchantment as exemplified in the church's priesthood correlation program and in the transformation of the display and understanding of charismatic spiritual gifts. On the other hand, we can also reflect on the ways in which Mormonism operates as a tremendous vehicle not only for individual and communal reenchantment *in* the modern age, but even potentially a platform for the reenchantment *of* the modern age.

Indeed, Mormonism does not operate as, nor can it be reduced to, merely a curious variety of the "purely self-sufficient humanism" or "exclusive humanism" that is the defining feature of our modern secular age.[20] Mormonism's exalted anthropology does not culminate in the death of God. Quite the opposite, it produces a universe full of exalted beings. Mormonism affirms that human flourishing is predicated on cooperation and partnership rather than on competition over scarce resources. Religiously speaking, Mormonism is the ultimate sharing economy. With its monistic erasure of the spirit-matter distinction as well as its virtually universalistic plan of salvation, Mormonism theorizes a universe predicated on *and* rather than on *or*. Joseph Smith's political vision, no matter how unworkable amid a modern political order (not to mention human nature), was "theodemocracy"—God *and* the people governing together.[21] Salvation is narrated via Jesus's condescension *and* Enoch's ascension. Brigham Young rejoiced that Joseph Smith "brought heaven and earth together," simultaneously bringing heaven down to earth and lifting earth up to heaven.[22] Mormonism does not simply offer new answers to old theological and philosophical debates, but changes the conversation altogether.[23]

Joseph Smith and all his successors have understood themselves to be establishing the church and kingdom of God in the last days. Translating that ambition into secular terms, we might say that they were not retreating from modernity but rather constructing an alternative modernity. Far from being an antimodern ideology, Mormonism in its most robust form represents a distinctive way of being modern—theologically, socially, culturally, and existentially. It stands to reason then that Mormonism's best conversation partners are not the premodern luminaries Plato, Aristotle, Augustine, and Aquinas—though they have much to teach us—but rather modern (and often non-American) thinkers such as Emerson, Weber, Einstein, James, Kierkegaard, Sartre, Gandhi, McIntyre, and Taylor. The next phase in Mormonism's engagement with and place in the academy may well come not by dehistoricizing a religion that insists on history, but rather in broadening our sense of just what that historicity entails. Twenty-first-century Mormonism might be content to be a church or a subculture, and scholars (LDS or not) will productively continue to analyze it as such. But it is not and never really was, at its heart, a mere Americanism.

Notes

1. Harold Bloom, *The American Religion: The Emergence of the Post-Christian Nation* (New York: Touchstone, 1992). For a critical

view of Tolstoy's supposed claim, see Leland A. Fetzer, "Tolstoy and Mormonism," *Dialogue: A Journal of Mormon Thought* 6 (Spring 1971): 13–29.

2. R. Laurence Moore, *Religious Outsiders and the Making of Americans* (New York: Oxford University Press, 1986); Nathan O. Hatch, *The Democratization of American Christianity* (New Haven, CT: Yale University Press, 1989); Jon Butler, *Awash in a Sea of Faith: Christianizing the American People* (Cambridge, MA: Harvard University Press, 1990); and William R. Hutchison, *Religious Pluralism in America: The Contentious History of a Founding Ideal* (New Haven, CT: Yale University Press, 2003).

3. For critical assessments, see Walter E. A. van Beek, "Church Unity and the Challenge of Cultural Diversity: A View from across the Sahara," and Wilfried Decoo, "Expanding Research for the Expanding International Church," in *Directions for Mormon Studies in the Twenty-First Century*, ed. Patrick Q. Mason (Salt Lake City: University of Utah Press, 2016), 72–131.

4. Weronika Iepure-Gorska, interview with the author, Cluj-Napoca, Romania, March 10, 2015.

5. It should be noted that the modernity of which I am referring to is primarily a Western, and especially North Atlantic, version of modernity, which Charles Taylor traces the genealogy of in *A Secular Age* (Cambridge, MA: Belknap Press of Harvard University Press, 2007). For a classic, albeit Marxist, analysis of the conditions of modernity, see Marshall Berman, *All That Is Solid Melts into Air: The Experience of Modernity* (New York: Simon & Schuster, 1982).

6. Talal Asad, *Formations of the Secular: Christianity, Islam, Modernity* (Stanford, CA: Stanford University Press, 2003), 13.

7. Taylor, *Secular Age*, 170.

8. See Gabriel A. Almond, R. Scott Appleby, and Emmanuel Sivan, *Strong Religion: The Rise of Fundamentalism around the World*

(Chicago: University of Chicago Press, 2003).

9. S. N. Eisenstadt, "Multiple Modernities," *Daedalus* 129 (Winter 2000): 1–29.

10. Sterling M. McMurrin, *The Theological Foundations of the Mormon Religion* (1965; repr., Salt Lake City: Signature Books, 2000), 2, 29, 35.

11. Terryl L. Givens, *Wrestling the Angel: The Foundations of Mormon Thought; Cosmos, God, Humanity* (New York: Oxford University Press, 2015), 101.

12. Givens, *Wrestling the Angel*, 51–65, quotations on 53, 59.

13. McMurrin, *Theological Foundations*, 77.

14. Taylor, *Secular Age*, 170.

15. McMurrin, *Theological Foundations*, 50, 54.

16. C. S. Lewis, *The Weight of Glory: And Other Addresses* (1949; repr., San Francisco: HarperCollins, 2001), 46.

17. See Jared Hickman, "*The Book of Mormon* as Amerindian Apocalypse," *American Literature* 86 (September 2014): 429–61. Hickman's approach departs from long-standing debates over whether or not the Book of Mormon is the product of ancient or modern authorship. However, even in that debate, both camps acknowledge the essentially human construction of Mormon scripture.

18. William Shakespeare, *Hamlet*, act 2, scene 2.

19. The two classic articulations are Hatch, *Democratization of American Christianity*, and Butler, *Awash in a Sea of Faith*. Not coincidentally, Mormonism features in both accounts.

20. Taylor, *Secular Age*, 18–19.

21. See Patrick Q. Mason, "God and the People: Theodemocracy in Nineteenth-Century Mormonism," *Journal of Church and State* 53 (Summer 2011): 349–75.

22. Brigham Young, "Testimony of the Spirit—Revelation Given according to Requirements—Spiritual Warfare and Conquest, Etc.," *Journal of Discourses*, 5:332.

23. Stephen H. Webb recognized this in his *Mormon Christianity: What Other Christians Can Learn from the Latter-day Saints* (New York: Oxford University Press, 2013).

6 | IT IS MUCH BETTER TO ERR ON THE SIDE OF GENEROSITY

SMOOTH STONES ROLLING: REFLECTIONS ON CRITICAL BELIEF IN SCHOLARSHIP

Section Introduction

GRANT WACKER

The papers by Armand Mauss, Laurel Thatcher Ulrich, and Claudia Bushman reflect on the intersection between academic work and religious belief in three very different ways. Even so, taken together, they make a powerful case that the line between objective findings "out there" and subjective interpretations "in here" is a porous one indeed.

In his exceptionally thought-filled paper, Mauss raises several critical issues, but for the sake of economy I will focus on just two. First, he tells us that he started college with an apologetic interest in Mormon studies, but by the time he finished his doctoral work at UC Berkeley, he had developed a model of social process that neither invoked nor ruled out divine intervention. He simply set that question aside. He would focus on data available to anyone and use explanatory frameworks

239

available to anyone, of whatever faith or none. He calls this approach, especially in the classroom, "pedagogical neutrality."

Mauss acknowledges that he might have fudged his principle a bit by consistently trying to give his subjects the benefit of the doubt. I appreciate his candor, but I would counter that there is nothing to apologize for here. Richard Bushman has said that someday we will meet our subjects in heaven, and when we do, we will have to look them in the eye and ask whether we have told their stories as truthfully and fairly as we could. It is much better to err on the side of generosity than of suspicion.

I suspect that pedagogical neutrality is the approach most believers must adopt for their academic work if they expect to be read outside church circles—or earn a PhD from UC Berkeley! Mauss does not explicitly say so, but there can be little doubt that for him pedagogical neutrality was not simply an intellectual principle but also a pragmatic judgment. The only way for multiple groups with multiple outlooks to get along in the university was to move onto this neutral territory.

Mauss's paper raises a second enduring question. He makes the refreshing claim that pedagogical neutrality actually *helped* him come to peace with the Mormon retreat from the assimilationist ideals that he had grown up with. He grew to understand that this retreat, which he calls retrenchment, was an impersonal one characteristic of most large-scale organizations. He may have been the victim of retrenchment, but he certainly was not the target. I say this claim is refreshing because believing academics usually allow that the encounter with naturalistic methods was an *unsettling* process for those who wanted to preserve their tradition, or an *exhilarating* process for those who wanted to free themselves from its shackles. Mauss's route of finding naturalistic methods helpful, rather than unsettling or exhilarating, is a path that many Christian academics have followed. Even so, it has received far too little attention.

In her similarly thought-filled paper, Laurel Thatcher Ulrich moves in a different direction, comparing Latter-day Saint identity with gender identity. Her story is rich with delicious ironies. At the University of Utah, she remembers, the purportedly free forum of college debate proved not free at all but restricted by gender. When she moved to the University of New Hampshire, pretty much the same thing happened. Male mentors encouraged her interests in the history of marriage and motherhood, but they assumed she had nothing to lose since she probably would not go on the job market anyway. The ironies grow. If she had finished her doctoral work at a major research institution, she suspects, her advisors would have tried to deflect her historical interest in the daily life of wives and mothers because that topic was (supposedly) too narrow and too political. Laurel is too kind to say so, but I suspect they would have assumed that their own fields were, in contrast, broadly based and antiseptically free of identity politics.

Ulrich's academic work—let's call it what it is, fame, for she has, after all, won a Pulitzer Prize, a Bancroft Prize, and a MacArthur Fellowship—rests on university press books. She paid her dues to the secular academy, following its rules about evidence, warrant, argument, conclusion—and good writing. Those books explored aspects of American culture associated with the feminine sphere: "sexuality, childbirth, mothering, housekeeping, community service," areas once considered narrow and political. But they came from the same pen that also wrote personal essays designed for Latter-day Saint readers, the "unsponsored sector," as she calls it elsewhere. So Laurel led two lives. Yet they were not two *distinct* lives, but one life with different emphases. "The historical is also personal," she concludes. "Whether or not we intend it, we reveal ourselves in the things that we write." In her original conference address, Ulrich made this point in a different way. We often think of history as "a dialogue between present and past," she rightly noted, but it also is a dialogue between "self and subject." With these words she shows that the best historians can use simple language to convey profound thoughts.

Claudia Bushman's delightful paper proves that historians can be funny as well as smart. She highlights a different kind of tension. That is the one between the nonprofessional and the professional scholar. "I've always been a scholar for fun and entertainment, and also pain and misery, rather than for fame, fortune, or food," she writes. "I am always an outlier." I am pretty sure this juxtaposition is a spoof, designed to make a serious point. Professional scholarship is often fun, and heaven knows it often involves pain and misery, especially when we see such adversity in the lives of the people we study and bear their burdens. And nonprofessionals can become very famous and make a very good living from history writing too. In real life the categories get all mixed up.

The second and larger aim of the paper is to highlight her experience of being a woman academic, and especially a Mormon woman academic, in a secular university environment that assumed that her primary identity would be in the home and Sunday School. The university's discomfort with the notion of cognitive or propositional revelation, which lies at the heart of Mormon theology, was not the issue here. Rather, the issue was the cultural stereotype that women's true vocation lay outside the academy. Women were free to join conversation, but only as nonprofessionals.

Claudia Bushman persuasively relates her fourth-generation Mormon status to her teaching methods. As a sympathetic outsider to the tradition, I never would have made that connection on my own. Her faith that the classroom should be a site of democratic leadership, her focus on writing as a means for encouraging students to embrace their own ideas, her conviction that personal experience beats grand theories (which always end up morphing anyway), and her willingness to admit that she has never flunked a student and that she practiced grade inflation before it was cool offer a crisp new way of thinking about how the nonprofessional or "unsponsored sector" of her life influenced the professional or "sponsored sector."

Her closing paragraphs actually bring all three papers together. She tells us that at the end of the day, all of her books and articles are "autobiography." "They are all my extended story, additional and alternative worlds that I appropriate and colonize." I propose that what we see here is something like Chalcedonian Christology: two distinct natures subsisting in one. Not two natures butting up against each other, nor even a mixture in which one shows up one day and the other another day, but truly a hypostatic union: one being, one heart, one mind, continuously suffused and empowered by distinct but overlapping impulses.

These thoughts bring us back to the reason for the conference and for this book: to honor Richard Bushman. I am not going to add to the encomia that have fluttered around this room for two days. All are richly deserved, and I do not have any more to toss into the mix. Rather, I want to talk about something else. Someday an ambitious scholar will write a biography of Richard. He or she will have to be skilled in economic history *and* social history *and* cultural history *and* religious history *and* intellectual history. But if the job is done right, that scholar will have to write about something else: Richard's influence on other Christian historians, including me. More precisely, he influenced us not only as a scholar and teacher and Christian public intellectual, but also and more important as a man who had *rightly ordered priorities*. To take a case in point, I have learned from friends inside the LDS Church that throughout his life Richard also has invested fifteen to twenty hours a week as a bishop, stake president, and advising patriarch for younger men and women.

Full disclosure: I have never been much impressed by theological apologetics. For every argument *pro* there is an argument *con*. For every shoe box filled with note cards, someone has a bigger shoe box filled with more note cards. Rather, I am impressed by the apologetic of a life well lived, day in, day out, through good times and bad times and all the times in between. Richard has mentored his peers and two generations of younger historians by the example of his scholarship, for sure, but also by his sense of priorities: always busy but never in a hurry, the courage to stand by his convictions, and humility in an academic world not famous for humility. One of the mottos of the Salvation Army is "keep the main thing the main thing." For five decades Richard has mentored us by his singular ability to keep the main thing the main thing.

THE PERSONAL
AND THE HISTORICAL

LAUREL THATCHER ULRICH

Can a good Mormon write Mormon history? At first glance, that is a silly question. It hints that there is something inherent in our faith that is at odds with scholarly practice—or vice versa. That cannot be true. We are here celebrating the work of a renowned historian who is also a very good Mormon.

From a broader perspective, however, the question isn't silly at all. It points to enduring dilemmas in the academy and in contemporary life, issues involved in scholarly debates over postmodernism and objectivity and in public arguments over "identity politics" of all sorts. For centuries, white men have been writing books about other white men and calling it "history." But when women, nonwhites, and religious minorities took up their pens, their own identities became entangled in the story. To write women's history in the 1970s was to be "present-minded." To write about Mormons, even today, risks being seen as an "apologist."

In some circumstances, being *too* professional may actually compound the problem. I am thinking of Larry McMurtry's infamous review of *Rough Stone Rolling*,[1] Richard Bushman's biography of Joseph Smith. That review was all about identity. It treated readers to an account of Mormon missionaries knocking on McMurtry's door, a description of an old capo sopping bread in the rooftop restaurant in Salt Lake City, and an allusion to "lost boys" foundering in contemporary polygamist communities. In a letter responding to outraged readers, McMurtry proclaimed that until church leaders apologized for the 1857 Mountain Meadows Massacre, Mormonism could not be considered an ethical religion.[2] None of this, of course, had any relationship to Bushman's biography. In that same letter, McMurtry insisted that he *had* read the book and that he did respect Bushman's scholarship but that he preferred Fawn Brodie's 1945 biography because it had more "kick." In other words, it took a position. In his review, McMurtry faulted Bushman for failing to address the question of whether Joseph Smith was "the mouthpiece of God" or "just a clever young man who babbled out a kind of trance-written novel." To use a Mormon term, he wanted Bushman to "bear testimony" for or against the appearance of angels.

Did the editors of the *New York Review of Books* display religious prejudice or bad judgment when they assigned a serious work of scholarship to a novelist and screenwriter? Did McMurtry dismiss Bushman's book because it was biased or because it was boring? Little matter. A person who presumes to write about topics close to his own identity risks becoming the story.

I have lived with these issues my entire academic career, not just as a Mormon but as a woman writing women's history. When I passed my PhD exams at the University of New Hampshire in 1976 and began casting about for a dissertation topic, I worried about pursuing what was by then my real passion—women's history. Through earnest and deep discussion with other LDS women in the greater Boston area and by working alongside them to publish the so-called pink issue of *Dialogue* and then *Mormon Sisters: Women in Early Utah,* I began to revise my sense of what it meant to be a Mormon woman.[3] Claudia Bushman was the guiding spirit of our publishing efforts, not only because she had already begun work toward a PhD in women's history (a field that, as she said, "no one had yet thought of") but also because she had connections in the right places and knew how to turn meandering discussions into projects.

By the time my husband and I moved to New Hampshire, I was fully committed to exploring women's issues in my private life, but I was not yet sure that this was the right thing to do academically. If I wrote about women, would anybody take me seriously? I told my mentor, Charles Clark, that I worried that writing a dissertation on early American women would forever confine me to "Women's Division."

That comment was a direct allusion to my experience with intercollegiate debate in college. I had won a lot of trophies—but always in "Women's Division," and as a budding feminist I had come to see that as a problem. My experience in high school had been different. My father, who had participated in both debate and theater in college, always made sure Sugar-Salem High School had a debate team. Among my most vivid memories of my high school years is getting up at 6:00 AM to practice the piano before going to school early to practice debate. My mother slept in while my dad made breakfast for the two of us. He sometimes listened to my speeches and gave me tips on how to make them better. I modeled myself on my brother Gordon, who, though seven years older than I, set standards I hoped to reach. He was a champion debater in high school and college and later won moot court competitions in law school. Although my younger sister Layle and I sometimes teamed up, most of my partners were male.

I was shocked when I arrived at the University of Utah in 1956 to discover that there were no coed debate teams at the "U," or apparently in any of the schools we debated, a consequence no doubt of some rule developed by the Western Speech Association. George Adamson, our debate coach, enforced that rule rigorously. He said that allowing women to compete against men would be unfair. Judges would be biased toward women, and teams with women would always win. I was puzzled by that, but I lived by the rules. I did not yet have a way of countering his argument. By 1975, my feminist consciousness had been raised. I wanted to write about women, but I did not want to be consigned to "Women's Division."

My mentor laughed at this story, chalking up my experience in Utah as a Mormon phenomenon. (Perhaps embarrassed a bit by the women's divisions that still persisted in the church, I quickly explained that the University of Utah was a public school.) He told me that it made perfect sense to write about what I cared about. He had been a journalist before becoming a historian and was then writing a book on early American newspapers. I was a housewife and mother. Surely I could capitalize on that by writing about "good wives" in early America.

Had I been at a major research institution, I doubt that I would have received the same advice. Many women have since told me how they were warned away from women's history in the 1970s (and beyond) under the assumption that they would hurt their chances in the job market by embracing a topic that appeared too narrow and at the same time too political. It was, of course, feminists who taught us that "the person is political," so we should not have been surprised when male academics who believed that their own standards were neutral were suspicious of our interests. Was writing about women genuine scholarship or a form of activism? If scholarship was gender- and color-blind, then women and racial minorities who proved themselves worthy would rise within the profession. Few men recognized how cultural assumptions and public policies had facilitated their own careers. When activists began to point that out, they bristled.

As I look back on my own career, I try to remember how much support—and mentoring—I received from men who were either bemused by or hostile to feminism. I recall my father puzzling over what he considered the very strange behavior of women who, as he supposed, "wanted to be men." It would never have occurred to him that teaching his daughter to debate had in any way encouraged such behavior. At UNH my two dissertation advisers were social historians with radically different approaches—one quantitative, the other cultural. Neither was particularly interested in women's history, but both encouraged me. I suspect they did so not only because I was a good student but because they thought I had nothing to lose. I was a faculty wife with children and unlikely to enter the job market. In fact, at a celebration dinner after I successfully defended my dissertation, one of my mentors said as much, arguing that for male students, getting a job was a "source of identity" in a way it could not be for me. (The two female historians at the table were horrified. I silently took note.)

A number of years ago, historian Joanne Meyerowitz published a fascinating analysis of the emergence of feminism in the 1960s based on the same periodicals that Betty Friedan had used in her landmark book *The Feminine Mystique.* Meyerowitz argued that "the problem that has no name," the female angst Friedan identified, was not produced by overt sexism but by a kind of double-think that assumed equality between men and women and encouraged female achievement and at the same time accepted the notion that adult women would spend most of their lives as wives and mothers.[4]

Those contradictory assumptions shaped my own Mormon upbringing. I loved school. I respected home and motherhood. I had no idea that social arrangements would make it extremely difficult for me to continue developing my gifts as a human being alongside my future responsibilities as a wife and a mother. It just never occurred to me to question the fact that almost all of my teachers in college were male and that the three female professors (there were only three) were single. I blissfully assumed that once I had my BA and my MRS, all other steps would unfold magically. It took me about six months after my first child was born to recognize that something had been missing in my education.

My decision fifteen years later to write a dissertation in women's history was in one sense foreordained—I was in a PhD program in part because of my involvement with other LDS women who had found validation from the study of Mormon history. We were surprised and enlivened to discover the protofeminist writings of our Mormon foremothers. I initially considered writing a thesis on Mormon history, but that was an impractical decision for a woman with five children living far from Mormon archives. I settled on early American history, a strength of the history program within walking distance of my house. Richard Bushman, in a message conveyed through Claudia, advised against a PhD, suggesting that it would "ruin my style." I considered this a compliment on my writing rather than a put-down. When I did it anyway, he welcomed me into the field and became a valued supporter. Claudia and her women's history group at Boston University and the cadre of women then working on Mormon women's history at the Church Historical Department became lifelong friends and allies.

Suspicious of tendentious writings that focused only on misogyny and oppression (in early America that meant witches), I embraced what some called "cultural feminism," that is, a belief that history had been impoverished by a failure to consider areas of common life marked "female"—sexuality, childbirth, mothering, housekeeping, community service. In my first published scholarly essay, a study of Puritan funeral sermons, I wrote, "Well-behaved women seldom make history." I wasn't encouraging misbehavior. I was arguing for more attention to the women Virginia Woolf called "Anon." My work on the eighteenth-century Maine midwife Martha Moore Ballard was in that vein.[5]

Meanwhile, I continued to write personal essays, most of them published in nonofficial Mormon periodicals, including *Exponent II*, the independent newspaper launched in homage to the *Woman's Exponent*, a nineteenth-century Mormon periodical devoted to the rights of women.[6] My historical works focused on colonial and revolutionary America and the material culture of rural New England. People who knew me through those books sometimes assumed I was a New Englander until they heard me speak in an Idaho accent. My personal essays and my scholarly writing were entirely separate, or so I believed.

In 2001 the *Journal of American History* asked seven historians to write short essays discussing the ways their personal lives had or had not influenced their scholarly work. I began my essay by proclaiming, "As a writer, I have led two lives." I explained that during the years I had published books in early American history, I had also been writing personal essays for Latter-day Saint publications. This was, I believe, the first time I had discussed my Mormon roots in an academic setting. I acknowledged that my experiences growing up in a small Mormon town "reading scriptures, learning to bottle fruit, knit, and embroider dishtowels, listening to my grandfather's stories about the old West, and hearing my grandmother talk about giving birth to twelve children in a homestead in Idaho surely had something to do with my ability to write about religion, frontier life, childbirth, housework, and community." But I insisted that my work as a historian was also an escape from domestic constraints and that I preferred writing about housework to doing it. I also alluded, subtly, to the burden of writing in first person singular and the liberation I felt in choosing to write about remote centuries rather than about the world I knew. "In personal essays, I was all-present, accountable to the world and people I loved. Moving backward in time, I was able to establish a critical distance on my own life and culture. There was no point in advocacy. I had to sit back and try to understand."[7]

Recently, Marion Rust, a specialist in early American literature, published a long article in a scholarly journal reinterpreting my best-known book, *A Midwife's Tale*, in the light of my personal essays. I was astonished that anyone would take the trouble to seek out my most fleeting work, some of it published in pretty obscure places, but I was intrigued by the result. Reading Rust's analysis was like looking at a candid photograph of myself taken on the sly by a friendly but penetrating observer. I was forced to think about myself in new ways. Apparently my two lives as a writer were more closely connected than I had imagined. Rust said that reading the essays helped her "tease out and begin to resolve" the seemingly contradictory elements of *A Midwife's Tale*: its celebration of ordinary life and its display of scholarly virtuosity.[8]

In my essay in the *Journal of American History*, I described my embrace of scholarship as a way of escaping the constraints of daily life. Rust helped me to see the contrary impulses in that decision: "As if to demonstrate that she belongs among the male historians who until recently had refused to grant women a place alongside them, Ulrich repeatedly declares her allegiance to the very model that kept both her and her subject matter out of the picture; precisely, it would seem, to bring them into the light." Although I resist the notion that scholarly standards are inherently male, I did embrace them. Although I like to describe my career as a happy accident, a patchwork composed of just what happened to come along, I chose to enter a PhD program even when wise people argued against it. I worked very hard to get my first seminar paper into print. I submitted grant applications. I got up at 5:00 AM to write books. I did all that knowing that good Mormon women do not seek the honors of the world.

The historical is also personal. Whether or not we intend it, we reveal ourselves in the things we write.

Notes

1. Larry McMurtry, "Angel in America," review of *Joseph Smith: Rough Stone Rolling*, by Richard Lyman Bushman, *New York Times Review of Books*, November 17, 2005.

2. Larry McMurtry, "'Angel in America,'" letter to the editors, *New York Review of Books*, March 23, 2006, http://www.nybooks.com /articles/2006/03/23/angel-in-america/.

3. *Dialogue: A Journal of Mormon Thought* 6 (Summer 1971); and Claudia Bushman, ed., *Mormon Sisters: Women in Early Utah* (Cambridge, MA: Emmeline Press, 1976). When our little feminist collective began, I was still trying to finish a part-time MA in English at Simmons College and had not yet taken the leap into history. My essay in *Mormon Sisters* was on twentieth-century historical novels. Note that the first edition of this anthology was self-published because no Mormon press was interested in it. It was later reissued by Utah State University Press.

4. Joanne Meyerowitz, "Beyond the Feminine Mystique: A Reassessment of Postwar Mass Culture, 1946–1958," *Journal of American History* 79 (March 1993): 1455–82.

5. Decades later, when my accidental slogan went viral, I explored the tension in the larger field of women's history between the self-assertion nourished by feminism and the rediscovery of the ordinary by social historians and feminist scholars. See Laurel Thatcher Ulrich, *Well-behaved Women Seldom Make History* (New York: Alfred A. Knopf, 2007).

6. On the founding of *Exponent II*, see essays by Claudia Bushman, Susan Kohler, Judith Dushku, and Carroll Sheldon in a forthcoming issue of *Dialogue*.

7. Laurel Thatcher Ulrich, "A Pail of Cream," *Journal of American History* 89 (June 2002): 43–47, quotations on p. 46.

8. Marion Rust, "Personal History: Martha Ballard, Laurel Thatcher

Ulrich, and the Scholarly Gaze in Early American Women Studies," and Laurel Thatcher Ulrich, "Looking at a Candid Photograph of Myself," *Legacy: A Journal of American Women Writers* 32/2 (2015): 147–66, 170–72.

ACTS OF FAITH . . .
AND REASON

ARMAND L. MAUSS

Only the last half of my academic career was devoted mainly to scholarly treatments of Mormon history and culture. My doctoral dissertation in sociology had been a major study of the race issue and the LDS Church of the 1960s, but I had felt obliged by strategic career considerations to put aside most of my interests in religion until I had established my credentials as a "mainstream" sociologist and full professor at a research university. By mid-career, I judged that such had been achieved, so increasingly I turned to sociological studies of religion, with special reference to the Mormons. Four of my books and scores of academic articles on Mormons issued from that career change.[1]

My teaching followed the same trajectory. I began with introductory courses in sociology, followed by upper-division and graduate courses in social deviance, social movements, and religious movements. All of these fields shared common or similar theoretical underpinnings. Later in my career, I focused more of my teaching on the sociology of religion, on the rise of new religious movements, and increasingly on the Mormons. These latter teaching opportunities were not all available at Washington State University, my main employer for most of my career, but they were offered at other universities where I taught as visiting faculty: University of California, Santa Barbara; University of Calgary; University of Lethbridge; and most recently Claremont Graduate University.

The Pull of Apologetics

In my teaching, as in my publications, I have neither announced nor tried to hide my own personal religious commitments. Yet I have always assumed that such would leave questions lurking in the minds of my students, whatever their own religious preferences might be. After all, few people who have ever heard of the Mormons are neutral about them. In my courses on religious movements, especially those on the Mormons, a regular source of delight for me was the occasional student who would approach me privately about halfway through a semester to ask privately about my own religion, having been unable to figure that out simply from the content of my teaching.

Such pedagogical neutrality on my part, however, did not come easily to me. As I began my own college education, I remember having had a strong apologetic bent toward all things Mormon, a tendency that stayed with me even as I began my graduate work at University of California, Berkeley. I think it had pretty well worn off by the time I finished my doctoral work, but even now I sometimes wonder if one or another of the explanations I have used in my teaching or publications on the

Mormon experience might have originated—however unintentionally—in an apologetic impulse.

Certainly by the middle years of my academic career, it had become my intention to avoid even the appearance of apologetics in framing my academic publications. Yet, in trying so to do, I have also wanted to avoid the *other* extreme of *foreclosing the possibility* of divine intervention, or of any other construction, as explanations for developments in the Mormon experience. For example, in some of my work, I have favored a theoretical model in which developments in the LDS Church and culture during the second half of the twentieth century are explained mainly as evolving through normal organizational responses to events in the American social and political environment. Such an explanation does not rule out divine intervention as the ultimate source of any decisions made in those organizational responses, but it simply leaves such intervention moot. Similarly, in my treatments of Mormons and race, I have interpreted the changing LDS understandings as the products of changing organizational imperatives across time, fully understandable without positing divine intervention for either the origin or the demise of the LDS racialist heritage. This approach neither invokes divine influences nor rules them out; nor does it rule out consideration of various other alternatives that might have occurred in the human decision-making process at either the individual or the collective level.

If any intimation of apologetics can still be found in my work, it might appear in my tendency to give the benefit of the doubt to the individual actors and players in Mormon history. I am well aware of the pettiness, meanness, and self-serving tendencies in the human condition, but my initial posture in a given analysis is not a cynical one. In general, my interpretations of

LDS historical developments have tended to assume that deci-sion-making among church leaders is typically well-intentioned and guided by fiduciary impulses, whatever the apparent out-comes of those decisions, and that ordinary church members too have usually tried to act in accordance with their religious com-mitments, if only imperfectly. To some extent, perhaps my pos-ture invokes the "hermeneutics of generosity" once attributed to Richard Bushman.[2] Of course, whatever the risk of apologetic interpretations in assessing the performance of actors in history, it is far greater in autobiographical *self*-assessments. In working on my latest book, a memoir, I was reminded constantly of the hazards in retrospective constructions of important autobi-ographical experiences, even with the help of good documen-tation; so I have proceeded here with some trepidation![3]

Theory versus Apologetics

Whether or not my academic work on the Mormons has in-deed freed itself from apologetic inclinations I will leave others to judge. Not that I have anything against apologetics, which is a perfectly legitimate category of theory, sometimes used with great erudition and sophistication.[4] Yet I have preferred, at least in my mature years, to seek explanations for the Mormon ex-perience that emphasize its basically *human* character—to see Mormons and their religion, in other words, *in comparison with* other social movements, especially those of a religious character. In this process I have favored theories that focus on the *shared reg-ularities* in the development of these movements as they occur in human societies, or at least in the American historical experience.

One of these theoretical frameworks portrays human so-cial organizations (including incipient organizations like social movements) as *tension management systems*, in which a variety of interests must be served and managed as an organization responds to external developments and pressures from the surrounding "host society" where it is trying to survive and prosper.[5] This approach tends to *deemphasize the intentionality of individual* actors in favor of *collective* processes and unintended consequences over which the players and actors (e.g., church leaders and members) have very limited control.

A second, and perhaps more controversial, theoretical framework I have favored seeks for *regularities in the life cycle of a movement* as it strives to achieve, and eventually maintain, a more permanent and settled organizational form. I have sometimes referred to this process as the *natural history* of a social movement. It is actually implicit in the well-known conceptualization of the typical transition of a new religious movement from "sect" to "church."[6] Natural history, or "life-cycle," conceptualizations have sometimes been used on a grand scale by historians of the past, including Crane Brinton in his classic study of revolutions.[7] More recently, such macroscopic theories seem to have been more common in the work of social scientists than in that of historians. Elsewhere Richard Bushman has offered a cogent critique of the uses of such theories in my work.[8]

Of course, any theoretical framework used by a scholar in his or her analysis constitutes, or at least implies, an underlying *ontology*, that is, a definition of ultimate reality or being. In the social sciences generally—or at least in sociology—all realities are typically considered *social constructions* and therefore have inherent biases in their very construction and not merely in the data that are selected or manipulated for a given analysis. As a believing Latter-day Saint, I was bothered in my younger days by this concept of the ultimate relativity in all reality until I finally realized an important corollary: if all realities are indeed social constructions (and thus not attributable to divine or other extra-human sources), then no reality can be privileged a priori over any other reality.[9] For me this has meant that any construction of reality—and any theoretical framework deriving from that construction, including apologetics—must be judged ultimately on its *explanatory usefulness*: How well does the theory explain the matter at hand? How much understanding does the theory yield? At the same time, we also need to recognize the biases in any theory, including what it fails to explain and *what interests are served* in choosing that theory over others, including "forgotten alternatives."[10]

Theory, Scholarship, and Personal Religious Challenges

I wish to return now to the original questions of how Mormonism has informed my scholarship and what challenges and complications have resulted. Of the books and articles I have published during the past several decades, I think my experiences with two of my books in particular would typify and suggest some answers to these questions. These were *The Angel and the Beehive* and *All Abraham's Children*. Both were the products of ongoing negotiations across time between my identity as a Mormon and my identity as a secular scholar. They both stand at the intersection of faith and intellect.

Interpreting Late Twentieth-Century Developments in Mormonism

The Angel and the Beehive was the combined product of scholarly curiosity and personal religious discontent. My upbringing and young adult years had occurred during the Americanization period in Mormon history. While a certain institutional defensiveness remained about the historical scandals and peculiarities sometimes haunting the public perception of the church and its members, institutional policies in those years generally favored rapid assimilation into normal American respectability. Increasingly the Mormon way of life converged with the American way, and even the doctrines and scriptures selectively emphasized in Mormon teaching tended to complement, rather than challenge, conventional Protestant American preferences. Then, beginning in the 1960s and increasingly thereafter, the church began to modify its assimilationist posture by recovering and reemphasizing some of the doctrines and policies from its more radical past and to impose them through a centralized organizational scheme called "correlation." I came to refer to this changed ecclesiastical culture as *retrenchment*, and it made my religious life seem quite different from, and much less comfortable than, the one in which I had grown up and served my mission. I needed to understand what was happening and why.

Meanwhile, in my graduate work, I encountered the conventional explanations from social science about the nature of religion, the understanding of all realities as socially constructed, and the natural and typical changes in religious movements as they are gradually transformed from radical sects into assimilated and respectable churches. While such sect-to-church

transitions historically seemed always to go in the same direction, it remained theoretically possible for this process to reverse
itself at some point so that a given religious movement, for its
own purposes, might turn away from assimilation and begin to
recover some of its earlier sectlike traits. The literature offered
no specific examples of this kind of reversal, but as I saw what
was happening in my own religious experience, it seemed to me
that Mormonism was just such an example. As I investigated
this prospect, I found ample empirical evidence of this retrenchment in LDS doctrine and scripture, pedagogy, family policies,
the missionary enterprise, and renewed emphasis on genealogy and temples. A more or less natural concomitant of all this
was a greatly reduced official tolerance for independent intellectual expressions and publications among the members. The
initial incentive for putting together a general theory about all
this occurred when I was invited to give a lecture at the Charles
Redd Center at Brigham Young University, out of which *The
Angel and the Beehive* was eventually born. Certain elements in
that lecture proved somewhat contentious when BYU's alumni
magazine undertook to publish it. Eventually certain cuts had to
be made and clearance received directly from the BYU president
before it could be published—rather an ironic illustration in itself of the retrenchment process![11]

From the 1960s through the 1990s, indeed, the retrenchment process was not merely a scholarly abstraction for me,
for it occurred in concrete and personal forms in my own life
and in the lives of my wife and children in the wards and stakes
where we lived. We saw it in the pedagogy of the high school
seminary program, in the policies relating to women's roles and
family obligations, in the content of the Relief Society curriculum, in the renewed emphasis on the Book of Mormon, and in

a new urgency about "following the prophet." I felt it personally on several occasions when I was summoned by my stake president (on orders from above) to explain some of my scholarly publications or lectures on Mormon subjects. In all these various manifestations of retrenchment, my faith was sometimes tested, but ultimately that faith—or at least my loyalty to the church—found an ally in my sociological understanding, for I realized that what was happening was essentially an impersonal process originating in well-intentioned policies, even if I didn't like them. I could either walk away or stay and try to help my family and others to understand and deal with the retrenchment process until it had run its course and the pendulum had begun to swing in the other direction. I remained in the church, and the retrenchment eventually did indeed begin to wane—or even retreat somewhat.[12]

Identity Construction and Deconstruction in LDS Racialist Teachings

All Abraham's Children had quite a different origin, one that derived from my efforts to understand and explain LDS policies toward African Americans. The project began with my doctoral dissertation comparing the consequences of LDS teachings about African Americans with those about Jews. When the project reached its final form some three decades later, it had turned out to be a book on the origin and consequences of the Mormon *racialist heritage more generally*, involving not only blacks and Jews but also American aboriginal peoples, or "Indians," plus the construction and implications of a superior ethnic identity for Euro-American Mormons themselves. During that entire period, of course, LDS Church policies and teachings toward all of these various ethnic identities were gradually evolving. The ethnic and racial heritage of potential converts had come to be understood as totally irrelevant in determining either their access to all salvific rituals or their eternal destinies. All peoples truly and finally could become "Abraham's children," as Paul had promised (Galatians 3:6–9, 26–29).

It must be remembered that my research and writing on such race-related questions occurred during that same retrenchment period analyzed in *The Angel and the Beehive*. It was also, as things turned out, a period of great sensitivity, both in the nation and in the church, about racial and ethnic differences and their various implications. In academia and in the mass media, there was little tolerance for actual or perceived racial discrimination based on religious doctrines or policies, especially on college campuses or in scholarly publications. The LDS leadership, for its part, seemed divided over how best to resolve its paradoxical teachings and policies not only in relation to people of African descent but even in its policies toward American Indians, where a long-standing and well-intentioned integration program was unraveling toward eventual termination. Among the leaders, as well as in the Mormon rank and file, there was little appreciation for the unsponsored and unapproved publications of pesky intellectuals like me. Many of us felt the pressures from such disapproval in one form or another. However, significant changes during recent years in church narratives and policies toward blacks, as well as toward certain other ethnic peoples, have left me feeling a degree of vindication and have reinforced my faith that perhaps divine revelation can eventually break through even the most entrenched cultural traditions.

Conclusion

Mormonism has been a formative influence on my scholarship in general, but especially in two main lines of inquiry: (1) the development of late twentieth-century LDS ecclesiastical culture and (2) the changing Mormon conceptions about race and lineage. Derivatively, my university teaching in the sociology of religion has been informed by my study of new religious movements, especially in offering a comparative context for the study of Mormons and Mormonism. The tensions and complications presented by these career choices have occurred mainly with LDS leaders and members who have found it difficult to reconcile my academic approach in religious studies with the more devotional approach so familiar to them. This predicament has occasionally led to challenges from "fireside" audiences where I have spoken, from LDS students in courses I have taught, and even from local or general priesthood leaders who have called on me to explain my ideas. My chief resort in dealing with all such challenges has been a continuing effort to educate church members and leaders about the value and complementarity of *both* the academic and the devotional approaches.

Notes

1. The four books were *Neither White nor Black: Mormon Scholars Confront the Race Issue in a Universal Church* (Salt Lake City: Signature Books, 1984), coedited with Lester E. Bush Jr.; *The Angel and the Beehive: The Mormon Struggle with Assimilation* (Urbana: University of Illinois Press, 1994); *All Abraham's Children: Changing Mormon Conceptions of Race and Lineage* (Urbana: University

of Illinois Press, 2003); and *Shifting Borders and a Tattered Passport: Intellectual Journeys of a Mormon Academic* (Salt Lake City: University of Utah Press, 2012).

2. Stuart Parker, "The Hermeneutics of Generosity: A Critical Approach to the Scholarship of Richard Bushman," *Journal of Mormon History* 38 (Summer 2012): 12–26.

3. I am referring here again to my *Shifting Borders*, which had a foreword by Richard L. Bushman.

4. In this connection, I would cite much of the work of Terryl L. Givens, especially his *By the Hand of Mormon: The American Scripture That Launched a New World Religion* (Oxford: Oxford University Press, 2003).

5. A good overview of this theoretical framework can be found in Wilbert E. Moore, *Social Change* (Englewood Cliffs, NJ: Prentice-Hall, 1963). How such an approach is used, for example, in my *Angel and Beehive* and in my *Abraham's Children*, is indicated in chapters 5 and 6 of my *Shifting Borders*.

6. This conceptualization, first advanced by Max Weber and Ernst Troeltsch, is analyzed by sociologist Benton Johnson in "On Church and Sect," *American Sociological Review* 28 (August 1963): 539–49, and in his "Church and Sect Revisited," *Journal for the Scientific Study of Religion* 10 (Summer 1971): 124–51. The theoretical framework of my *Angel and Beehive* starts with this classical evolutionary idea and traces its implications as later spelled out by Rodney Stark and colleagues (e.g., in Rodney Stark and Roger Finke, *Acts of Faith: Explaining the Human Side of Religion* [Berkeley: University of California Press, 2000], especially chapter 10).

7. Crane Brinton, *The Anatomy of Revolution*, rev. ed. (New York: Vintage Books, 1965).

8. See Bushman's "Theory and Interpretation in Mormon Studies," in *Directions for Mormon Studies in the Twenty-First Century,*

ed. Patrick Q. Mason (Salt Lake City: University of Utah Press, 2016), 223–33.

9. For a discussion of this issue in my intellectual development more generally, see my book *Shifting Borders*, especially chapter 3 and pp. 187–88.

10. Here I am alluding to an important idea (adapted from C. Vann Woodward) in Patrick Q. Mason, "Scholars, Saints, and Stakeholders: A Forgotten Alternatives Approach to Mormon History," *Journal of Mormon History* 41 (January 2015): 217–28, especially 225ff. As though to recall some "forgotten alternatives" in LDS history, Ethan R. Yorgason published an intriguing "counterfactual" treatment of the Mormon experience with the "Americanization" process in *Transformation of the Mormon Culture Region* (Urbana: University of Illinois Press, 2003).

11. See my "The Angel and the Beehive: The Mormon Quest for Peculiarity and Struggle with Secularization," *BYU Today* 37 (August 1983): 12–15, for the version that survived the editorial cuts after approval by BYU president Jeffrey R. Holland. The entire incident is briefly described at the beginning of chapter 5 in my *Shifting Borders*, where I mistakenly confuse President Holland with a later BYU president, Rex Lee.

12. In an article intended as a partial revision and update of this argument in the book, I found evidence that the retrenchment process had begun to yield once again to new assimilationist tendencies in Mormonism. See my "Rethinking Retrenchment: Course Corrections in the Ongoing Quest for Respectability," *Dialogue: A Journal of Mormon Thought* 44 (Winter 2011): 1–42.

MY LIFE AMONG THE SCHOLARS

CLAUDIA L. BUSHMAN

How does being a Mormon influence my teaching and my scholarship?

I was a Mormon long before I was a scholar. I was a late and longtime graduate student who accumulated credits slowly. Then I spent my working years as the wife of a successful and ambitious academic, moving frequently, never going on the market or actually applying for a job. No one ever depended on me to provide bread. I've always been a scholar for fun and entertainment, and also pain and misery, rather than for fame, fortune, or food. I teach and I have taught and I write books because that is what I do.

I am a serious Mormon but a tenuous scholar who has never really identified with the academic life. I am always an outlier. I am participating in this conference not because of my academic record but because of my identity as the wife of a significant person. But I do have some things to say.

One of my all-time best stories is that I graduated from college in maternity clothes; began my master's degree, when we could afford tuition for me, with two children and finished with three; and began my PhD with five children and finished with six. This was a long time ago when things were very different than they are today. No one ever encouraged me to go to graduate school. My MA adviser never had time to talk to me because I wasn't a real student. He was shuttered in his office with real students, weeping undergraduates. When I applied for a doctoral program and the English department chair was pressured to accept me, he said in consternation, "Oh, Mrs. Bushman, why don't you just go home and take care of your children?"

So why did I do it?

Well, I was bored. I kept house and tended to my children. I read a lot, but I had nothing to lay my mind on. As a housewife in those days I had no status, no respect. I had no sense of progress. My husband had a rich life as a graduate student and then as a young professor with lots of compelling friends, new discoveries, and opportunities. He was out conquering the world, bringing home his honors and setting out again, coming home exhausted and going to sleep immediately. He had little interest in domestic life. He was understandably bored with a wife who had no conversation.

All I could see ahead was more of the same. Going to work was unthinkable then, certainly not desirable. Besides, I had too much work at home. What to do? I decided to go back to school, and when it was possible, I became a student again. Richard was always very helpful about that, advising me, discussing paper topics, talking ideas and books because those interested him.

My classes became extensions for him, and he became my great teacher. I made a place for myself in his life. Eventually we collaborated on some projects. We read and edit each other's work and have been mutually helpful.

I think I was always smart enough, but I never really got it in school. At my high school, it was the thing to be disdainful of study and learning. I did accidentally get all As in my freshman high school year, but I took care not to let that happen again. It was so uncool. I did get into some very good colleges, but that was a long time ago and almost a fluke. My guidance counselor gave me some excellent advice, and I took it. At my high school graduation, I was voted most likely to succeed, but I thought that was an insult. I would have preferred best dancer or best hair. School did not influence me to become a scholar. I just did not see any other options.

How has my Mormonness influenced my teaching, or in my case, how does it not? I'm such a Mormon, a so-deeply-encased third and fourth generation of active Latter-day Saints, with grandparents from different countries who met and married in Utah, who would never have met without the church. How could my whole life not be deeply influenced by the church?

So how am I influenced? Teaching for me began with church teaching, and so I still feel that the classroom benefits from discussion rather than lecturing. I went to Primary back in the days when we met during the week and learned skills and performed pageants, so I tend toward the theatrical and the crafty. I went to the Mutual Improvement Association when we had speech contests, three-act plays, and weekly dances, so I like to incorporate singing and dancing into discussion. In fact, I think that everything benefits from singing and dancing. I grew up before seminary and institute were available in my area and did not go to Brigham Young University, so I do not think much about the scriptures. The church is more social and cultural for me than theological.

I did not always find my church and academic lives compatible. My experience includes being forbidden to teach a class because I was a Mormon. I was an early student of women's studies and was teaching a class on the history of women in the United States for a university's honors program. The women's studies department refused to cross-list the class because I was a Mormon and therefore unqualified to teach that subject.

That was a pretty horrendous crisis for me. But I managed to reinvent myself as a local and public historian. I taught classes about my town and state and began a local historical society with my students. I was eventually drafted to direct a state agency that celebrated things. I had a great time doing that. Discipline drift and shifting emphases are common for scholars like me.

I've always been a tenuous academic. I hang on by my fingernails to the academic life until I fall off. Then I get a little purchase and hang on for a while again. Many years ago I was teaching freshman English when I began to expect my fourth child. I was told then that I could teach no more.

But I persevered. Anybody can teach a class at church and everyone does, including me from an early age. In the church we believe that all are equal, except for leaders viewed from afar, and that we are all above average. I feel the same in the classroom. I have never flunked a student, and I practiced grade inflation before it was popular. I think that once a student has been admitted to a program, all involved should help that student get through. Flunking out graduate students two or three years along seems terrible to me, defining them as lifelong failures.

I once had a football player in a freshman composition course who was pretty obviously plagiarizing his papers. His own weren't very good, and the substitutes were pretty bad too. I called him in and said I knew these were not his papers but that I didn't want to try to prove him a cheater. I said that I would not turn him in if the rest of his papers sounded as if he had written them. They pretty much did. He passed the course.

I want all the students to do well and graduate, just as I want all members of the congregation to be good and to be saved. That's definitely a result of my LDS upbringing. I don't think I have much to teach students, but I do think I can put them into environments where they can teach themselves something. And the things that students teach themselves are much more memorable and useful than those learned through lectures. So the effort is to get students to read some document, ask some kind of question, and then formulate an oral or written answer. I don't think people know what they think until they have to say it or write it. And expand on it. And defend it. And generally make it their own. But I was slow to learn this principle. I spent four years at a very good college where the professors tried to get me to think of answers to the questions they posed and to speak them or write them, and I wanted none of it. My ingrained experience from high school led me to say, "Just tell me what this is all about. I'll write it in my notes, and I'll learn it." I didn't want to hear the puerile comments of my fellow students. I didn't want class discussions. I wanted lectures. It took me a long time to change my mind as to what a real education consisted of.

I believe that knowledge and learning start at the bottom level, the individual experience. The individual story is the basis of literature. The one is the important unit, and that's why I love autobiography and oral history, why I think everyone should write daily in a journal, creating their own personal scriptures. I distrust the big ideas of history and literature. Those change. They differ from age to age. They are interesting to discuss, but they don't last. The careful or accidental arrangement of words on paper by a single individual does last. I privilege that writing over the interpretation of some later scholar. Another reason I think students should be treated generously and individually is that I am really a religious universalist. I think everyone will be saved. I don't believe that some postdeath judgment will consign individuals forever to some limited rank. I don't believe in permanent placement in the three degrees of glory. I think we just keep moving along, some more quickly than others. I don't believe that a third of the hosts of heaven were just discarded, as Mormons teach. I think they went into some remedial program and will be peopling other earths and working out their salvation somewhere else. I even have my doubts about truly evil historical characters. They have been important players in the scheme of things and certainly are spirits of merit and ability. My view is one of total Mormon optimism: there is no beginning and no end, and we are all getting better and better with more and more experience. I have faith that there will be success ahead and that it will all work out.

I know that being Mormon in an academic world is considered problematic. Our membership as Mormons precedes us into new worlds, and people have strong feelings about it, even as they refrain from mentioning it. I almost never have the occasion to mention that I'm a Mormon. There have been dramatic instances of this. Richard and I recently spent a year as senior scholars at the American Antiquarian Society in Worcester, Massachusetts. We have been members of that institution for a long time, and I was a resident fellow there a long while back when I worked on my book about the changing perception of Christopher Columbus in the Americas over the years.[1]

I still knew some of the old-timers, and one of them asked, shortly after our arrival back there, if I was related to Serge Bushman. I said yes, he was my son, but how could she know him? He works on telephone apps in Kansas City and has lived there for many years. There could certainly be no other person of that name, which I had hesitantly bestowed on him, naming him for my father who was named for the LDS missionary who had converted his father. She said it was her husband who knew the name. Her husband does taxes for people, and he remembered doing the taxes of one Serge Bushman in connection with two facts: that Serge Bushman had been born in Utah and that he had given a lot of money to charity. Therefore he must be Mormon. And here we were, decidedly Mormon with the same surname. We figured out that Serge had his taxes done in Massachusetts about twenty years previously when he was in business school. This man had remembered that name and a couple of related facts for a very long time. That tithing business is a very strong marker.

As is that alcohol business. One of the things that senior long-term scholars at the Antiquarian Society are supposed to do is to involve the short-term fellows in social experiences, which experiences generally include alcohol. But we Mormons just do not do alcohol. I am grateful that alcohol is not part of my life. I am protected from the problems of its overuse. I don't think of alcohol as evil, but I do see it as a major marker, a notable boundary. So I don't drink alcohol.

I was at a very elegant dinner recently when the French man sitting next to me noted that I was not drinking and asked if I knew that in a number of civilizations it was considered very disrespectful not to drink with your companions. I said I knew that and that I wanted him to know that I was not offended that he was not not-drinking with me, whereupon he turned away and did not speak to me for the rest of the dinner. I had identified myself in his eyes as an uncivilized boor. But I didn't think that he looked very good either.

As to scholarship, I know that my choices are informed by my Mormonness. I don't like to write; I don't like to do research. I occasionally enjoy reading a few chapters of a monograph, but I would much rather read nineteenth-century novels than history. And though I do not like to write, I have written quite a bit. My CV lists many books and quite a few selected articles. I've been at it for a long time. A couple of my books are edited documents, a couple are edited essays, and there are some long and serious books over which I struggled for many years. But they are all autobiography. I am always writing my own story. Someone would have to know me pretty well to see all the relationships and justify the choices, but they are all there. Like the voyaging explorers to other continents, I have discovered and been drawn to my topics and made them my own. They are all my extended story, additional and alternative worlds that I appropriate and colonize.

As Richard and I share our writing, so we sometimes share our teaching. Our most recent and potentially final teaching experience came recently when we cotaught a class on contemporary Mormonism. This was an undergraduate seminar at Columbia University. The idea came from a book of that name I had written fairly recently, and the idea was to talk about the church today rather than beginning with Joseph Smith, the gold plates, the trek west, and so on. The class was wildly popular, filling the first day with a wide variety of religion majors and practitioners of various stripes—Catholics, Protestants, Jews, agnostics, former and closet Mormons, people who had known Mormons before. This undergraduate seminar was meant for fifteen students, but we eventually took twenty and had a number of auditors as well. We were absolutely open and straight about all topics, without the traditional pieties that such classes have included in the past. We invited in a number of guest speakers such as the bishop, the temple president, the missionaries, a gay man, male and female bedrock types, less-active Mormons, and so on. They made brief presentations and then answered all questions, absolutely open about their pasts, volunteering such unknown information as previous disfellowshipments, excommunications, and divorces to our very great surprise. Of course the class was enthralled. The students were required to attend a three-hour church service, which they dreaded and survived. It was all a great experience, bringing Mormonism and the classroom so close together. The class made a fitting conclusion to a life of sporadic Mormon-influenced teaching and of living Mormonism itself.

That's where I'll start in another life.

Note

1. Claudia L. Bushman, *America Discovers Columbus: How an Italian Explorer Became an American Hero* (Lebanon, NH: University Press of New England, 1992).

BENEDICTIONS

BLESSING OF—AND FOR—
THE ACADEMIC LIFE

TONA HANGEN

I count myself fortunate to be in the penumbra of Richard Bushman's mentorship, and one of the things I have learned there is the power derived from particularity, the joy of things concrete and specific. Richard's optimistic, expansive view of Mormonism grants authenticity to anyone who speaks from lived experience, and I'm grateful to have my perspective welcomed and validated. I came of age in the Washington, DC, suburbs enjoying every advantage of the American dream, a Reagan-era Generation X child in an era of seemingly limitless prosperity and personal freedom, but also of deteriorating social contracts and Cold War fear of impending apocalypse. I'm part of what Richard calls the Mormon diaspora, the twentieth-century out-migration from the Mormon culture region for education and jobs that (re)planted Zion far away from the Wasatch Front. I have LDS ancestors who settled Farmington and Brigham City,

Utah, but their descendants left long ago for Southern California and then northern Virginia, and I went to New England for my education and put down roots there. With one of my sons now marrying and settling near Palmyra, New York, my own life has darn near inscribed the Mormon epic migration in perfect reverse. Mine is the generation of women wedged between the fierce fighters of second-wave feminism and the culture wars of yuppies versus stay-at-home mothers. My husband and I have built a beautiful, busy, and fulfilling life that includes a family of four children, two advanced graduate degrees, and two full-time careers while one or the other of us nearly always serves in a major church role. I have been called—by virtue of circumstances that landed me the rare plum of a tenure-track job in a unionized faculty in a stable public university system—to engage the intractable and monumental problems of my time and place as a person of faith. Put differently, I am a "professor" in both senses of the word.

Every graduate school story is a nonlinear journey. For me, I began at Brandeis with an interest in labor and social history and then branched out into media studies and religious studies. My doctoral dissertation considered Protestant evangelical radio pioneers of mass media religion in the pretelevision age and became my first book, *Redeeming the Dial*. I was drawn to the intersection of media, religion, and culture and sought to understand the performance of religious identity in the public sphere. I suspect this is true for other LDS historians, but at least for me, studying a different religious tradition's beliefs and practices was a way to study Mormonism by proxy (how very Mormon!). I could think about the coalitions and tribal loyalties fostered by religious media, about trajectories of religious institution building in the twentieth century, and about how religious conservatives and liberals approach the challenges and existential crises of secular modernity. Much of my intellectual work since has been in the same vein, particularly in recovering marginalized voices and groups in the American past and peopling history with a more diverse (i.e., more authentic and accurate) cast of characters, ideas, and organizations.

Billy Graham's popularity really kicked off with a big Los Angeles tent revival in 1950, and something he told the crowds there stuck with me since I first read about it. "Listen," he said, "it's not how many souls you've won; how big the meetings were that you had. It's whether you are faithful in the place where God puts you. If God puts you to selling automobile tires and you sell them faithfully as unto the Lord and witness for Christ at every opportunity . . . you'll get that crown."[1] Somehow, for some reason, God put me in this history department, and it's up to me to be faithful in that place, especially since I end up representing my faith whether I like it or not as the one token Mormon in my workplace. Instead of selling automobile tires, I'm teaching, but I'm under the same mandate to do it "as unto the Lord." And to a great extent, the Mormon skill set is a tremendous asset in academia. I've found that many of the talents developed in a lifetime of Mormonism seamlessly transfer into my work as a college professor. Some of those are generic effectiveness skills, such as goal setting, running a meeting, being part of a small team or committee, putting on events, recruiting and welcoming new members of the community, and having accountability within a vertically organized reporting hierarchy. Others have been honed in the interpersonal aspects of Mormon life, like being responsible and genial, getting along even when you disagree, sublimating one's ego to a common goal, returning and reporting, and giving others the benefit of the doubt.

All that said, higher education today is a bizarre place, and not all days are good days. Being a public university professor is a high status but relatively low-paying job, and the cultural landscape is a disorienting blend of idealism and crass corporate commercialism. In their marvelous, thought-provoking book, *The Slow Professor*, Maggie Berg and Barbara Seeber speak for many of us who "wanted to become professors because of the joy of intellectual discovery, the beauty of literary texts, and the radical potential of new ideas"[2] but who find the lived reality of higher education mind-numbingly unradical. It's easy to generate a high-minded list of the academy's core scholarly values: open-ended inquiry, peer review, collective governance, academic freedom, discovery and exploration, integrity, expansive critical thinking, taking intellectual risks, the ability to suspend initial judgment and to change one's mind based on new evidence, and active affirmation of diversity and pluralism. When I look at that list, I think it's all deeply compatible with the rock-solid core of my faith, and that is the tribe I want to be part of.

But let's be honest. That idealism runs smack into the unvarnished realities of higher education today: corporate doublespeak, byzantine assessment imperatives, administrative bloat, miles of red tape, and Kafkaesque internal politics played by personalities straight out of central casting. "Liahonas" and "iron rod" types are actually universal archetypes not unique to Mormonism. And Laman and Lemuel seem to have jumped the bounds of their scriptural framework straight into committee meetings. There were whole parts of the actual job description of being a twenty-first-century academic that never got covered in graduate school and for which I was wholly unprepared: advisement, curriculum development, accreditation, program leadership, managing budgets, dealing with students not yet ready for college-level work, and lots and lots of negotiating ideological and interpersonal minefields. There is, shall we say, opposition in all things.

While I know we are commanded to "give thanks in all things" (Mosiah 26:39), for a long time I forgot to give thanks for being hired into a deeply fractured department that was managed like a mafia ring. The department's culture actively minimized women's voices, was generationally and ideologically divided, and had allowed personality differences to fester into full-blown animosity. Being grounded in both my faith and my family saved my sanity on many occasions and helped me make sense of the tragicomic parts of academia. I determined to wait it out, knowing the culture would slowly tip in a more collegial direction if we hired well and let retirements take their course. And, eventually, the tipping has begun.

Partway through thinking about and writing this essay, I unexpectedly became the chair of that same department—first by assignment (which felt a little like receiving a very unexpected and unpopular church calling) and later by being elected on the narrowest of margins. I can now appreciate how my initial situation was an opportunity in disguise to forge friendships and cross-disciplinary collaborations and to take chances to reach outside my department in a search for allies—opportunities that I might not otherwise have sought out and that have enriched and expanded my thinking immensely. And I *am* grateful.

As I navigate the transition from junior to midcareer scholar, I hope to promote creative solutions to some of the long-standing obstacles to women's success and advancement at my university and in the academy more generally: more ways to blend careers with family life, more flexibility and humanity in allocating time and resources, more opportunities for holistic thinking about career and scholarship "stages"—especially for women—rather than just pulling up the ladder after me. I find those desires to be in deep (internal) dialogue with the ongoing current conversation about women's participation, voices, and perceived value in the church. At the same time, in higher education today tenure is precarious and increasingly unprotected, and a majority of current faculty do not have access to it at all. Thinking of students primarily as "consumers" encroaches on the classroom, on hiring, and on which buildings do and do not get built. Learning is being reconceptualized into something that can be chopped into media modules and measured by sophisticated algorithms and assessment tools.[3] Not all the change is bad, of course: there are more models than ever for how to be scholars in different contexts, including the rise of alternative academic ("alt-ac") careers and public intellectuals in social media, the blogosphere, and podcasting. But the academy itself is not static. One might say it's open to continual revelation, and therefore it needs clear-eyed prophets and prophetesses.

Received wisdom suggests that academia seeks to partition intellect and faith. Maybe this is true within the disciplines themselves and maybe in classrooms in the strictest sense, but I think it a false dichotomy. "The academy," after all, includes niches of appreciation for the holistic person. I find little partitioning of scholarly self and soul in places like the Disability Services and Academic Success offices, campus counseling center, deans' offices, or my own office when the conversation leaves the abstract world of ideas and turns suddenly real. I'm thinking of the student who lived an entire semester in his car rather than spend time with his abusive father. Another student who shyly confessed she wasn't doing the reading because she couldn't afford the textbook. One who was in such emotional distress over a recent abortion that I personally walked her into the counseling office. What about the student who misses class for a cancer treatment or a court appearance or because her boyfriend died of a heroin overdose? What can I give in such situations? I offer affirmation of their humanity and pain; I offer tissues, chocolate, sympathy, campus resources, a reality check, basic human compassion. "I'll walk with you." I believe it's no accident I'm who I am, positioned where I am at this point in time, if I can just hear the heavenly cues I'm supposed to be following.

I rarely teach Mormonism as a topic in my classes, although in much of my teaching I try to explicitly make room for religious worldviews in a general way since most of my students are unfamiliar with them (whereas I believe I have the precise opposite problem from my colleagues who teach in Mormon educational settings or in regions where religion is more culturally present). But I do think I have a "stealth curriculum" in my everyday teaching through which runs a deep, rich vein of Mormon doctrines. "The worth of souls is great," for example, resonates with my training in social history and with my wish to foster a community welcoming of diversity and difference. It is the beating heart of my Christian faith that also informs my reflexive feminism, my commitment to being an LGBTQ ally, and my grasp of the urgency of the Black Lives Matter movement. "O Remember, remember" is another guiding doctrinal principle because this is the basic work of history—to keep the past from receding out of living memory. "If any of you lack wisdom, let him ask of God" informs my sense that learning and faith are both processes of active experimentation and that curiosity and questioning can open the windows of heaven for personal revelation, discover truth, and radically reenvision a better society.

One of Mormonism's most beautiful and true doctrines is that creation is unfinished. Thomas S. Monson phrased that idea this way:

> God left the world unfinished for man to work his skill upon. He left the electricity in the cloud, the oil in the earth. He left the rivers unbridged and the forests uncut, and the cities unbuilt. God gives to man the challenge of raw materials, not the ease and comfort of finished things. He leaves the pictures unpainted and the music unsung and the problems unsolved, that man might know the joys and glories of creation.[4]

Some things in that quotation I object to, starting with the environmentally exploitative "dominion" theology and the unvaried male gendering of his language. But I do love the underlying idea, which is that we are all partners in an ongoing work of creation; the universe is ever expanding. Mormons understand creation as both a physical reality, accomplished in successive stages, and as a spiritual reality, a pattern for living and being in the world. We are creation and creators, usually acting in partnership rather than acting alone. Creation is a cycle, an eternal round of endless variety. I love the commandment given to Eve and Adam (and therefore to all of us) to "multiply and replenish the earth" because I believe it has meaning far beyond human reproduction and childbearing. A book, an article, an essay, a lecture, a syllabus, even the arc of an entire academic life—these are things that multiply the earth and replenish its goodness and abundance.

This essay was written as one academic year frantically galloped toward its close: the high season of finals, grading, awards ceremonies, honor society inductions, hooding, and commencement. Outside the classroom windows, the trees exploded into blossom and the campus reveled in the scent of fresh-mown grass. All the colored velvet robes, ceremonial maces, arcane symbolism, and rhetorical ritual put me in mind of how limited the liturgical tradition in Mormonism is (outside the temple, of course). For me, a religious reading of the seasonal rhythms of academia supplies some of that missing liturgy. The summer is the academic year's premortal existence, the time for spiritual creation of the future semester. The word becomes flesh in September with convocation and all-college meetings, fresh pencils and notebooks on the first day of class, hope springing eternal. Then there's a dark Lenten period of teaching, down in the trenches, sleep-deprived and time-starved, traveling through a wilderness with only a Liahona for guidance. Come May, we all stagger across the finish line with grades in hand ("it came to pass"), some weary and some triumphant. Commencement has two meanings, an end *and* a beginning, starting the calendar all over again. And we, the robed ones, stand as sentinels to admit the next generation with the signs and tokens they'll need to progress from novices to professionals, to ensure the future of knowledge when we are gone.

Perhaps you'll indulge me in closing with a benediction, as befits any good Mormon meeting. I have in mind the gloriously overwrought closing to Norman Corwin's radio special "On a Note of Triumph," which aired just days after the Second World War ended in May 1945. Over a dramatic, crescendoing organ solo, narrator Martin Gabel first calls upon the "Lord God of trajectory and blast" to "sheathe now the swift avenging blade and . . . assist in the preparation of the ploughshare." He beseeches the "Lord God of fresh bread and tranquil mornings" to make "tokens of orange juice and a whole egg appear now before the hungry children." He asks the "Lord God of the topcoat and the living wage" to bless the assembly line, factory smoke-stack, and farmer's field. And he hopes that the "Lord God of test-tube and blueprint" will appear in the parliaments and laboratories of the postwar generation to bring a lasting peace, "that man unto his fellow man shall be a friend forever."

As my more modest prayer, let me offer this one. (Imagine, please, a solo organ crescendo.)

Lord God, giver of life to the mind. Bring us an office with windows, the book rightly shelved, research grants that fall like ripe fruit into our outstretched hands, colleagues worthy of the description "collegial," and a comfortable chair to sit and think in. Grant us wide-awake students, fresh whiteboard markers, and classroom workstations without technology glitches. Enliven our minds that we may enliven others.

Lord God of abundance and creation, whose elegant signature is variety and diversity. Teach us to "strengthen and nourish" those who are different from us rather than try to re-make students in our own image. Give us mercy toward tardy students, delinquent assignments, loners, and those in crisis. Lend us your eyes to see the divine spark in everyone around us, kindling genuine and lasting human warmth against the cold and darkness.

Lord God of silent prayers, offered in times and places when we cannot pray openly. Fill our mouths with right words in the very hour we need them. May our lamps and cruses of oil never fail. Lift us to teach and not be weary and to talk and not faint. May this academic life (such as it is) be a well-tended vineyard in thy kingdom and a branch of the true vine.

Can I get an amen?

Notes

1. Joel A. Carpenter, ed., *The Early Billy Graham: Sermon and Revival Accounts*, Fundamentalism in American Religion, 1880–1950 (New York: Garland, 1988), 131.

2. Maggie Berg and Barbara K. Seeber, *The Slow Professor: Challenging the Culture of Speed in the Academy* (Toronto: University of Toronto Press, 2016), 3.

3. See, for example, James E. Côté and Anton L. Allahar, *Lowering Higher Education: The Rise of Corporate Universities and the Fall of Liberal Education* (Toronto: University of Toronto Press, 2011); Frank Donoghue, *The Last Professors: The Corporate University and the Fate of the Humanities; The Twilight of the Humanities in the Corporate University* (New York: Fordham University Press, 2008); Benjamin Ginsberg, *The Fall of the Faculty: The Rise of the All-Administrative University and Why It Matters* (Oxford: Oxford University Press, 2011); Christopher Newfield, *Unmaking the Public University: The Forty-Year Assault on the Middle Class* (Cambridge, MA: Harvard University Press, 2008); Jeff Selingo, *College (Un)bound: The Future of Higher Education and What It Means for Students* (Boston: New Harvest, 2013); Jennifer Washburn, *University Inc.: The Corporate Corruption of American Higher Education* (New York: Basic Books, 2005); and Robin Wilson, "The Ivory Sweatshop: Academe Is No Longer a Convivial Refuge," *Chronicle of Higher Education*, July 25, 2010, http://www.chronicle.com/article/The-Ivory-Sweatshop -Academe/123641.

4. Thomas S. Monson, "In Search of an Abundant Life," *Liahona*, August 1988.

FINDING THE RIGHT WORDS

Speaking Faith in Secular Times

RICHARD LYMAN BUSHMAN

It warms my heart to sense the friendship of so many people at this conference. When I was young and had published only one book, I used to dream of a funeral where people would talk of my scholarship in the presence of my children. If I was not to be around, I wanted them to know that their father's work was honorable. This symposium fulfills that dream.

Jerry Bradford was the one who thought up the idea of a festschrift. At first I had reservations. Grant Underwood had already organized a celebratory event at the American Historical Association complete with a reception afterward. My eightieth birthday was marked by a two-day symposium at the Springville Art Museum, generously lent us by Vern Swanson. I was beginning to feel overexposed. It was not my intent in living so long to give people additional opportunities to plan another conference on my behalf.

But when Spencer, Jed, and Kathleen began putting plans together, I saw the possibilities. I have long been interested in how Mormons integrate, exploit, elucidate, get around, or overcome their faith when writing and teaching. Ours is supposedly an encompassing religion. The word *consecration* plays a big part in Mormon worship. What would it mean to consecrate our scholarship? Is there any way we can integrate our personal religious lives and our work as scholars and teachers? Does our belief make any difference at all in our scholarship?

Sometimes I have dreamed that Mormonism could function as Marxism does in providing a set of issues and categories to be explored. What would be the Mormon equivalent of class or hegemony? Do Mormons have a conception of human nature that would play out in history?

None of these lines of thought have gotten me very far. In an essay entitled "Faithful History," I speculated on possible approaches to history derived from the scriptures, but none of them held up. I eventually concluded that we will know what a Mormon historiography will look like only when Mormons write it. I could find no systematic framework for approaching historical issues.[1]

The best I can come up with is an attitude toward the subjects of my historical inquiries—an impulse to take people on their own terms. At the conference for my eightieth birthday, Stuart Parker proposed that I practice a hermeneutics of generosity as contrasted with a hermeneutics of suspicion.[2] I try to think the best of people, to understand the world as they see it. I once told a graduate student, Lauren Winner, in a moment of candor, that my belief in an afterlife affected my attitude toward historical subjects. I had to picture myself at some point talking face-to-face with the people I write about.

When my own deliberations did not take me very far, I was still interested in hearing what others would have to say. I thought it would be particularly delicious to have Mormons reflect on the interplay of their personal religious belief and their scholarship and teaching in the presence of non-Mormon scholars—not in the privacy of the Mormon ghetto but before a sympathetic but skeptical non-Mormon public. That would be a useful exercise for everyone: for Mormons to state their perspectives in a public, academic language, and for non-Mormon scholars to seek understanding of a religious outlook that may be foreign to them. And so the project was launched. Spencer Fluhman sent out the invitations, you accepted, and here we are.

As it turned out, the exercise proved to be rewarding for me. Working up my own comments for the occasion, I began to see my experience in a new light. I discovered that my search for a Mormon attitude toward writing history was entangled with my personal search for faith. The stories I planned to tell about how my attitudes about scholarship were formed actually were stories about working out my personal religious convictions.

I have told many times the story of how I lost my faith in God during my sophomore year at Harvard. By that time, I had decided to declare history and science as my field of concentration. It was a tiny concentration, newly put together by various people at Harvard, among them I. B. Cohen and Thomas Kuhn. At my request, Cohen took me on as a tutee if I would agree to read the things he was reading. Every few weeks we got together for an hour to talk over the readings. Cohen took a kind of fatherly interest in me and at one point chose to give me some advice. Knowing my background, he observed that people around here, meaning Harvard, thought Mormonism is garbage. It was not a malicious comment; he was simply trying to help me grow up.

I was set back a little, but his observation was not news to me. I had been hearing a lot about logical positivism, then current among undergraduates, and could see the implications for religion. I was in hostile territory, but I certainly was not going to back away from my faith on the advice of a Harvard professor or the positivist Bertrand Russell. Cohen was challenging everything I stood for, my people, my family, my friends back in Portland. I could not give all that up on the basis of one comment.

Looking back now, I realize that I was not just encountering one professor or one philosophy or even the intellectual culture that reigned at Harvard. I was encountering modernism itself with its skepticism about all things religious. I was glimpsing a world where, as Richard Rorty has said, the universe does not speak. Only we speak.[3] There is no friendly intelligence beyond our own, nothing like spirit or soul, no angels, no gold plates, no divinely inspired prophets, no listener to our prayers. That empty universe was the modernist world I was called upon to confront.

As I have told the story for many years, the pressure of all these influences wore me down. By the end of my sophomore year, I had to admit that I was no longer sure that there was a God. Religious agnosticism seemed like the only viable position given what we know for sure. Before this loss of faith, I had been interviewed for a mission and was to enter the field in June. I carried through on my commitment and left for New England, my assigned mission field. Soon after arriving, I was asked by my mission president if I had a testimony. I told him no. I did not know there was a God or that any of the things Mormons believe had actually happened.

Then in the usual telling of the story, I go on to relate how during my first three months in the mission field I wrestled with my doubts, asked all the difficult questions, and prayed the agnostic's prayer for light. When the mission president arrived for the first conference and I was asked to speak, I said that at last I knew that the Book of Mormon was right. End of story.

That is a story Mormons like to hear, faith overcoming doubt and the doubter ending up in the right place. But I have always been troubled by one inconsistency in my own story. If I was such a doubter, why did I go into the mission field where I would be called on to testify of my beliefs virtually every day? At the time, I recognized there was a problem, but there was no anguished debate about going or not. I did not worry about being hypocritical or misleading people. I was up front about my skepticism, but I did not hesitate to go. How could that be?

Not until a few years ago did I face up to this contradiction and reformulate the story. I have come to believe that in actuality my problem was not faith but finding the words to express my faith. The problem was that when Cohen said that Mormonism was garbage, I did not know how to reply. I knew that the words I had been taught in Sunday School or in my home would sound silly to him. I was left speechless.

Harvard is all about talking. Much of the education takes place at the dinner table where undergraduates yak on endlessly about everything. There was an unwritten rule that you could believe nearly anything, but you had to explain why. You did not need to persuade everyone, but you had to make sense. I needed a way to state my beliefs that would sound reasonable even if they were more than a little weird.

That was what I lacked at the end of my sophomore year. I had no critique of Russell or Nietzsche and no language for Mormonism that made sense over the dinner table. I think I believed all along through that year—why else the mission?—but I was dumb, unable to speak.

Over the years, what can be thought of as a growth in faith can be thought of as an improvement in language. I have learned to speak in a way that can be understood in a secular time. There is nothing particularly clever or overpowering about this speech. It just comes out of a perspective. Soon after I arrived at Claremont, the man soon to be dean of religious studies asked me to lunch. A Catholic himself, we had no sooner sat down than he blurted out his question: "How can you believe in Joseph Smith?" I replied in one sentence: "I find that when I live the Mormon way, I am the kind of man I want to be." That was anything but a noble defense—there was nothing deep or clever—but the words did the trick.

Often I find the language only after I have muffed an occasion to use it. At the time, I fumble a reply and work out what I should have said only later. My colleague Ken Jackson runs a lunch table for scholars at Columbia's Herbert H. Lehman Center for American History. Soon after *Rough Stone Rolling* came out, he asked me to lead a discussion. I made some comments about Joseph Smith, and then Andy Delbanco, the literary historian, asked what my personal relationship to the Book of Mormon was.

It was a logical point of inquiry and one I should have been able to answer in a second, but I froze. I was obviously paralyzed, and Jackson had to come to my rescue by saying a few words about his own religious belief. I froze because Mormons know precisely what they should say when asked this question. They should bear their testimony about the Spirit revealing the truth of the Book of Mormon. The answer is prescribed.

I froze because I knew that such an answer would not work. It would be like a lawyer defending the church in court. When the lawyer was asked why he knew the church was in the right in the case, it would not do to say it was because he knew that this was the true church of God. A testimony of that kind would not work in a courtroom. It would weaken the lawyer's case rather than strengthen it. I felt the same way at the lunch table. Testimony was not the answer. The "I know" formula would not do.

Later I worked out another answer. I could simply say that I read the Book of Mormon as informed Christians read the Bible. As I read, I know the arguments against the book's historicity, but I can't help feeling that the words are true and the events happened. I believe it in the face of many questions.

Searching for the right words may seem like a simple and trivial response to the profound questions about religion coming out of modernism. Saying that living the Mormon way helps me be the kind of man I want to be does not begin to deal with the complexities of the modernist challenge. They may seem like a dodge, but I don't think the right words are trivial. They are not merely a gambit.

Words are our entry into another culture. They are the way we make ourselves intelligible in a strange land. They not only allow us to connect, to make ourselves understood. They show respect. We are making an effort to communicate in a way that can be understood. If we insist on using standard church language, we are in effect declaring our indifference. We force people to learn our language in order to understand us. We don't go halfway.

Out of this inquiry came questions about the nature of my faith. Was I really doubting during my sophomore year? Or was I only lacking for words? I think that by nature I am a believing person. It is the point of rest in the oscillations of my soul. But does that faith take a workable form until I find the right words? Do I need to speak it before it is real?

One thing I know is that I could not have written *Rough Stone Rolling* without decades of practice in speaking my faith among colleagues of all persuasions. *Rough Stone Rolling* is not notable for its research. There are lots of people who know more about Joseph Smith than I do. What distinguishes the book is its tone, its language. It is written in the vocabulary that I learned at Harvard at the dinner tables and in Cohen's tutorial. That is its primary virtue. The book is autobiographical in the sense that it comes out of a lifelong effort to make myself intelligible to unbelieving listeners. If you look closely at the book, you can see my personal faith and my scholarship intersecting.

Rough Stone Rolling may have been the culmination of a quest, but it is not the end. Learning how to speak the right words continues down to this very day, to this very moment when we have collected to talk to one another about what we believe. After Cohen, a number of people in this room have been my tutors. I learned to talk from them.

Some of these relationships go back a long way. I have known David Hall since he was a senior in history and literature at Harvard and I as a graduate student sat on his oral examination committee. David does not know how much of an influence he has been. We worked together for nearly a decade on developing the American and New England Studies Program at Boston University. We brought together local institutions like the Boston Museum of Fine Arts (MFA) and Old Sturbridge Village to help us investigate material culture. A lot of the funding came from the National Endowment for the Humanities. Jonathan Fairbanks, then curator of American art at the MFA, said that David could press his hand on a blank sheet of paper and a grant application would appear. What I learned from David is how to do projects, that you can make something out of almost nothing. The summer seminar and many of the other projects I have been involved in are really an outgrowth of what I learned from David during those Boston University years.

Richard Brown and I came together through early American history projects we were involved in. I took to him and his wife, Irene, right away. I have many times told a story on Richard that he may not remember. Years ago when I was a Mormon bishop in Cambridge, I invited the Browns to come to dinner and meet the missionaries. I asked the elders, two young men, to present a filmstrip on the Granite Mountain Records Vault and the church's record-collection program. I thought the story of Mormon record keeping would appeal to an early Americanist. When the missionaries arrived, they did not bring a Granite Vault film but one on ancient America. Lacking a script to match the pictures, they asked me to narrate the story. That out of the way, they asked if they could have a prayer. Richard agreed, but then they asked him to kneel, and at that he bridled. Next they asked, "Do you believe in God?" Richard drew himself up a little and said, "If you were a person of age and wisdom, I might talk about my belief, but not here." The meeting was a disaster. But the strange thing is that the very broad-minded Browns seemed to tolerate the young men, and it did not damage our friendship. To the contrary, whenever we meet, we talk candidly about the things that matter most to us. We connect at a deep level, partly I think because I let him see my Mormonism in the raw.

We first got to know Grant Wacker through a group of evangelical scholars that included Mark Noll, Skip Stout, and Nathan Hatch. We felt a kinship because we were all believers making our way through a secular landscape. I did not realize how generous and kind Grant was until we spent a year at the National Humanities Center when he was teaching at Duke. He went out of his way to welcome us and give us a chance to talk to his students. Since then many things have bound us together. The strange thing is how a very small item formed my early impression of Grant. After a scholarly conference, I joined a group of his evangelical friends for dinner—I am pretty sure Mark and Skip were there too. As we sat down to eat and our food was before us, Grant looked around at his colleagues and asked, "What about grace?"—which we proceeded to offer right there in the restaurant. I remembered that moment. It showed that Grant's belief had a little edge to it.

I first became acquainted with Laurie Maffly-Kipp through Mormon students like Reid Neilson who flocked to the University of North Carolina at Chapel Hill because Laurie was interested in Mormon topics herself. She and I have had an ongoing exchange over her review of *Rough Stone Rolling* for *Books & Culture*. In it she said something about how modern scholars will not take the book seriously because it does not offer a material explanation of Joseph Smith. For some reason that comment stuck with me, and I have brought it up in public various times when she was present. I think there has been a misunderstanding on my part. Laurie was not speaking for herself, I now realize, but for a consensus of academic readers. So for any undeserved barbs, Laurie, I hereby apologize, and thank you for your many valuable observations about Joseph Smith and Mormonism. For wisdom and good judgment you can't beat Laurie.

Not all of you will know that Ann Taves played a large role in establishing the Mormon studies program at Claremont Graduate University. She taught American religion at the Claremont School of Theology, a closely affiliated school, and masterminded the intellectual structure of the Mormon studies program. When she left for the University of California,

Santa Barbara, I took over the American religion program at Claremont. Ann is working on a problem raised by Laurie Maffly-Kipp. On a panel I chaired, Laurie gave a talk on Joseph Smith's sincerity. Can we believe in the religious sincerity of a man who claimed he possessed gold plates? Is there a way to approach Mormonism, Laurie asked, other than going through this disruptive story? Ann has been trying to preserve Joseph Smith's sincerity by arguing there are ways of conceiving the plates that are religiously valid and do not presume any form of fraud on Joseph's part. Joseph was not trying to deceive his followers. If the plates were not real in the usual sense, religiously they were. This is a bold and noble effort and an indication of Ann's goodwill.

I have known Bob Goldberg for less time than any of the others, but I heard of him many years before we met. Bob tells a story of driving in from the airport when he was being interviewed for a job at the University of Utah. As they passed the Salt Lake Temple, the driver made some comment about the temple being a local version of Disneyland architecture. Bob was astonished at this cavalier treatment of a religious monument. He took the job and since then has taken on the task of mitigating if not dispelling the animosity between the church and the university's faculty, a divide that has prevailed for a long time. Only he knows the battles he has fought, but he has successfully made Mormon scholars feel at home at "the U" and has raised money for scholars in residence programs. The U has now become a venue where the best work on Mormon subjects can be presented and Mormons can be themselves.

As for my comrades in Mormon studies, I can only take pride in all you have accomplished. When the Mormon History Association was formed a half century ago, there was only a tiny handful of historians with PhDs. Now there are scores and scores in many humanistic and social science fields. Mormon studies and Mormon scholarship are thriving.

We are all over the map in our interests and approaches to the issues raised in this symposium. We pursue our investigations idiosyncratically, as I think we should. But I sense one common theme. I think we all feel some tension between our religious convictions and the secular times in which we live. In one way or another, modernism invades and unsettles our thinking, perhaps our thinking about our fields, perhaps our personal beliefs. What I hope we all realize is that this tension is not to be suppressed or regretted. Unanswerable as some questions are, we need not lament the discomfort they bring. The strain of believing in unbelieving times is not a handicap or a burden. It is a stimulus and a prod. It is precisely out of such strains that creative work issues forth. And we can take satisfaction in knowing that we are in this together.

Notes

1. Richard L. Bushman, "Faithful History," *Dialogue: A Journal of Mormon Thought* 4 (Spring 1969): 11–25.
2. Stuart Parker, "The Hermeneutics of Generosity: A Critical Approach to the Scholarship of Richard Bushman," *Journal of Mormon History* 38 (Summer 2012): 12–27.
3. Richard Rorty, *Contingency, Irony, and Solidarity* (Cambridge: Cambridge University Press, 1989), 6.

APPENDIX
The Academic Achievements and Publications
of Richard Lyman Bushman

Education

Undergraduate: Harvard College, AB, magna cum laude, Phi
Beta Kappa, 1955
Graduate: Harvard University, AM, history, 1960; PhD,
history of American civilization, 1961

Teaching

Harvard University, tutor in American history and literature,
1957–58
Brigham Young University, assistant professor, 1960–63,
1965–66; associate professor, 1966–68
Brown University, interdisciplinary fellow, 1963–65
Boston University, professor, 1968–77
Harvard University, visiting professor, 1973

University of Delaware, professor, 1977–85; H. Rodney Sharp
Professor of History, 1985–89
Columbia University, professor, 1989–91; Gouverneur Morris
Professor of History, 1991–2001; Emeritus 2001–
Bard Graduate Center for Studies in the Decorative Arts,
1993; instructor in material culture
Claremont Graduate University, Visiting Howard W. Hunter
Chair of Mormon Studies, 2008–2011

Fellowships and Awards

Interdisciplinary Fellow in history and psychology, Brown
University
Bancroft Prize
Phi Alpha Theta Prize
American Council of Learned Societies Fellowship
Charles Warren Center Fellowship
John Simon Guggenheim Fellowship
National Endowment for the Humanities Research Fellowship
David Woolley Evans and Beatrice Cannon Evans Biography
Award (twice)
Regents' Fellowship, Smithsonian Institution
Fellowship, Center for Advanced Studies, University of Delaware
National Humanities Center Fellowship
E. Harold Hugo Memorial Book Prize of the Old Sturbridge
Village Research Library Society
R. Stanton Avery Distinguished Fellow, Huntington Library
Bellagio Residency Fellowship, Rockefeller Foundation
Shelby Cullom Davis Center Fellowship, Princeton University
Presidential Teaching Award, Columbia University
Best Book Award, Mormon History Association

Biography Award, Association of Mormon Letters

Research Fellowship, Huntington Library

Leonard Arrington Award for Distinguished Service to Mormon History

Mellon Distinguished Senior Scholar in Residence, American Antiquarian Society

Editorial and Administrative

Associate director, Honors Program, Brigham Young University, 1965–68

Book review editor, *Dialogue: A Journal of Mormon Thought*, 1965–68

Bishop and stake president, Church of Jesus Christ of Latter-day Saints, 1968–72 (bishop), 1972–77 (stake president), 1981–86 (bishop)

Acting director, American and New England Studies, Boston University, 1973–74

Chair, Department of History, University of Delaware, 1977–83

Coordinator, History of American Civilization Program, University of Delaware, 1984–89

President, Mormon History Association, 1985–86

Member of the board of editors, *Encyclopedia of Mormonism*, 1989–91

Council member, Institute of Early American History and Culture, 1982–84, 1989–92

President, Society for Historians of the Early American Republic, 1997–98

Chair of the advisory committee, Smith Institute, Brigham Young University, 1999–2004

Co-general editor, Joseph Smith Papers, Church History Department, 2004–12

Chair of the board of directors, Mormon Scholars Foundation, 2007–16

Mormon Studies Council at the University of Virginia, 2013–

Books

From Puritan to Yankee: Character and the Social Order in Connecticut, 1690–1765. Cambridge, MA: Harvard University Press, 1967. Awarded the Bancroft Prize and Phi Alpha Theta Prize.

Edited: *The Great Awakening: Documents on the Revival of Religion, 1740–1745.* New York: Atheneum, 1970.

Edited: *Uprooted Americans: Essays to Honor Oscar Handlin.* Boston: Little, Brown, 1979.

Joseph Smith and the Beginnings of Mormonism. Urbana: University of Illinois Press, 1984. Awarded the History Book Club selection and Evans Biography Award.

King and People in Provincial Massachusetts. Chapel Hill: University of North Carolina Press for the Institute of Early American History and Culture, 1985.

The Refinement of America: Persons, Houses, Cities. New York: Alfred A. Knopf, 1992. Awarded the History Book Club and Book of the Month selections.

Mormons in America. With Claudia Bushman. New York: Oxford University Press, 1999. New edition titled *Building the Kingdom of God: A History of Mormons in America* published by Oxford University Press, 2001.

Believing History: Latter-day Saint Essays. Edited by Reid L. Neilson and Jed Woodworth. New York: Columbia University Press, 2004.

Joseph Smith: Rough Stone Rolling. New York: Alfred A. Knopf, 2005. Awarded the Association of Mormon Letters Best Biography Award, Evans Biography Award, and Mormon History Association Best Book Award.

On the Road with Joseph Smith: An Author's Diary. Limited edition. New York: Mormon Artists Group Press, 2006. Paperback edition. Salt Lake City: Kofford Books, 2007.

Mormonism: A Very Short Introduction. New York: Oxford University Press, 2008.

Select List of Articles

"English Franchise Reform in the Seventeenth Century." *Journal of British Studies* 3/1 (November 1963): 36–56.

"On the Uses of Psychology: Conflict and Conciliation in Benjamin Franklin." *History and Theory* 5/3 (1966): 227–40.

"Jonathan Edwards and Puritan Consciousness." *Journal for the Scientific Study of Religion* 5/3 (Fall 1966): 383–96.

"Corruption and Power in Provincial Massachusetts." In *The Development of a Revolutionary Mentality*, 63–91. Washington, DC: Library of Congress, 1972.

"Massachusetts Farmers and the Revolution." In *Society, Freedom, and Conscience: The American Revolution in Virginia, Massachusetts, and New York,* edited by Richard M. Jellison, 77–124. New York: W. W. Norton, 1976.

"Caricature and Satire in Old and New England before the American Revolution." *Proceedings of the Massachusetts Historical Society* 88 (1976): 19–34.

"Freedom and Prosperity in the American Revolution." In *Legacies of the American Revolution,* edited by Larry R. Gerlach, 61–83. Logan: Utah State University Press, 1978.

"This New Man: Dependence and Independence in 1776." In *Uprooted Americans: Essays to Honor Oscar Handlin,* edited by Richard L. Bushman, 79–96. Boston: Little, Brown, 1979.

"Family Security in the Transition from Farm to City, 1750–1850." *Journal of Family History* 6/3 (Fall 1981): 238–56.

"American High-Style and Vernacular Cultures." In *Colonial British America: Essays in the New History of the Early Modern Era,* edited by Jack P. Greene and J. R. Pole, 345–83. Baltimore: Johns Hopkins University Press, 1984.

"Regional Material Culture: A Review of 'The Great River: Art and Society of the Connecticut Valley, 1635–1820.'" *William and Mary Quarterly* 43/2 (April 1986): 245–51.

With Claudia L. Bushman. "The Early History of Cleanliness in America." *Journal of American History* 74/4 (March 1988): 1213–38.

"Opening the American Countryside." In *The Transformation of Early American History: Society, Authority, and Ideology,* edited by James A. Henretta, Michael Kammen, and Stanley N. Katz, 239–56. New York: Alfred Knopf, 1991.

"Portraiture and Society in Late Eighteenth-Century Connecticut." In Elizabeth Mankin Kornhauser, *Ralph Earl: The Face of the Young Republic*, 69–83. New Haven: Yale University Press, 1991.

"Public Culture and Popular Taste in Classical America." In Wendy A. Cooper, *Classical Taste in America, 1800–1840*, 14–23. New York: Baltimore Museum of Art and Abbeville Press, 1993.

"Shopping and Advertising in Colonial America." In *Of Consuming Interests: The Style of Life in the Eighteenth Century*, 233–51. Charlottesville: University Press of Virginia for the Capitol Historical Society, 1994.

"The Rise and Fall of Civility in America." *Wilson Quarterly* 20/4 (Autumn 1996): 13–46.

"Markets and Composite Farms in Early America." *William and Mary Quarterly* 55/3 (July 1998): 351–74.

"A Poet, a Planter, and a Nation of Farmers." *Journal of the Early Republic* 19/1 (Spring 1999): 1–14.

"Farmers in Court: Orange County, North Carolina, 1750–1776." In *The Many Legalities of Early America*, edited by Christopher L. Tomlins and Bruce H. Mann, 388–413. Chapel Hill: University of North Carolina Press, 2001.

"Cultural Orientations: Migrations West, Migrations North." In *Planter Links: Community and Culture in Colonial Nova Scotia*, edited by Margaret Conrad and Barry Moody, 1–11. Fredericton, NB: Acadiensis Press, 2001.

"The Complexity of Silver." In *New England Silver & Silversmithing, 1620–1815*, edited by Jeannine Falino and Gerald W. R. Ward, 1–15. Boston: University Press of Virginia, 2001.

"The Place of the Eighteenth Century in American Agricultural History." In *The World Turned Upside Down: The State of Eighteenth-Century American Studies at the Beginning of the Twenty-First Century*, edited by Michael V. Kennedy and William G. Shade, 40–77. Bethlehem, PA: Lehigh University Press, 2001.

"Puritan and Polite: Virtuous Youth in Eighteenth-Century New England." In *Cheiron: Materiali e strumenti di aggiornamento storiografico*, 187–204. Rome: Bulzoni Editore, 2003.

Mormon Studies

"Mormon Persecutions in Missouri, 1833." *Brigham Young University Studies* 3/1 (Autumn 1960): 11–20.

"Inspired Constitution." *Brigham Young University Studies* 4/2 (Winter 1962): 158–63.

"Faithful History." *Dialogue: A Journal of Mormon Thought* 4/4 (Winter 1969): 11–25.

"The First Vision Revisited." *Dialogue: A Journal of Mormon Thought* 4/1 (Spring 1969): 82–93.

Joseph Smith and Skepticism. Commissioner's Lecture Series. Provo, UT: Brigham Young University Press, 1974.

"The Book of Mormon and the American Revolution." *Brigham Young University Studies* 17/1 (Autumn 1976): 3–20.

"The Character of Joseph Smith: Insights from His Holographs." *Ensign*, April 1977, 10–13.

"My Belief." In *A Thoughtful Faith: Essays on Belief by Mormon Scholars*, edited by Philip L. Barlow, 17–28. Centerville, UT: Cannon Press, 1986.

"The Book of Mormon in Early Mormon History." In *New Views of Mormon History: A Collection of Essays in Honor of Leonard J. Arrington*, edited by Davis Bitton and Maureen Ursenbach Beecher, 3–18. Salt Lake City: University of Utah Press, 1987.

"Treasure-Seeking Then and Now." *Sunstone* 11/5 (September 1987): 5–7.

"The Crisis in Europe and Hugh B. Brown's First Mission Presidency." *Dialogue: A Journal of Mormon Thought* 21/2 (Summer 1988): 51–60.

"Joseph Smith's Family Background." In *The Prophet Joseph: Essays on the Life and Mission of Joseph Smith*, edited by Larry C. Porter and Susan Easton Black, 1–18. Salt Lake City: Deseret Book, 1988.

"The Lamanite View of Book of Mormon History." In *By Study and Also by Faith*, edited by John M. Lundquist and Stephen D. Ricks, 2:52–72. Salt Lake City: Deseret Book and FARMS, 1990.

With Dean C. Jessee. "Smith, Joseph: The Prophet." In *Encyclopedia of Mormonism*, edited by Daniel H. Ludlow, 1331–39. New York: Macmillan, 1992.

With Larry C. Porter. "History of the Church: C. 1820–1831, Background, Founding, New York Period." In *Encyclopedia of Mormonism*, 598–604.

"The Quest for Learning." *BYU Today*, November 1991.

"Joseph Smith in the Current Age." In *Joseph Smith: The Prophet, the Man*, edited by Susan Easton Black and Charles D. Tate Jr., 33–48. Provo, UT: Religious Studies Center, Brigham Young University, 1993.

"The Social Dimensions of Rationality." In *Expressions of Faith: Testimonies of Latter-day Saint Scholars*, edited by Susan Easton Black, 69–77. Salt Lake City: Deseret Book and FARMS, 1996.

"The Secret History of Mormonism." *Sunstone* 19/1 (March 1996): 66–70.

"Making Space for the Mormons." Leonard J. Arrington Lecture, Utah State University, Logan, Utah, October 22, 1996.

"The Visionary World of Joseph Smith." *Brigham Young University Studies* 37/1 (1997–98): 183–204.

"Joseph Smith as Translator." In *The Prophet Puzzle: Interpretive Essays on Joseph Smith*, edited by Bryan Waterman, 69–86. Salt Lake City: Signature Books, 1999.

"Was Joseph Smith a Gentleman? The Standard for Refinement in Utah." In *Nearly Everything Imaginable: The Everyday Life of Utah's Mormon Pioneers*, 27–46. Provo, UT: Brigham Young University Press, 1999.

"The Little, Narrow Prison of Language: The Rhetoric of Revelation." *The Religious Educator: Perspectives on the Restored Gospel* 1 (Spring 2000): 90–104.

"The Colonization of the Mormon Mind." In *Annual of the Association for Mormon Letters 2000*, edited by Lavina Fielding Anderson, 14–23. Salt Lake City: Association for Mormon Letters, 2000

"A Joseph Smith for the Twenty-First Century." *Brigham Young University Studies* 40/3 (2001): 155–71; reprinted in *Lives of the Saints: Writing Mormon Biography and Autobiography*, edited by Jill Mulvay Derr, 9–18. Provo, UT: Joseph Fielding Smith Institute for Latter-day Saint History, Brigham Young University, 2002.

"The Theology of Councils." In *Revelation, Reason, and Faith: Essays in Honor of Truman G. Madsen*, edited by Donald W. Parry, Daniel C. Peterson, and Stephen D. Ricks, 433–46. Provo, UT: FARMS, 2002.

"Would Joseph Smith Attend the New York Stake Arts Festival?" *Dialogue: A Journal of Mormon Thought* 35/3 (Fall 2002): 212–20.

"The Character of Joseph Smith." *Brigham Young University Studies* 42/2 (2003): 23–34.

"Joseph Smith and Abraham Lincoln." In *Joseph Smith and the Doctrinal Restoration: The 34th Annual Sidney B. Sperry Symposium*, 89–108. Salt Lake City: Deseret Book and Religious Studies Center, Brigham Young University, 2005.

"Joseph Smith's Many Histories." In *The Worlds of Joseph Smith: A Bicentennial Conference at the Library of Congress*, edited by John Welch, 3–20. Provo, UT: Brigham Young University Press, 2006. Also published in *Brigham Young University Studies* 44/4 (2005): 3–20.

"The Inner Joseph Smith." *Journal of Mormon History* 32/1 (Spring 2006): 65–81.

"The Balancing Act: A Mormon Historian Reflects on His

Biography of Joseph Smith." *Common-Place* 7/1 (October 2006). www.common-place.org.

"The Archive of Restoration Culture, 1997–2002." *Brigham Young University Studies* 45/4 (2006): 99–106.

"What's New in Mormon History: A Response to Jan Shipps." *Journal of American History* 94/2 (September 2007): 517–21.

"Joseph Smith and Creation of the Sacred." In *Joseph Smith Jr.: Reappraisals after Two Centuries*, edited by Reid L. Neilson and Terryl L. Givens, 93–106. New York: Oxford University Press, 2009.

"Oliver's Joseph." In *Days Never to Be Forgotten: Oliver Cowdery*, edited by Alexander L. Baugh, 1–14. Provo, UT: Religious Studies Center, Brigham Young University, 2009.

"The Historian's Craft: A Conversation with Richard Lyman Bushman," by Jed Woodworth. *Mormon Historical Studies* 10/2 (Fall 2009): 135–74.

"Joseph Smith and Power." In *A Firm Foundation: Church Organization and Administration*, edited by David J. Whittaker and Arnold K. Garr, 1–13. Salt Lake City: Deseret Book and Religious Studies Center, Brigham Young University, 2011.

"After the Golden Age." *Journal of Mormon History* 38/3 (Summer 2012): 225–31.

"Reading the Gold Plates." *Journal of Mormon History* 41/1 (January 2015): 64–76.

"Joseph Smith and His Visions." In *The Oxford Handbook of Mormonism*, edited by Terryl L. Givens and Philip L. Barlow, 109–20. New York: Oxford University Press, 2015.

"Joseph Smith and the Study of Antiquity." In *Approaching Antiquity: Joseph Smith and the Ancient World*, edited by Lincoln H. Blumell, Matthew J. Grey, and Andrew H. Hedges, 3–22. Salt Lake City: Deseret Book and Religious Studies Center, Brigham Young University, 2015.

"Joseph Smith and Money Digging." In *A Reason for Faith: Navigating LDS Doctrine and Church History*, edited by Laura Harris Hales, 1–6. Salt Lake City: Deseret Book and Religious Studies Center, Brigham Young University, 2016.

"Theory and Interpretation in Mormon Studies." In *Directions for Mormon Studies in the Twenty-First Century*, edited by Patrick Q. Mason, 223–33. Salt Lake City: University of Utah Press, 2016.

Current Projects

The American Farmer in the Eighteenth Century. New Haven: Yale University Press, forthcoming.

"Joseph Smith's Gold Plates: A Cultural History"

CONTRIBUTORS

Philip L. Barlow is the Leonard J. Arrington Professor of Mormon History and Culture at Utah State University. His writings on religion have contemplated belief (*A Thoughtful Faith: Essays on Belief by Mormon Scholars*, editor), geography (*New Historical Atlas of Religion in America*, coeditor), and scripture (*Mormons and the Bible: The Place of the Latter-day Saints in American Religion*). With Terryl Givens he is the editor of *The Oxford Handbook of Mormonism*. His current project contemplates a "war in heaven" in the history of ideas.

Brian D. Birch is the director of the Religious Studies Program and Center for the Study of Ethics at Utah Valley University, where he teaches philosophy of religion, ethics, and Mormon studies. He is the founding editor of *Element: The Journal of the Society for Mormon Philosophy and Theology* and coeditor of the Perspectives on Mormon Theology series. His recent projects include *The Expanded Canon: Mormonism and Sacred Texts*. He has served on the boards of trustees of the Parliament of the World's Religions and *Dialogue: A Journal of Mormon Thought*.

Matthew Bowman is associate professor of history at Henderson State University. He is the author of *The Mormon People: The Making of an American Faith* (Random House, 2012) and co-editor of *Women and Mormonism: Historic and Contemporary Perspectives* (University of Utah Press, 2016).

Richard D. Brown is Board of Trustees Distinguished Professor of History, Emeritus, at the University of Connecticut. He is the author of *Self-Evident Truths: Contesting Equal Rights from the Revolution to the Civil War* (Yale University Press, 2017), *The Strength of a People: The Idea of an Informed Citizenry in America, 1650–1870* (1996), and *Knowledge Is Power: The Diffusion of Information in Early America, 1700–1865* (1989) and coauthor of *The Hanging of Ephraim Wheeler: A Story of Rape, Incest, and Justice* (2003). He serves on the board of the American Antiquarian Society and is president and board member of the *New England Quarterly*.

Claudia L. Bushman holds degrees from Wellesley College, Brigham Young University, and Boston University. She has taught at many colleges, most recently at Claremont Graduate University and Columbia University. Her books include *Mormon Sisters: Women in Early Utah*; *Contemporary Mormonism: Latter-day Saints in Modern America*; *Mormon Women Have Their Say: Essays from the Claremont Oral History Collection*; and such monographs as *In Old Virginia: Slavery, Farming, and Society in the Antebellum Journal of John Walker*; *America Discovers Columbus: How an Italian Explorer Became* *an American Hero*; and, most recently, *Going to Boston: Harriet Robinson's Journey to New Womanhood*. She is currently writing her autobiography to be titled *I, Claudia*.

Richard Lyman Bushman is Gouverneur Morris Professor of History Emeritus at Columbia University and author of *Joseph Smith: Rough Stone Rolling*.

Kathleen Flake is the Richard Lyman Bushman Professor in Mormon Studies at the University of Virginia. She is the author of *The Politics of Religious Identity: The Seating of Senator Reed Smoot, Mormon Apostle*. She has published in several scholarly journals and is on the editorial boards of *Religion and American Culture: A Journal of Interpretation* and the *Mormon Studies Review*. Her current project is "Mormon Matriarchy: A Study of Gendered Power in Antebellum America."

J. Spencer Fluhman is executive director of the Neal A. Maxwell Institute for Religious Scholarship and associate professor of history at Brigham Young University. He is the author of *"A Peculiar People": Anti-Mormonism and the Making of Religion in Nineteenth-Century America* (University of North Carolina Press, 2012) and editor-in-chief of the *Mormon Studies Review*.

Terryl L. Givens did graduate work in intellectual history at Cornell University and in comparative literature at the University of North Carolina at Chapel Hill. He teaches courses in nineteenth-century studies and religious themes in literature at the University of Richmond, where he is professor of literature and religion and Jabez A. Bostwick Professor of English. His published books include *By the Hand of Mormon*, *When Souls Had Wings*, *People of Paradox*, and a two-volume history of Mormon thought: *Wrestling the Angel* and *Feeding the Flock*

(Oxford University Press). With his wife, Fiona, he has written *The God Who Weeps*, *The Crucible of Doubt*, and *The Christ Who Heals*.

Robert A. Goldberg is professor of history and director of the Tanner Humanities Center at the University of Utah. He is the author of eight books, with his last two, *Barry Goldwater* and *Enemies Within: The Culture of Conspiracy in Modern America*, published by Yale University Press. He has won twelve teaching honors, including the Distinguished Honors Professor Award and University of Utah Distinguished Teaching Award. In 2003 he held the Fulbright Distinguished Chair in American Studies at the Swedish Institute for North American Studies, Uppsala University. He was awarded the Rosenblatt Prize for Excellence in 2008.

Deidre Nicole Green is currently a postdoctoral fellow at the Neal A. Maxwell Institute for Religious Scholarship. She is the author of *Works of Love in a World of Violence* (Mohr Siebeck, 2016). Deidre has also published in *Journal of Religion* and *Hypatia*, as well as in a number of anthologies. She has held a postdoctoral fellowship from the American-Scandinavian Foundation to conduct research at the Søren Kierkegaard Research Centre in Copenhagen, Denmark, and has been a House Foundation Fellow at the Hong Kierkegaard Library, St. Olaf College.

Matthew J. Grow is director of publications at the Church History Department of The Church of Jesus Christ of Latter-day Saints and a general editor of the Joseph Smith Papers. He leads a team of forty historians, editors, and web specialists writing historical publications for academic and popular audiences. He has written or cowritten biographies of Thomas L. Kane and

Parley P. Pratt, as well as coedited documentary histories of the Relief Society and the Council of Fifty.

David D. Hall was educated at Harvard College and Yale, where he earned his PhD in American studies and taught history and American studies until moving to Boston University and subsequently to Harvard Divinity School, from which he retired in 2008. Outside the university context, he founded (with others) the Program in the History of the Book at the American Antiquarian Society and served as general editor of the five-volume series A History of the Book in America (2009–2010). Beginning in the 1980s, he focused on popular religion in early New England, including witch-hunting, an approach complemented by the possibilities for studying "lived religion." Currently he is completing a comparative history of Reformed Protestantism as a force in the making of the English and Scottish reformations and their development into the mid-seventeenth century.

Tona Hangen is a professor of history at Worcester State University. She is the author of *Redeeming the Dial: Radio, Religion, and Popular Culture in America* (University of North Carolina Press, 2002). Her research and teaching interests explore intersections among media, religion, culture, and civil rights in twentieth-century America.

Jared Hickman is assistant professor of English at Johns Hopkins University. He is the author of *Black Prometheus: Race and Radicalism in the Age of Atlantic Slavery* (Oxford University Press, 2016) and the coeditor of two essay collections, *Abolitionist Places* (Routledge, 2013) and *Americanist Approaches to the Book of Mormon* (Oxford, forthcoming). He has published articles in

American Literature, Early American Literature, Nineteenth-Century Literature, PMLA, and other venues.

Kate Holbrook is managing historian of women's history at the LDS Church History Department. She is coeditor of *At the Pulpit: 185 Years of Discourses by Latter-day Saint Women* and *The First Fifty Years of Relief Society: Key Documents in Latter-day Saint Women's History.* She also coedited *Women and Mormonism: Historical and Contemporary Perspectives.* Her dissertation, "Radical Food: Nation of Islam and Latter-day Saint Culinary Ideals, 1930–1980," explored the everyday theological priorities carried in food, and she received the first Eccles Fellowship in Mormon Studies at the University of Utah for that work.

David Holland is John A. Bartlett Professor of New England Church History at the Harvard Divinity School. His book *Sacred Borders: Continuing Revelation and Canonical Restraint in Early America* was published by Oxford University Press in 2011. His current project, *A Particular Universe: Ellen Gould White, Mary Baker Eddy, and the Nineteenth-Century United States,* will be published by Yale University Press.

Melissa Wei-Tsing Inouye received her PhD in East Asian languages and civilizations from Harvard University. She is a lecturer in Chinese studies at the University of Auckland. Her forthcoming first book, *China and the True Jesus,* is a study of the True Jesus Church, a restorationist Pentecostal church founded in Beijing in 1917. She coordinates the Global Mormon Studies Steering Committee and is currently engaged in research on the economy of charisma within global Mormonism. In 2017 she received the Early Career Teaching Excellence Award from the University of Auckland Faculty of Arts.

Laurie F. Maffly-Kipp received her PhD from Yale University and holds the Archer Alexander Distinguished Professorship at the John C. Danforth Center on Religion and Politics at Washington University in St. Louis. She coedited *Proclamation to the People: Nineteenth-Century Mormonism and the Pacific Basin Frontier* (University of Utah Press, 2008) and authored *Setting Down the Sacred Past: African-American Race Histories* (Harvard University Press, 2010) and *American Scriptures*, a Penguin Classics anthology of sacred texts (Penguin, 2010). She is currently writing a survey of Mormonism for Basic Books.

Patrick Q. Mason is Howard W. Hunter Chair of Mormon Studies and dean of the School of Arts and Humanities at Claremont Graduate University. He is the author or editor of several books, including *What Is Mormonism? A Student's Introduction* and *Planted: Belief and Belonging in an Age of Doubt.*

Armand L. Mauss is professor emeritus of sociology and religious studies at Washington State University. After retirement at WSU, he taught the earliest courses in Mormon studies at the Claremont Graduate University and helped establish the Howard W. Hunter Chair there, first occupied by Richard L. Bushman. He is the author of many articles and four books in Mormon studies, the most recent being *Shifting Borders and a Tattered Passport: Intellectual Journeys of a Mormon Academic* (University of Utah Press, 2012).

Adam S. Miller is a professor of philosophy at Collin College in McKinney, Texas. He earned a PhD in philosophy from Villanova University and is the author of seven books, including *Speculative Grace, Letters to a Young Mormon*, and *The Gospel*

According to David Foster Wallace. He also directs the Mormon Theology Seminar.

Mauro Properzi is associate professor of world religions, religious outreach fellow, and moral education professor at Brigham Young University. He received graduate degrees in theology and religious studies from Harvard, the university of Cambridge and Durham University in the UK, and the Pontifical Gregorian University in Rome. He is the author of *Mormonism and the Emotions* (Fairleigh Dickinson University Press, 2015) and several articles in *Journal of Research on Christian Education, International Journal of Religion and Spirituality in Society, Journal of Mormon History, Journal of Ecumenical Studies, Issues in Religion and Psychotherapy,* and *BYU Studies.*

Jana Riess has a PhD in American religious history from Columbia University and is a senior columnist at Religion News Service. She is the author or coauthor of many books, including *Mormonism and American Politics, Flunking Sainthood, The Prayer Wheel,* and the forthcoming study *The Next Mormons: The Rising Generation of Latter-day Saints* (Oxford University Press, 2019).

Ann Taves is professor of religious studies at the University of California, Santa Barbara. She is the author of several books, including the forthcoming *Revelatory Events: Three Case Studies of the Emergence of New Spiritual Paths* (Princeton University Press, 2016), the first of which is Mormonism.

Laurel Thatcher Ulrich is past president of the Mormon History Association and a professor of history at Harvard University. She is the author of many works on early American history. Her most recent book, *A House Full of Females: Plural Marriage and*

Women's Rights in Early Mormonism, 1835–1870, was published by Alfred A. Knopf in 2017.

Grant Underwood is professor of history and holder of the Richard L. Evans Chair of Religious Understanding at Brigham Young University. He is the author or editor of a number of books and articles pertaining to Mormonism, including, most recently, volumes 1–3 of the Documents series of *The Joseph Smith Papers* (Church Historian's Press, 2013–2014). From 2006 to 2013 he was founding codirector of the American Academy of Religion's Mormon Studies Group, and he has served the Mormon History Association in a variety of capacities over the past thirty years.

Grant Wacker is the Gilbert T. Rowe Professor Emeritus of Christian History at Duke Divinity School. He is the author of *Heaven Below: Early Pentecostals and American Culture* (2001) and *America's Pastor: Billy Graham and the Shaping of a Nation* (2014), both published by Harvard University Press.

Jed Woodworth is a historian for the Church History Department of The Church of Jesus Christ of Latter-day Saints. He assisted Richard Bushman in the research and editing of *Joseph Smith: Rough Stone Rolling* (2005) and is a coeditor of Bushman's *Believing History: Latter-day Saint Essays* (2004).

INDEX

Bushman, Richard (*continued*)
  psychohistorical period of,
    62–63
  response to Sterling McMurrin,
    199
  scholarly humility of, 197
  scholarly works of, ix
  on stewardship of historians, 87
  summer seminar program led
    by, 167
  teaching philosophy of, 152,
    160–61
  work and integrity of, 196
Bushman, Richard and Claudia,
  as hosts, 155, 162
Bushman, Serge, 277
Butler, Jon, 181, 223
BYU Board of Trustees, female
  leaders on, 129n44

C

Calvin, John, 6
Cardinal Egidio da Viterbo, 180
Caspary, Mary Humiliata, 183
Catholic Church, 149. *See also*
  Second Vatican Council;
  Vatican II
  hierarchy of, 182
  reforms, 183
  women educators within, 183
Chalcedonian Christology, 243
character
  Mormon experience explained
    in terms of human, 260
  scholarly perspective affected
    by, 11
Chamberlain, Cathy, 120

charismatic ideals, 76
charismatic spiritual gifts, 232
choices, difficult, 78
Christ, body of, 108
Christian discipleship, effect on
  scholarly rigor, 31
Christian epistemology, 202
Christianity and Marxism, 131–32
Christian theology, dilemma in,
  59
christo-fiction, speculative inquiry
  of, 107–8
Christopher Columbus, changing
  perception toward, 277
Christ's church, restoration of, 41
Church, LDS
  defense of, 300
  exhorting the, 112
  loyalty to, 265
  now open to professional histo-
    riography, 175
church, institutional, working for,
  170
church and kingdom of God,
  established in last days, 233
Church Educational System, disputes with historians, 174
churches as mix of humanity and
  divinity, 40
church hierarchy, 181
church historian, early role of
  LDS, 85
Church Historian, 174–75. *See
  also* Historian, Church
  as member of the First Quorum
    of Seventy, 174
  revival of position of, 174
Church Historian's Press, 170, 176

faith-promoting, 172
honest and scholarly, 171
human forces in, 56
as inspiration to action, 82
interpretations of, 153
larger purpose of, 4
messiness of, 51, 76
moral, 10
narrative, 152
personal accountability and, 49
problems of insiders, outsiders, 54
purposes of, 53
salvific qualities of, 81
secular ideas about, 179
storytelling aspect of, 172
tension with faith claims, 199
through God's eyes, 10
tidiness in, 78
transparent, 151
history, LDS
narratives from, 160
transparency in, 159
History Division as predecessor of
Publications Division, 169
Holbrook, Kate, 49
holistic person, appreciation for,
288
Holland, David, 49
Hollinger, David, 219
Holy Spirit, witness of, 204
humans
characteristics of, 37
dynamic vs. static beings, 39
enemies to God, 38
social organizations of, 260–61
teleology, 24
human soul in Mormon theology,
228

humility, 16
Hunter, Howard W., 170
Hutchinson, Anne, 5
Hutchison, William, 223

I

immunity principle, 202
incarnation, doctrine of, 60
indigenous critical theory, 141n7
individual and society, 39, 40,
229
individual intentionality vs. collective processes, 261
Infinite, human understanding
of, 218
Inouye, Charles Shiro, Mormon
and Buddhist influences on,
70
Inouye, Dillon Kazayuki,
speed-reading classes of, 70
Inouye, Melissa Wei-Tsing, 49
intellect
academia's partitioning of faith
and, 288
irrelevant in matters of faith,
163
intellectual community, idealized,
207
intellectual integrity, 29–31
intellectuals, Mormon, role of, 44
interdisciplinarity in scholarship,
208
interpretation, notion of, 78
I-witnessing, 26

reason, magisterial and ministerial uses of, 203
reason and faith, 151, 172
record keeping, LDS, 303
records, accurate, 81
Reeder, Jennifer, 87
Rees, Martin, 26
Relief Society
documentary history of, 170
potential of, 90
religion
in age of printing, 30
academic study of, 214
certainty and uncertainty of, 40
epistemology of, 40
relation to social science, 257,
263
as relationship with God, 153
and science, 37
religious belief, secular challenges
to, 200, 306
religious community, 5
religious experiences, 202–3
religious freedom, Catholic concept of, 182
religious history, as credible, compelling, 220
religious identity in public sphere,
284
religious media, 284
religious movements, "life cycle"
of, 263
religious studies, complementarity of academic, devotional
approaches, 267
apologetics and, 206
religious tradition, beliefs and
practices of, 284

"ressourcement," Catholic leaders
embracement of, 183
restorationism
in Catholicism and Mormonism, 182, 184
retrenchment, 263
within Mormonism, 240
process of, 264–65
revelation
divinity of, 64
LDS belief in, 117
women's participation in, 96
Ricoeur, Paul, 31
Riess, Jana, 152
Robinson, Marilynne, 31, 107, 136
Romney, Marion G., 185
Rorty, Richard, 298
Rough Stone Rolling
reflections on, 64
review of, 246
tone of, 302
Rushforth, Brett, 85
Russell, Bertrand, 298
Rust, Marion, 252

S

Salt Lake Temple, 305
salvation
and knowledge, 10–12
narratives of, 232
plan of, 228
Salvation Army, motto of, 244
Saul, King, 151
Scheler, Max, on prejudice, 22
Schmidt, Leigh, 57
scholarly self and soul, partitioning of, 288

words, meaning of, 6
writing, accountability in, 51
writing history, Mormon attitude
    toward, 297

Y

young Mormon adults, loss of,
    157
Young, Brigham, 77, 115, 126n22,
    232
    documentary series on, 171
Young, Zina Diantha Huntington,
    113

Z

Zion as the community of the
    pure in heart, 77
Žižek, Slavoj, defense of Christian
    legacy by, 131

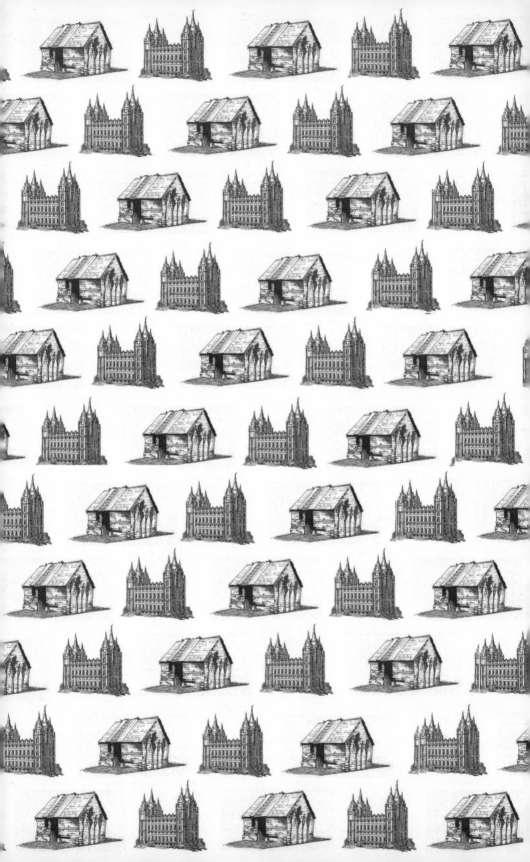